D1622453

THE
ART AND
ETIQUETTE
OF
GIFT GIVING

DAWN BRYAN

BANTAM BOOKS
TORONTO · NEW YORK · LONDON · SYDNEY · AUCKLAND

THE ART AND ETIQUETTE OF GIFT GIVING
A Bantam Book / November 1987

*Grateful acknowledgment is made for permission to reprint the excerpt from:
MIDDLETOWN FAMILIES by Theodore Caplow. University of Minnesota Press,
Minneapolis. Copyright © 1982 by the University of Minnesota.*

Library of Congress Cataloging-in-Publication Data

Bryan, Dawn.
  The art and etiquette of gift giving.

  Includes index.
  1. Generosity.   2. Gifts.   3. Etiquette.
I. Title.
BJ1533.G4B79   1987   395   87-47576
ISBN 0-553-05223-3

Published simultaneously in the United States and Canada.

PRINTED IN THE UNITED STATES OF AMERICA

DH   0   9   8   7   6   5   4   3   2   1

This book is dedicated to
MY PARENTS

The only gift is a portion of thyself.
—R.W. EMERSON

ACKNOWLEDGMENTS

T his book would not have been possible without the gifts of knowledgeable advice, cooperation, and assistance from many people. I am sincerely grateful to each of the following:

Kenneth L. Albrecht, National Charities Information Bureau; Barbara Alpert, Bantam Books; American Museum of Natural History Library; Dr. James D. Anderson; Susan Anderson; Sylvia and Richard Anderson; Stephen Arruda; Elaine Asch, *Revista Aerea*; John Baker, *Publishers Weekly*; Arlene Belzer; Rabbi Arnold Mark Belzer; John Anderson Bryan; Laura Bryan; Raymond Caldiero, Marriott Corporation; David Carey; Norine P. Carey; Albert V. Casey; Mary Casey; Children's Book Council; Victor Cherkashin, Counselor, Embassy of the Union of Soviet Socialist Republics; Harriet Choice; Lawrence R. Churchill, Pratt & Whitney, United Technologies; Connie Clausen, Clausen Associates; Marshall Coyne, Madison Hotel; Robert Cuomo; Madeleine de Vries, Madeline de Vries, Limited; Richard G. Ebel, Specialty Advertising Association International; Joan Edson; Endicott Booksellers; Laura Erickson; Fei Zhengxing, Shanghai International Studies University; R. Scott Fitzsimmons, Society Expeditions; Francine and Luc Forbin, France; Dene Garbow, National Building Museum and Mt. Vernon Inn; Melvin C. Garbow, Arnold & Porter; Carmella Garcia, Spanish Consulate, New York; Theresa Gilardi; Joan Giurdanella, The Franklin Library; Ingeborg Godenschweger,

German Information Center; Evan Goldfisher; Marjorie Goldstein, The Doubleday Large Print Home Library; Mary Gremmler, Campbell-Mithun Advertising; Lis Hansen, Danish Consulate, New York; Jill and Robert Held, Australia; Diane Herman, Book-of-the-Month Club; Roger Horchow; Jai Weidong, Jiang Wei, Shanghai International Studies University; Ruben H. Johnson; Michael Jolley, Rolls-Royce, Inc.; Patricia Kasamatsu, Japan; Jean Keith; Kate T. Kestnbaum, Kestnbaum & Company; Guy Kettlehack; Jane Klein, Creative Resources; Sergey B. Komslov, Embassy of the Union of Soviet Socialist Republics; B. C. Kovach; Trina Koykka, Finnish Consulate, New York; Warren E. Kraemer, McDonnell Douglas; C.J.M. Kramers, former Consul-General of the Netherlands; Sergio Barriga Kreft, Chile; Judith Kuriansky, Ph.D.; Doe Lang, Charismedia; Martin Levin; Suzanne Levitt; Nancy A. Link; Lu Weiguang, Shanghai International Studies University; Stanley Marcus; Charles McCabe, Manufacturers Hanover; William McGrail, Habitat; Andrew Morgan; Robert G. Neumann, Center for Strategic & International Studies, U.S. Department of State and former U.S. Ambassador to Saudi Arabia; New York Public Library; Joon Oh, Republic of Korea Mission to the United Nations; Katie O'Meara; Bettie Bearden Pardee; Charles Plante; Nathaniel Polster; Julie Prosser, Embassy of Australia; Jack Schwartz, American Association of Fund-Raising Counsel; Yang Soonja; May Lee Soong; Leta K. Stathacos, *Artnews*; James W. Symington, Former U.S. Chief of Protocol; Gregge Tiffin, G Systems; Jeffrey Todrys; Jo-Von Tucker, Jo-Von Tucker and Associates; Bretta Weiss, American Montessori Society; Glen Wiggins; Peter Workman, Workman Publishing; Yuan Shi-yun, Shanghai International Studies University; personnel and libraries of numerous embassies and consulates.

My very special appreciation for Robin Mays.

CONTENTS

Preface / xiii

PART ONE: GIFTING / 1

THE ART OF GIFT GIVING, OR GIFTS AS COMMUNICATORS / 3
GIVING GIFTS / 5
RECEIVING GIFTS / 9
THE METAPHYSICAL ASPECTS OF GIVING AND RECEIVING / 12
EASY WAYS TO MAKE YOUR GIFT GIVING SPECIAL / 15
    Start A Collection for Someone / 15
    Create Your Own Occasion / 16
    Combine Items / 19
    "A Portion of Thyself" / 21
    Special Touches / 22
INEXPENSIVE GIFTS / 25
EXTRAVAGANT GIFTS / 28

PART TWO: AMERICAN GIFT GIVING HOLIDAYS / 35

TRADITIONAL AMERICAN GIFT GIVING HOLIDAYS / 37
    Saint Valentine's Day / 37
    Easter / 38
    May Day / 39
    Mother's Day / 39
    Father's Day / 40
    Halloween / 41
    Thanksgiving Day / 42
    Christmas Eve and Day / 43
ROMANTIC VALENTINE'S DAY GIFTS / 44
CHRISTMAS—THE PLEASURES OF GIVING / 48

PART THREE: OCCASION GIFTS / 53

BIRTHS AND CHRISTENINGS / 55
BIRTHDAY GIFTS / 59
WEDDINGS / 62
    Wedding Gifts / 63
    Bridal Showers / 65
    Encore Weddings / 66
    Receiving Wedding Gifts / 66
    Exchanging Wedding Gifts / 68
    Returning Wedding Gifts / 68
    Bridal Couple's Gifts to Each Other / 68
    Gifts for Wedding Attendants / 69
    Gifts to Bride and Groom from Wedding Party / 69
ANNIVERSARY GIFTS / 71
HOUSEWARMING GIFTS / 74
PARTY GIFTS / 76
STOCKING GIFTS / 78
INTERIM GIFTS / 81

PART FOUR: BUSINESS GIFTS AND OFFICE PRESENTS / 85

SUCCESSFUL BUSINESS GIFTS—CLIENTS, CUSTOMERS, AND SPECIAL
   INDIVIDUALS / 87
GIFTS FOR THE OPENING OF A NEW OFFICE OR BUSINESS / 95
JOINT OFFICE GIFTS / 97
GIFTS FOR THE BOSS / 100
GIFTS FOR EMPLOYEES / 103
    Service Awards / 103
    Incentive Gifts / 104
    Holiday Gifts / 104
    Retirement Gifts / 105
    Special Occasion Gifts / 106
PRODUCT PROMOTIONS AND PREMIUM GIFTS / 108
BUSINESS GIFTS: SPECIALIZED APPLICATIONS / 110
CORPORATE GIFT CONSULTANTS/SHOPPING SERVICES AND HOW TO
   USE THEM / 112

PART FIVE: INTERNATIONAL AND ETHNIC GIFTS / 115

INTERNATIONAL AND ETHNIC GIFT GIVING AND RECEIVING / 117
JEWISH GIFT GIVING CUSTOMS / 121
GIFT GIVING CUSTOMS IN FRANCE / 129

Gift Giving Customs in Britain / 134
Gift Giving Customs in Japan / 137
Gift Giving Customs in China / 149
Gift Giving Customs in West Germany / 161
Gift Giving Customs in Italy / 166
Gift Giving Customs in the Arab World / 170
Gift Giving Customs in Scandinavia / 177
Gift Giving Customs in Korea / 181
Gift Giving Customs in the Soviet Union / 187
Gift Giving Customs in Australia / 190
Gift Giving Customs in the Netherlands / 193
Gift Giving Customs in Spain / 197
Gift Giving Guidelines in Latin America / 199
Gift Giving Customs in Venezuela / 201
Gift Giving Customs in Brazil / 205
Gift Giving Customs in Chile / 207

PART SIX: WHEN YOU CHOOSE ... / 209

Books as Gifts / 211
Museum Gifts / 220
Flowers and Plants as Gifts / 223
Gifts from Catalogs / 230
Philanthropic Giving / 234
Gifts of Money / 238
Liquor, Wine, and Bar Accessories as Gifts / 240
Pets as Gifts / 243
Gifts You Should Never Give / 245

PART SEVEN: SPECIAL INTERESTS AND SPECIAL
    RECIPIENTS / 247

Gifts for Families / 250
Gifts for Teens and Graduations / 253
Entertaining Ideas for Hosts/Hostesses and Gourmet Cooks / 258
Gifts for the Elderly or Disabled / 265
Gifts for Ill Persons / 270
Gifts for the Traveler / 273
Gifts for the Office / 278
Gifts for Those with Sports Interests / 280
Gifts for Gardeners / 289
Gifts for the Clergy / 293

GIFTS FOR THOSE INTERESTED IN THE ARTS / 295
GIFTS FOR SOMEONE AWAY FROM HOME / 299
GIFTS FOR PETS AND THEIR OWNERS / 301
GIFTS FOR NEEDLEWORKERS / 303
GIFTS FOR ROCK, MINERAL, AND GEM ENTHUSIASTS / 305
GIFTS FOR TEACHERS / 308
GIFTS FOR CHOCOHOLICS / 309
GIFTS FOR DEBUTANTES / 311
GIFTS FOR CHILDREN / 313
GIFTS FOR LEFT-HANDED PEOPLE / 320
FOR CHILDREN ONLY / 321

PART EIGHT: PRESENTATION / 327

SIGNATURE WRAPPING / 330
TRADITIONAL JAPANESE PACKAGING / 331
STORE WRAPS / 332
CONTAINERS AS PACKAGING / 334
BASIC AND CREATIVE GIFT WRAPPING / 336
AVAILABLE GIFT WRAPS / 338
GIFT CARDS / 342
GIFT PRESENTATIONS / 344

APPENDICES / 347
SENDING GIFTS / 349
GIFT GUIDELINES / 353

INDEX / 357

PREFACE

Although the idea for this book has been with me for many years, it became a necessary reality when I found myself writing lengthy gift protocols for clients who were unable to find information of this depth from any other source. Personal, business, and international gift etiquette and suggestions were simply not compiled anywhere.

Modern corporate and public sector life increasingly demands more international and social sophistication from its managers and their families. However, the gift exchange as a mode of international communication—particularly in business settings—has seldom been explored or explained. Understanding something about the culture and customs of a foreign country is key to understanding the business within that culture.

How would you react upon unexpectedly receiving an elaborate gift from a newly married Japanese couple to whom you'd recently sent a wedding present?

Why should you not take a half-dozen roses to your French hostess?

What would you do if your negotiations with an Arab came to an immediate halt after you had presented a lovely gift of food to your host?

Would you send flowers to an Orthodox Jewish funeral?

One section of this book, then, describes proper gift giving and (of equal importance) receiving in foreign cultures. Special emphasis is given to those countries in which entire systems of gift giving are woven into the fabric of everyday social and business behavior, such as Japan, the Arab countries, and China.

At the same time I became concerned that crass commercialism, along with the complexity and busyness of our lives today, has enervated the art of gift giving. So many of the gifts we give are obligatory and/or regulated by holidays and occasions; we seldom enjoy the luxury of spontaneous giving. I decided a comprehensive resource was required that could answer gift giving needs in a highly personal way—from discussing issues of propriety and protocol to teaching presentation strategy and ways of increasing creativity in choosing gifts. It is time to put thoughtfulness and charm back into gift giving.

The joy of successful gifting comes from choosing, from preparing, from presenting—and from the pleasure you share with someone you want to please. I hope that in addition to providing a vital resource and helping you to avoid the commonplace, *The Art and Etiquette of Gift Giving* brings you moments of pleasure and leaves you feeling more generous of spirit.

Your pleasure is a gift to me.

PART ONE

GIFTING

THE ART
OF GIFT GIVING, OR
GIFTS AS COMMUNICATORS

How often have you asked yourself, "What in the world can I get for——?"

The ideal gift communicates the appropriate and desired messages about both the giver and the receiver. A well-selected gift paints a picture of you as you want to be regarded. It makes a statement. It tells the receiver what you want him or her to see in you—a loving relative, a grateful employer, a passionate devotee, a friend, an admirer, a thankful and appreciative person, a sly tweaker, a figure of elegance and taste, or a person who knows how to end a relationship with a smile. More important, it makes a statement about the recipient: his loyalty is recognized, his fortitude deserves recognition, he is dear, his leadership is significant to the board, he is esteemed by his colleagues, his good health is important to us, he makes business transactions a pleasure, he has achieved a higher status, or, simply, he deserves thanks.

Everyone gives and receives gifts. Whether the gift giving is voluntary or involuntary, each gift must be selected and presented. And each gift becomes an extension of your taste, a measure of your interest in the recipient—even an indication of your knowledge and personal power. How and what people give makes an impact, a lasting impression. How they receive a gift can be just as telling.

Whether we acknowledge it or not, all gifts have meaning for those who give as well as for those who receive. They play an important role in our lives: our hunger for gifts is also our hunger for approval, affection, importance, love ... and people need to give because they need to give of themselves. Our abilities to give and to receive touch on many other aspects of our lives.

We use gifts to dominate and control, to motivate, to compensate, to teach, to secure a relationship, to demonstrate love and caring, to display our knowledge and sophistication, to help others, to express goodwill, to cheer, to extend our personal power.

A gift can establish a relationship, move it off dead center, transform it, or end it. For many people, thoughtful gift giving can help with business and personal relationships. Unfortunately, much time, energy, thought, and money are invested daily in uninspired, lackluster, often unappreciated or inappropriate gifts.

Today's affluent society spends more and more money on gifts each year; and each year seems to bring more gift occasions—from a national Grandparents' Day to your friend's dog's birthday party. Many people feel they must compensate for their lack of time and creativity by purchasing gifts that are needlessly expensive. Others buy multiples of the same item—fifty mini-food-processors!—often ill suited for many of the recipients. Thus, the concept of making gift giving less time-consuming and more personalized is especially enticing.

The person who masters the art of gift giving will not use gifts simply to make someone feel good or to repay an obligation; he will be sending precisely the message he means to communicate in an appropriate manner.

GIVING GIFTS

Although gift giving is one of the warmest and most pleasant of international customs, the ritual of gift exchange involves more than unselfishness. Stimulated by complex motivations, it is seldom an act of spontaneous largesse but one calculated to cement or change a relationship or to improve one's status.

The elements of power and prestige have long been important in gift giving. Native American tribes in British Columbia threw potlaches—occasions of feasting, dancing, sports events, public ceremonies, and gift exchange for their friends, their enemies, and other tribes. The prestige that the host acquired came not only from hosting the event but from the quality and lavishness of the gifts he distributed to his guests. He would confirm his status within the tribe or strike for higher status by inundating his guests with gifts. As recently as 1921, Daniel Cranmer of the Nimpkish clan gave away twenty-four canoes, two pool tables, three hundred oak chests, five gasoline-powered boats, four hundred Hudson's Bay blankets, one thousand sacks of flour, cash, and an indeterminate number of gramophones, bedsteads, sewing machines, and bureaus. Sometimes a chief—to add luster to his name—would deliberately and publicly destroy very valuable gifts given to him, thus proving how great and wealthy a man he was.

In the Solomon Islands, the Buin used gifts also as competition for status. In aristocratic marriages the ambitious father of the bride would deliberately return more pigs than corresponded to the proferred shell money customarily sent by the groom's family when requesting a young lady in marriage. The groom's father, if similarly competitive and wealthy enough, would send back more currency. This would continue until the resources of one competitor were exhausted, and his rival became the victor by default.

In mythology and folklore, most gifts of revenge were meant to inflict vengeance: Medea, when Jason deserted her for the princess of Corinth, sent her rival the gift of a poisoned robe. On the other hand, giving a generous gift to one who has hurt you can be spiritually freeing, healing. The act can also restore your self-esteem, giving you a sense of power.

Certain societies have used competitive gift giving as revenge, shaming those who have hurt or insulted them. Members would hold elaborate feasts at which they would sing challenges to accompany their gifts of revenge. Those who had derided the host would receive the most lavish gifts; those who could not reciprocate were the losers. One notable example—Head Chief Sharp-Teeth, whose pride was deeply wounded by his wife's desertion to a Hudson's Bay Company fur trader named Captain McNeil—decided to erase his shame in a way his people would understand. His bountiful feast and gifts of expensive skins were meant to humiliate her and to regain his pride. She reciprocated with a magnificent trade canoe emblazoned with her heraldic emblem. The gifting continued until she erected a magnificent totem pole that put her on a par with her estranged husband. Her totem pole remains one of the finest in North America.

Apparently some tribes that had long practiced barter had difficulty understanding the concept of a gift. For example, at an isolated settlement on Victoria Island in about 1850, Commander Robert McClure (who discovered the Prince of Wales Strait) wrapped a scarf about the neck of a young Eskimo woman who appeared to be suffering from the cold. She reacted by becoming upset and gesturing that she had nothing to give in return; then she drew her small child from her hood where she was keeping it warm, offering it in payment. She was delighted to learn that she could keep both scarf and child. In more modern society, the difference between barter and gift exchange is sometimes equally nebulous. Although in barter the exchange of one commodity for another is by mutual agreement, many gifts clearly imply the need for reciprocity.

Much of what we may think of as essentially voluntary gift giving is, in fact, prescribed behavior. Consumer psychologist Russell Belk tells us that we maintain and define friendship by giving gifts.

In his study of the festival cycle and family symbolism in *Middletown Families,* (Bantam Books, 1982) which focused on Muncie, Indiana, sociologist Theodore Caplow points out that most gift giving is part of an exchange and can be justified on rational grounds. "Social ties and gift giving go hand in hand: neither exists without the other. The gift affirms the relationship and symbolizes the kind of relationship it is." Caplow goes on to say that most festivals today are celebrated in part by gift giving and that most of the gifts are chosen and given by women. Gifts, especially Christmas gifts, symbolize and reinforce every social relationship; thus, the women in Middletown, more than the men, define and maintain social relationships, even those of their husbands.

"Gifts are given on many occasions in Middletown, but only at Christmas is it obligatory to give one to nearly every close relative, friend, and associate. Ideally, each gift given should differ from all the others given by that person. This unwritten (indeed, generally unstated) rule is burdensome, but Middletown people obey it remarkably well. The Christmas present not only reaffirms each relationship, it also specifies what that relationship is, while it flatters, if possible, the recipient's taste and personality. That each gift must convey so much and that overt speculation about the motives for choosing any gift is taboo explain why Christmas shopping is such a problem. Yet it must be done. Social cohesion depends on this annual reaffirmation of relationships."

To those who cry, "Christmas is too commercialized!" Caplow replies that extensive gift giving serves an important purpose by maintaining all sorts of personal relationships, and that the message of secular Christmas is not really different from the message conveyed by the traditional Christmas story. "The episodes of the Nativity convey the necessity for looking after a child's, and a family's, welfare. In a sense, we can say that God the Father is caring for His creation, the human race, as parents should care for their own creations, their children. This message is repeated on a smaller scale in the story of the Holy Family itself. . . ."

Interestingly, he points out that Santa Claus, a giver of specific gifts to children, receives nothing for his generosity. He "epitomizes the generosity, particularism, and nurturance of Christmas," while emphasizing the predominantly one-way flow of gifts from parents to children. This observance about our celebrating the nurturing of children helps to support his conclusion: Middletown's festival cycle celebrates family matters because the family is the institution most at risk in the community.

Our reasons for giving are diverse and often unacknowledged even to ourselves: a man chooses an unusual, personal gift for a woman because it signifies a greater commitment; parents may give too many feminine gifts to a young boy because they wanted a girl; we may choose a very beautiful gift because it enhances us in our own eyes as well as in those of the recipient.

Many favors we do for others are actually gifts to ourselves, either because of the pleasure that their doing affords us or because of a pleasure that we would not allow ourselves without such a pretext.

Sometimes our giving seems intrinsically bound to our feelings about ourselves. At Christmas, especially, we may measure our personal worth—or feel that others are doing so—by how much we spend or how lavish our gifts are. But we need to remind ourselves that money does not equate with personal value.

The truly spontaneous gift, the unexpected gift, the one with no specific reason, is a gift of the heart and is the best kind of gift. However, even as we present it, we may gain a feeling of power to hear the surprised exclamations.

I truly enjoy selecting and giving gifts. I usually give because it makes me feel good to do so; and I like to think I am giving without any demands. What does this person want or need? How can I best delight this person? But, is it really to make others happy, or is it for my own satisfaction in making others happy? Is it mainly in order to be appreciated by others? Perhaps, but I believe the goal of the true giver is to give pleasure to another. A well-selected present, given in the right spirit, will delight the recipient, making the giver into a receiver, too.

All people have the need to give their affection and to feel that their love is needed and appreciated. No matter what the gift, the true meaning is in the love it expresses.

RECEIVING GIFTS

The receipt of a gift is usually followed by an acknowledgment. As young children, we learn to accept a gift "with grace." Mother whispers, "Don't forget to tell Uncle Perry how much you love the paper dolls." There is a family rule that all holiday thank-you notes must be mailed before January first.

Sometimes "with grace" means with a smile even if it's an exceptionally ugly pillow or you already have three Belgian waffle irons. In the interest of integrity, you can thank the donor for his or her remembrance or thoughtfulness without specifically praising the gift.

At the same time, our culture teaches us to look for ulterior motives: not to accept gifts from strangers; not to take expensive or personal gifts from persons we do not know well. We are particularly suspicious of the unexpected gift—often making an ungracious response.

According to psychologists and psychiatrists, gifts can arouse complex responses in the recipient. The same gift can have different meanings for each of us. Gifts of clothing, for example, often carry a special significance related to our past experiences. Clinical psychologist and television and radio personality Dr. Judith Kuriansky explains why a young woman becomes unduly upset when her mother buys her clothes she doesn't like, things her mother would clearly choose for herself. The recipient attaches a deeper meaning to this gift: all her life she has resented her mother's desire to make her daughter more like her, while the young girl was struggling to establish her own identity. A stylish woman who receives a conservative-looking dress from her husband might interpret this gift as a criticism of her fashion choices, of her personal taste—and feel she is once more trying to please her parents by "dressing the part" of a finishing-school graduate. Kuriansky tells us that "by accepting a gift, you are not agreeing to be what the other person wants you to be. And by the opposite token, don't expect others to give you permission to be what you want: give that to yourself."

There are certain gifts that many of you may feel uneasy about accepting:

- A gift from a parent that makes you question your independence, especially if it's something you couldn't have gotten yourself

- A gift that implies the need for a return gift or obligation, which you had not intended

- A gift that you feel the giver really did not want to give

- A gift that you feel was given in order to demonstrate superiority or to control you

- A gift that you think you don't deserve

- A gift that the donor selected for him- or herself rather than for your tastes or lifestyle

- A gift of conscience or forgiveness—a defense mechanism

- Gifts as extortion (some parents call them rewards)—such as a new bicycle for a good report card

- A gift that is meant primarily to flatter the pride of the giver

In the case of all of these possibilities, you can accept the gift graciously if you manage to view it as a transaction that has no power over you and does not change you. Try to separate the act of giving from the specific item that is given. Kuriansky suggests that you appreciate the giving and consider liking the gift as a bonus. If you don't like it, don't treat it as a loss. Imagine it's something you wouldn't have had anyway. You are free to do what you want with it: put it in the back of the closet, give it away, or return it. Choice always takes the edge off upset.

Acknowledging gifts has in parts of our society become a matter of a thank-you phone call. Seldom is this sufficient—and it is never proper in business. As a matter of fact, a phone call can have the opposite effect if you interrupt an important meeting or disturb someone during his dinner hour.

The social thank-you letter should be written on proper note paper or stationery with matching envelope, and should be handwritten. It should, when possible, tell how the gift will be used or mention something noteworthy about it, and should be sent promptly. The business thank-you should be a brief and separate communication— not an addendum to a letter about another subject. It should be written on proper stationery—preferably personal rather than corporate—and may be typewritten. If the gift will be used in your office, you might want to invite the donor to visit one day to see how it looks.

Do not accept a present if your instincts tell you not to. Gifts that are too expensive or extravagant when seen in terms of your relationship with the giver, like a fee that is too large for a service you have performed for someone, can be returned with a polite "thank you anyway for your thoughtfulness or kindness." Remember that the sender may feel personally rejected, so tact is called for; you should explain why you cannot accept the gift, either in person or in an accompanying note. Refusing an expensive business gift can be accomplished by praising the gift, then explaining that your company (or you) has a strict policy governing the acceptance of gifts. The return of a gift that has sexual overtones, is a bad joke, or is an obvious bribe does not require either tact or kindness; they are, however, still appropriate.

THE
METAPHYSICAL
ASPECTS OF GIVING AND
RECEIVING

Man has always responded to the end of the annual planetary cycle with ceremonies or other observances that included—and often centered around—the exchange of gifts. Early man's mystical services included gifts that represented the good of the planet presented to all participants; North American Indians danced, feasted, and exchanged ceremonial gifts. The winter solstice, today celebrated in many different fashions, continues to symbolize a time for giving and receiving. And the concept of giving gifts at a time of renewal or beginning is a universal common denominator in the recognition of the ongoing cycle of life.

At this season Jews, for example, commemorate the rededication of their temple to Jewish worship and celebrate the ideal of Jewish identity and distinctiveness with the lighting of the Hanukkah menorah and the exchange of gifts among family and friends. Christians, who rejoice in God's gift of His Son to the world, repeat this act of giving many times over at Christmas, the time of Christ's birth. The most important gift giving holiday in Japan is Oseibo; this celebration continues through December, to New Year's, when they visit a Buddhist temple or Shinto shrine to pray for happiness and longevity.

Metaphysicist Gregge Tiffen tells us that man celebrates the time when the earth both finishes its cycle and begins a new cycle with an entire symbology relating to gifts—on mental, physical, and spiritual levels. The solstice is the celebration of the beginning and the end: the person who gives the gift represents the end of the cycle; the receiver accepts the gift as a new beginning. The giver, who knows what the gift is, hands it to someone who doesn't know what it contains; and in that instant two people share the beginning and end of the cycle. One of the joys of the season is the repeating of this symbolic act over and over.

We live in a creative, bountiful universe. Religions are built on the belief that God gives abundantly and willingly. The essence of giving is the essence of the creative force—not only of the universe, but of us as individuals. It isn't the gift that we give, it is the force that we use as the perpetuation of an infinite condition.

Tiffen reminds us that the important gift (and one that we often ignore or avoid) is that of our own spirit—our own consciousness. Each year we are given the opportunity to renew ourselves. We plant, fertilize, grow, flower, and harvest; but before we plant again, we must renew—that is, we must recognize that we have grown and developed, heeding in some way our own experience, our own awareness, our own newness, and our new beginning in that cycle. That recognition can be likened to a field's fallow period. The human spirit needs the same period of renewal. New seeds cannot grow, new experiences cannot happen, unless one celebrates by connecting with the cycle of the planet and saying "I am now ready to renew myself, to accept new seeds (gifts)."

Unfortunately, we have been born into a very commercial era, in which the idea of gift exchange is often far removed from the actual essence of the season. During our own gift periods (be it Christmas or Hanukkah or Oseibo), we attempt with gifts to symbolize the physical, mental, and even spiritual aspects of the solstice. And, as we find giving much easier than receiving, we are better givers than we are receivers. Too often we greet a proffered gift with, "Oh, you shouldn't have."

Why is it that we are so willing to give, so eager to make the gift available? For many of us, it is because we are looking for recognition, for acclaim, for love. What we do not understand is that the only gift we can truly give is that which we have already accepted for ourselves.

How can one be a gracious receiver? The good receiver believes that he has the right to use his own gifts. Have you ever given a very special present, one that required your time and money and that you felt represented your love and caring, then discovered that the giver either gave the gift away or put it in a drawer, closet, or safe deposit box? How did you feel about this? If there is no receiver, there is no gift. By not allowing our consciousness to give to ourselves, however, we stop the natural flow of the universe. We clog up the drain and stagnation occurs. We can't give to someone anything we've refused to accept ourselves.

What is post-Christmas depression, and why are we relieved each time the season is over? Is it surveying the broken toys, trying to find the missing pieces, and standing in line to exchange too-small sweaters for larger ones? Perhaps this is part of it, but, more significant, it is our realization that all our desires to celebrate our attempts to please others with our gifts meant nothing at all. According to Gregge Tiffen, we have not fulfilled the cycle of the universe. We are the same the day after Christmas as we were the day before. We have not accepted the symbol of the Christ Child, the Spirit, as the ultimate love gift of the universe.

It is difficult for us to understand the story of the Christ Child as the symbol of spirituality that manifests itself when it is received as a gift. The symbolism continues with the Wise Men. They came from the East, the beginning, where the sun rises and the new day begins; and they brought with them spiritual gifts of frankincense and myrrh. The story of the Baby, a most vulnerable and fragile symbol, tells us that all gifts are beautiful, none need be measured against others, and the only necessary response from the receiver is to use it.

Solstice should be that moment when you recognize that you are the giver, the gift, and the receiver; that all that transpires between you and others is but a symbol of your own gift to yourself—your own uniqueness. Recall how you consider yourself a successful giver when you find the unusual, the rare, the original, the one-of-a-kind gift for someone. We value objects that are originals, signed by the maker. You cannot be a receiver until you can find and accept the same qualities in yourself—your singularity, your uniqueness. Turn yourself over, look inside yourself to find your most precious gift—your own hallmark.

(Material in this chapter has been adapted from Gregge Tiffin's lectures on the Winter Solstice.)

EASY WAYS
TO MAKE YOUR GIFT GIVING
SPECIAL

Gifts have meanings, deep and subtle, both for those who receive and for those who give. There are ways to add more thoughtfulness and pleasure to your gift giving, while at the same time often spending less time and money. Individuality and originality in giving are possible for anyone who employs any of the following strategies:

Start a Collection for Someone

People collect everything—antique cameras, matchbooks, dolls, thimbles, porcelain, pictures of something they're fond of, books, autographs, mirrors, baskets, scarves, pillows, ornaments, and much more.

- For a bride and groom or for a first anniversary, you might select their first crystal, straw, or silver Christmas tree ornaments, and then add to their collection annually.

- Starting a collection for the typically hard-to-buy-for father who "has everything" will go a long way toward solving future gift problems. If he's a workaholic, start by assembling a group of antique paperweights, or choosing something relating to his profession, such as first-edition books in his field of interest; old medical instruments; photos, models, or paintings of old aircraft or hunting dogs; autographs of famous people he admires; antique ink blotters (glass or crystal). So he's interested only in his woodworking shop? Find interesting old or antique tools and help him display them on a pegboard above his workbench.

- For the hard-to-please woman who seems not to need or desire anything personal, begin a collection of pewter, silver, or ceramic picture frames—all sizes—or of unusual bookmarks or signed pottery of a certain period.

- The teenager who looks forward to receiving a record/tape/disc from you on each gift giving occasion will promptly relay his or her requests to the right person in time for the event.

- People who travel widely might be enthused about receiving a rock, a vase, a basket, or a mask from an exotic locale, along with a book about collecting such items. They will soon enjoy finding their own in their travels as well as receiving other specimens from you.

- The elderly, who may no longer be interested in accumulation, will look forward to your annual restoration of favorite old family photos.

The type of collection you choose will be influenced by the interests and situation of the recipient—his lifestyle, his space, his appreciation of the beautiful, the amusing, the old, the rare.

Introducing someone to collecting demonstrates your interest in him and his life, solves your future gift problems, and may teach you a great deal about a fascinating new subject. In addition to purchasing the objects themselves, you can give your new collector display shelves, containers, albums, tickets to collections and fairs, subscriptions to collectors' magazines, registry books, or an offer to photograph his collection.

Create Your Own Occasion

Do you have red hair and freckles . . . and you're Irish, too? Purchase some small decorative pots or containers, a bag of potting soil, and a packet of seeds. Plant the seeds right after Christmas, and by the dreary middle of March you can present shamrock plants to your friends, relatives, and co-workers for Saint Patrick's Day. (If you're not Irish, well, there are always Caesar salads for the Ides of March.)

As a young child I decorated wooden berry baskets (the same ones I dreaded having to fill with strawberries many early June mornings), covered the bottoms with fresh ferns, filled them with wildflowers—Dutchman's-breeches, violets, spring beauties—and placed them on the doorsteps of all my neighbors and friends each May Day morning. It's a delightful and unique surprise, and many of my friends continue to receive flowery remembrances on the first of May.

People who really enjoy others and like to give parties can initiate an annual party, dinner, brunch, soiree—a wonderful gift for all who attend. I recently went to a wonderful picnic—celebrating the dedication of a treehouse. It was so successful both for adults and for children that the hosts are making it an annual anniversary event. They even decided to repeat the menu, from the *calientitas* to the corn on the cob to the chocolate soufflé cake. From high teas and garden parties to husking bees and square dances, special occasions make special gifts.

• When people are wondering what to do with the long summer weekends after the Fourth of July, an exciting celebration of Bastille Day would be eagerly awaited each year.

• The commemoration of Beethoven's birthday if you are musically inclined (it's the favorite celebration of a Washington, D.C., antique and art gallery each spring), or the marking of the original publication of Marshall McLuhan's first book if you're in the media business, can make an impressive gift for your friends as well as fulfill an accumulation of social obligations.

• Even the birthday of a pet can be the genesis of a festive occasion. A Texas physician who heads one of the state's biggest departments, invites hundreds of friends to his ranch each September to celebrate his dog's birthday (and the birthday boy's a mutt!); for ten years my Burmese cat Rangoon entertained people from all over the world at his birthday parties. The unusual nature of such parties produced invitations requesting that the guests not bring live gifts, and inspired the hostess to provide foods such as poached salmon and caviar as well as chocolate petit fours in the shape of tiny mice.

• One can create an occasion for any date. A couple of years ago a party was called for April 27—an inauspicious date for most people. The hosts made it both important and exciting by sending this invitation:

1822 Ulysses S. Grant, 18th President of the United States, is born at Point Pleasant, Ohio.

1844 Martin Van Buren and Henry Clay announce they oppose President Tyler's proposal to annex Texas, unless Mexico agrees to the annexation.

1850 An American-owned steamship, *The Atlantic,* inaugurates a schedule of regular transatlantic passenger service, the first American ship to offer competition to British liners.

1882 Ralph Waldo Emerson, essayist, poet, and philosopher, dies at his home in Concord, Massachusetts.

1897 The body of former President Ulysses S. Grant is removed to the tomb bearing his name on New York's Riverside Drive. (The mausoleum was built by popular subscription, some ninety thousand citizens contributing $600,000 of the cost.)

1898 The American fleet under the command of Commodore Dewey leaves China for the Philippines.

1906 The United States Steel Corporation begins to break ground along Lake Michigan for the construction of a new Indiana town, to be known as Gary, Indiana.

1937 The first Social Security payment is made in accordance with the provisions of the Social Security Act of 1935.

1941 Athens falls to the German invaders. The Nazi swastika is hoisted over the Acropolis after 180 days of heroic Greek resistance to the invaders.

1947 Baseball fans observe "Babe Ruth Day" throughout the nation in honor of the seriously ill former "Sultan of Swat." The largest observance is held at Yankee Stadium, where 58,339 persons tender the Babe the greatest ovation in the history of the national pastime. Barely able to speak, Babe thanks the cheering crowd.

1965 As the revolution in the Dominican Republic grows more intense, the U.S. aircraft carrier *Boxer* and two transports move into offshore positions to begin the evacuation of U.S. civilians there.

1985 **In New York City at 5 P.M., Janet Casey, Neal Todrys, and their friends will celebrate Spring.**

For those who need another reason to celebrate on April 27—Annual Events include Texas Wildflower Day, Togo's Independence Day, Tallahassee's Spring Farm Days, Polk County Ramp Tramp (always at Big Frog Mountain), and the World Cow Chip Throwing Championship (Beaver, Oklahoma).

RSVP: (212)555-9148

The creator of gift occasions may also find himself giving gifts for small, unheralded successes; as solace for a loss—a job, a pet, a friend, a prize; to friends on their arrival in a new city rather than their departure from yours; to new business associates who helped with a contract; to the deserving spouse or parent of a graduate.

Creating occasions as gifts identifies the creator as more original than his peers, more thoughtful of others, and more exciting in his lifestyle. And the creator will become more caring, more interesting, and have more fun!

Combine Items

Any gift becomes more distinctive and personal when paired with something that individualizes it. This is particularly true when you select a utilitarian gift or one that is already expected in a certain situation. Once you begin to employ this device of combining, you will frequently find yourself inspired.

Almost any occasion or recipient may call for an original combination:

- For a graduate, the usual attaché, portfolio, or briefcase—but with an appropriate subscription tucked inside, such as *The Wall Street Journal,* or a membership in an alumni or professional organization, or a gift certificate to a medical, architectural, or office-supply house.

- For a housewarming, a cookie jar filled with gooey cookies, or a homemade pie paired with a pastry cookbook.

- For a wedding anniversary, a picnic basket for two, a bottle of wine, and perhaps a book of poetry.

- For a wedding shower, a set of canisters filled with food items, or glass containers filled with many different kinds of beans, noodles, or pastas.

- For a teenager, a purse or billfold with tickets to a favorite rock concert, sporting event, or ballet; or a telephone accompanied by the *Toll-Free Digest* (over seventeen thousand listings for free, informative calls) and/or a gift certificate from the telephone company.

- For someone who enjoys entertaining, a wonderful serving basket brimming with colorfully patterned or lavishly lace-trimmed napkins.

- For a hardworking couple, a new pocket or desk calendar or date book, with tickets to a special entertainment—and maybe a gift certificate for dinner—inside.

- For any adult, a book about a favorite hobby, craft or other subject, with a notice of prepaid tuition for a related class as the bookmark, or perhaps tickets to a visiting show or exhibition.

- For a child, a small change purse containing a book of passes to an ice cream parlor, hamburger chain, or miniature golf.

- For the recent retiree, a hammock and a subscription to a special leisure or travel magazine.

- For the homebound elderly or physically handicapped, a new radio or a television remote-control unit, along with a membership to a local educational television or radio station that sends monthly program listings; or a book accompanied by an automatic page turner or lighted magnifying glass; a telescoping magnet and reaching tongs; a fishing pole and a harness for one-handed fishing.

- For a grandparent, a wallet filled with lots of family photos.

- For the cook, a beautifully bound cookbook with a lucite cookbook holder or an apron.

- For the two-career family, a time-saving appliance and a book on time management.

- For a person living abroad or far away at holiday time, a small cassette-tape player accompanied by tapes from family and friends.

- For a Bar or Bat Mitzvah, a savings bond and a savings account book.

A commonplace and tasteful gift is a basket of fruit or gourmet food items. The enterprising giver, however, can invent more imaginative assemblages for various occasions:

- For the new homeowner, a box of household adhesives—Super Glue, masking tape, cellophane tape, Elmer's Glue-All, silicone sealer, duct tape, wood glue, electrical tape—and perhaps a friendly note that says "Let's stick together!"

- A large wastebasket filled with an assortment of high-quality paper products—notepaper, cocktail napkins, paper doilies in various sizes, shelf paper, wrapping and tissue paper, paperback books (on household hints or home management).

- For an ill or hospitalized person, a large satin or linen pillowcase containing a small bell, pajamas or gown, a paperback book or magazine, lip balm, lotion, and a pen or pencil with notepad. (For a maternity hospitalization, add a small bottle of champagne.)

- For the new dormitory or apartment dweller, a plastic container of nails, tacks, screws, picture hangers, studfinder, a small hammer, and a screwdriver.

- For moving day, an emergency kit containing Band-Aids, paper towels, paper cups, napkins, soap, scissors, rags, all-purpose cleaner, pen and notepad, and instant coffee supplies.

- For children (and parents) going on a car trip, a small cooler packed with origami book and paper, comic books, small games, hand puppets, and crayons and coloring books.

- For the newly promoted manager, a collection of desk accessories and organizers.

- A wooden crate or a basket filled with ingredients for a noteworthy meal—pasta, sauces, mushrooms, cheeses, wine, and maybe an Italian cookbook; or go Chinese and put appropriate foods in a large wok. (If you like, include a handwritten copy of a favorite recipe.)

- In a gardening basket: garden gloves, sun hat, knee pads, markers, and some special seeds or bulbs.

- Inside a copper kitchen pan: a recipe holder, recipe box, recipe cards, and plastic sleeves for the cards.

- For the college student or close friend moving far away, a plastic crate or storage container filled with stationery (some addressed to you and stamped), a roll of stamps, stamped postcards, an assortment of occasion cards, and an address book (with important addresses filled in).

"A Portion of Thyself"

A gift that you have made is usually a welcome gesture. As a token of your inventive skill and imagination it can be infinitely adapted to suit individual tastes and preferences.

For most active people, making gifts is not always possible, and the options are not very elegant when contrasted with the quality and quantity of handmade items you can buy. We may agree with Emerson that "the only true gift is a portion of thyself," but most of us cannot find the time to do all that is demanded of us today. You can, however, produce many desirable gifts with relative ease and inexperience. I'm not suggesting that you make cookie jars from coffee cans, bake your own yeast breads, construct bird feeders from milk cartons, or create dough ornaments or felt backgammon sets. I *am* envisioning exotic vinegars in attractive bottles, potted Stilton cheese in an interesting crock, or a miniature herb garden.

The concept is not to create a product from "scratch," but to enhance a product, then package it more attractively. Although this is more easily accomplished with foods, there are other items that can be transformed to "homemade" merely by repackaging.

Examples of distinctive "homemade" gifts of food include:

Potted Stilton (mashed with butter, moistened with port or
    Madeira, and pressed into a small pot or crock)
Garlicked or spiced olives (rebottled with herbs/spices/dressings)
Raisins in rum
Mulled cider mix
Herbed wine vinegars or raspberry vinegar
Flavored butters—caper, mustard-shallot, green peppercorn, dill
Brandied fruits
Stuffed dates
Flavored nuts—orange, chocolate, sugar, toasted, spiced
Liqueurs bottled with fresh fruit
Mayonnaise with capers or dill
Mustard with spices or champagne

And wondrous results can be achieved merely by repackaging:

- Place flavored coffees or teas in a charming teapot or new glass and brass coffeemaker.

- Repot small herb plants into a large terra cotta container for a miniature herb garden. Tie a gingham ribbon around the pot or basket.

- Repot a large rosemary plant (bush). As the meaning of rosemary is friendship, this gift has added significance.

- Design a miniature rock garden by making holes in a piece of feather rock (available in builders'-supply stores). Insert small plants from florist, garden, or woods.

- Place a mixture of delicatessen olives in a crock or bowl with sprigs of fresh herbs or leaves.

Special Touches

Certain gifts can be of lasting significance. They need not be extravagant or expensive. Most of these gifts are special because they are also gifts of ourselves. Such gifts can touch the heart because they are not necessary, conventional, or traditional, but do show special thoughtfulness. They are gestures of appreciation.

- Plant a tree at a local park, church, or school with your friend's name on a plaque.

- Write a poem, limerick, song, or story for someone.

- Ask an older member of your family to talk on tape about his childhood in another country, early remembrances of his parents, or other almost-forgotten bits of interesting family history. Send copies to family members.

- For the eightieth and subsequent birthdays, and fiftieth and subsequent anniversaries, request a card from the recipient's mayor, governor, or from the President. For the President's greeting, write four weeks in advance to Greetings Office, The White House, Washington, D.C. 20500. Include recipient's name, address, and date (including year) of birthday or anniversary.

- Arrange a surprise conference call with family or old friends.

- Prepare a calendar for the new year marked with all the birthdays, anniversaries, and special occasions of family and good friends.

- Give something that will remind the recipient of your thoughtfulness each month, week, or periodically throughout the year—subscriptions, memberships, Dessert of the Month (one to twelve month programs, 16633 Ventura Boulevard, Suite 550, Encino, California 91436 (818) 501–6363; toll free outside of California (800) 423–3091), pasta of the month, wine of the month, fruit of the month, chocolate of the month, bulb of the month—or offer to prepare a meal, wash a car, or drive someone somewhere each month for six months or a year.

- Arrange for a special sketch, painting, or photograph of a meaningful house, church, vacation spot, or pet.

- Prepare an elegant breakfast in bed (including all cleanup).

- Obtain a copy of a newspaper or magazine from the day of a birth or a wedding—if possible, from the same city.

- Tape, photograph, or video-record a party or celebration.

- Give a leatherbound, personalized atlas to the armchair traveler.

- Find an antique fish server set in its original box and have the server's blade engraved with the date of the occasion.

- Donate a particular book in someone's name to a local library, school, or church.

- Present a catalog and tuition for one week at Elderhostel (a program of more than four hundred colleges and universities in the United States and abroad that offers low-cost residential academic study in diverse areas for persons over sixty years of age and their spouses). The maximum weekly fee of $180 includes room, board, and tuition. (Elderhostel, Suite 200, 100 Boylston, MA 02116. $10 for year's catalog.)

- Order special stationery on laid paper with hand-set pedigreed type, printed on an antique letterpress, or engraved stationery on fine quality paper.

- Offer a charming gift certificate for an hour's ride in a refurbished antique carriage (with modern horse).

- Plant a tree in Israel in a Jewish child's name.

- Print "good for" cards or coupons that promise personal services such as baby-sitting or foot massage.

- Present a fluffy, luxurious monogrammed bath sheet in someone's favorite color.

- Give a proof set of coins or commemorative stamps issued the year of birth (a terrific gift for a new baby).

Remember that the addition of a legend that gives the history or concept of the gift and/or a personal message also helps to make it special.

The variety of ways to improve gift giving and the suggestions presented here are intended to provide a catalyst for your future gift giving. I hope that reading this chapter will inspire original ideas and make your giving more enjoyable.

INEXPENSIVE
GIFTS

Our materialistic society has trained us to equate the amount of money spent on a gift with its value to the recipient. But for an effective gift, timing, presentation, and a warm note are by far more significant than its actual cost.

The range of interesting, inexpensive gifts is almost endless and can be appropriate for every type of person and every age group. Inexpensive gifts can be extravagantly unessential or usefully utilitarian. Combining a related group of several small items can be a most effective solution for the person who is difficult to buy for; and a note explaining why or how you chose the gift gives it a special cachet.

Some suggestions to get you started—all available for under twenty-five dollars, and many for a lot less:

Humorous/Whimsical

A kaleidoscope
Fanciful kites with twine
"Money to burn"—fake wads that will burn for thirty minutes
Bright, attractive mittens in the shapes of animals
A dozen pencils with recipient's name, favorite saying, or logo
Realistic black or red rubber ants or spiders
Playing cards from interesting places (my favorites are from my brother's trip to Russia)
Set of miniature soldiers

Old medals
Gourmet pizza
Pens or pencils topped with dolls or woolly lambs
Jigsaw puzzles
A beautiful rock or mineral—a slice of geode or piece of crystal
Pajama pillow
Sand castle (the lasting ones you can buy in gift shops)
Wind-up toys
Pool games or toys
Balloons
Song books or sheet music
A dramatic fun mask
Paper napkins with recipient's name or name of boat or vacation
home

Little Luxuries

Antique, unique collectible buttons (try Tender Button, 143 E.
62nd Street, New York, NY 10021)
Football flask
Pine-scented balls for starting barbecues or fireplaces
Popcorn popper
Cedar shoe trees
Bath salts and oils, or scented soaps
Silk pocket squares for men or women
Linen hand towels
English shortbread and marmalade
Beautiful lace-edged linen handkerchief
Small leather agenda or diary
Crock or jar of special honey such as acacia
Earrings—wonderful gift for preteen and teenage girls
Candles—beeswax, scented, or wrapped raffia
Solar watch
Decorative lunchbox with thermos bottle
Straw packets or lush pillows filled with sachet
Bowl of potpourri
Egg cup (Royal Copenhagen sells a beautiful one for just seven-
teen dollars)
Great junk jewelry—check flea markets
Dinner bell
Jewelry case
Lingerie bags
Good scissors or shears

Padded hangers
Bath pillow or festive shower cap
Calligraphy pen and ink
Fan—decorative hand or functional electric
Wind chimes
Antique hat pin
One long-stemmed rose or perfect orchid
Brandy snifter

At Home or Away

Tool kit for glove compartment
Nightlight headgear for reading in bed
Sunglasses
Bookends—theme-related, or for office
Bottle of wine, port, or sherry
Travel iron or steamer
Unusual pancake mix with maple syrup
Pottery
Passport case
Stainless steel orange peeler
Basket of bulbs such as freesia
Belt buckles
Earthenware or glass pitcher
Bunch of dried spearmint, basil, or chamomile
Wreath of bay leaves
Ceramic boxes or handpainted tiles
Set of place-card holders
City guides and maps
Large serving tray
Wood for fireplace and long matches
TV tables
Bird feeder or bird house with supply of bird seed
Hickory or mesquite chips for barbecue
Tie rack
Travel clock
Decorative light plate switches
Watering can or garden hose
Sprayer or plant light for indoor plants
Model of recipient's favorite car or pet

EXTRAVAGANT
GIFTS

W hat is an extravagant gift?

Extravagance is extraordinary. Extravagance is hyperbole. Extravagance is immoderate. Extravagance is lavish. Extravagance is fun.

Extravagance can be excessive. Extravagance can be preposterous. Extravagance can be outrageous. Extravagance can be exorbitant. Extravagance can be wasteful. But extravagance should always be your own individual definition, your own idea of supreme indulgence.

Some extravagant gifts are uncommon gestures: Goethe's Dr. Faust contracted to give his soul to the devil, Mephistopheles, for the love of Margaret. There are memorial gifts such as the Taj Mahal (for the Mogul Shah Jahan's favorite wife, who died giving birth to her fourteenth child), or Joe DiMaggio's gift of fresh roses to Marilyn Monroe's grave three times a week. There are publicly noted extravagant gifts, such as Anna Jarvis's creation of Mother's Day in honor of her own mother, and the fortune James Smithson left to the United States in 1829, which founded the Smithsonian Institution. And there are privately extravagant gifts, such as when Della and Jim sacrificed what they held dearest for each other in O. Henry's famous story "The Gift of the Magi."

Some extravagant gifts are suited to significant occasions—the birth of a first grandchild, a special anniversary, a sweeping declaration of love, or a new invention. Donald Trump's gift of Mar-a-Lago

(Marjorie Merriweather Post's Palm Beach fantasy eighteen-acre estate and 110-room residence) to his wife, Ivana, was meant to be a symbol of his love and appreciation for her. The proper truly extravagant gift should not require great sacrifice of the giver or create any guilt feelings in the recipient. The giver of the perfect extravagant gift experiences great pleasure and delight.

Neiman-Marcus has for years created great interest in extravagant gift giving with its dramatic luxury catalog items and fantasy His & Hers gifts. From a black Angus steer and white mink cowboy chaps to His & Hers camels and Hoverbugs, this retailer has always excelled in finding the unusual and the extravagant.

There are, however, many ways to demonstrate extravagance. For example, giving a large quantity of anything can be a wonderfully extravagant statement. Portugal's prince regent put 120 goldsmiths and silversmiths to work for four years making a huge silver and gilt table service of more than a thousand pieces (the centerpiece itself is twenty-eight feet long) as a part of his thanks to the Duke of Wellington, who routed the French from Portugal in the early 1800s. One of Stanley Marcus's favorite gifts was the presentation of eighty Hermès ties for his eightieth birthday. However, a large quantity of something need not necessarily be expensive—for a young girl, a collection of hair ribbons in a profusion of colors and designs; for a couple with a garden full of aphids, a container filled with a million lady bugs; for a tea lover, an amazing variety of exotic teas; for a vegetable gardener, an array of catalogs and seed packets; for almost anyone, masses of flowers. . . .

"Extravagant" can also be defined as "rare." In sixteenth-century England, among all the golden objects, blazing gems, and embroidered mantles that were presented to Queen Elizabeth for New Year's, the rarest of them was what pleased her most—a pair of silk stockings. The most famous gifts of all—gold, frankincense, and myrrh borne to the Christ Child by the Wise Men—were notable for their rarity. All the jewels that Richard Burton purchased for Elizabeth Taylor were especially rare gems—the 33.9 carat Krupp diamond and the $1,050,000 Cartier-Burton diamond, as well as various sapphires and emeralds.

A custom-made or one-of-a-kind item can be most extravagant. Quality objects that are signed, numbered, hallmarked, or have other distinguishing features to mark them as limited in quantity often have great value. But those that are truly unique have the greatest potential as extravagant gifts. Diamond Jim Brady presented actress Lillian Russell with a gold-plated bicycle complete with mother-of-pearl handlebars and spokes encrusted with chips of diamonds, emeralds, rubies, and sapphires. When Miss Russell went on tour, the bicycle, kept in a blue plush-lined Morocco case, traveled with her. Artist Marc Chagall's gift to the Jewish people—twelve stained glass windows—was created for the synagogue of the Hadassah-Hebrew University Medical Center in Jerusalem. The first Imperial Easter Egg was commissioned from Fabergé by Alexander III. It was to look exactly like a real hen's egg on the outside, but actually contain a delightful surprise, a special gift for the empress. The egg's gold yolk held a colored hen inside which a tiny diamond imperial crown lay concealed; a miniature ruby egg was hung within this crown. Then, of course, there was the specially commissioned colossal statue presented to the United States by the people of France—our Statue of Liberty.

Another type of extravagance is the fun or fantasy gift. Why not a custom-made boat-shaped lamp based on a photograph of a dear one's boat? Rather than arranging an ordinary holiday, what about offering a journey around the world by luxury private jet for only thirty persons—a flying penthouse experiencing a different world each day. (Society Expeditions, in Seattle, Washington can provide this. (800) 426–7794) Fulfill a fantasy of training and playing baseball with the pros at spring training sites (several teams offer week-long packages) or a secret desire to star in a Western movie. Or purchase an island for someone special—from a tiny, uninhabitable haven to Marlon Brando's 17½-mile-long coral atoll near Tahiti composed of twelve islands—eleven of them unpopulated—a small hotel, and an airstrip (recently for sale at $1.5 million).

Some gifts are just out of this world—for the adventurous, a space-ship reservation to orbit Earth beginning in 1993 (Society Expeditions reports that reservations for 1992 are already filled). The recipient will receive a PROJECT SPACE VOYAGE registration certificate with priority number, flight number, and expected departure date, an information and documentation packet, a list of recommended reading and preparation, a current copy of the Countdown newsletter, and something to think and talk about for the next ten years.

Rules for extravagant gifts:

- Do not give such a gift unless you feel entirely comfortable about it (this includes financial considerations).

- Be certain that the gift is presented at the appropriate time and in a suitable place.

- Do not be afraid to make a spontaneous, extravagant gesture.
- Do not confuse extravagance with ostentation unless that is your goal.

To give you some idea of the range of gifts that would—in most circumstances—be extravagant, I've listed below some that my clients have recently either given or received.

Custom footwear, with made-to-measure wooden last

Special or custom-made umbrella or umbrella handle with fabric to be chosen; handles of silver, carved rosewood, ebony, ash, chestnut, or rhinoceros horn—sticks can be measured to fit the client

Suit of armor from a master couturier of ironwork

Hot-air balloon with carpeting, cellular telephone, wet bar, radio, and television

Teakwood enclosed bath that creates various environments—dry heat, tropical breezes, steam, misting rain—and has whirlpool jets, shower heads, and sun lamps

Sport Sub, a recreational underwater vehicle for five people; the submarine, which has plastic bubbletop windows, can go down 250 feet for two to ten hours and travels at one to two knots per hour

Twenty or more ounces of pure foie gras in a porcelain pâté box

Individualized canvas floor cloths (colorful, stenciled, painted, and sealed—will do various designs to match color samples) by Joan Dworkin (212) 661–0006, by appointment

A life-size replica of Rome's Trevi Fountain erected in the backyard of your choice

Long-stemmed red roses delivered each week for a year

A car "stretched" to a limo and customized with anything from Baccarat crystal and oriental rugs to VCR and color television

New full-size carousel horse carved out of solid oak or a restored old one

Buy or charter (for a special dinner or trip) a reconditioned and refurbished "varnish"—old private wooden railroad car complete with chandeliers

Liveried butler/waiter/maid for a special occasion

Designed and stocked wine cellar

A week at a health spa

Fulfilled-fantasy gifts—cut your own record with back-up band; appear on stage at the Met

Lease a billboard or wall and have your message painted on it

Electronic desk blotter with calculator, clock, and telephone with digital readout

Robot with talking cassettes, which can be programmed for
  seven days
Electrically heated towel rack
Ultralight airplane
Automatic crepe maker
A musical work commissioned from an accomplished composer
Hire a landscape architect (for an herb garden) or an outside
  lighting design specialist
Rent Princess Margaret's or Lord Lichfield's vacation home on
  the island of Mustique
For a yacht—custom-designed nautical rug or catered gourmet
  meals
Hand-sculpted pipe with specified theme such as science, sports,
  or technology
Custom-designed illusions or magic show
D. Porthault linens
Restored antique stove or range
Telescope—the most powerful one for amateurs (nine feet tall
  with an eighteen-inch aperture) has magnification powers
  in excess of 1,000
Custom-made, hand-crafted sneakers
Rent an Irish castle for a week, complete with antiques, art,
  staff of eight, and exclusive salmon-fishing rights
"Starlight scope"—small binoculars for seeing in the dark, amplifies
  light by over 40,000 times and can be attached to cameras
  for night photography
A 12,000-piece, 5½' x 8' jigsaw puzzle
Custom-made, individualized weather-prediction system
Workaholic's bed—a mahogany bed with shelves, attached table,
  adjustable headboard, lights, and two swinging/pivoting
  tables that tilt up
Radio-controlled toy submarine for the swimming pool
Sky-written message
Caviar in crystal server
An Early American log cabin dollhouse, outfitted with furniture,
  wrapped Christmas gifts and a tiny gingerbread house
Larger-than-life mythical topiary figures for the garden
A full-length feature movie or mini-series about the recipient's life
Limited edition, authentic handcrafted reproduction sword, i.e.,
  Sam Houston's
Rent a cruise ship for a week
A housculpture—handmade miniature replica of one's private
  home, complete with shrubs and snow

Personalized, handcrafted notecards from Posh Papers (Liberace's had a chandelier on a grand piano, complete with rhinestones and sequins)

An aristocratic title ($15,000–25,000 for an English lordship—Lord of the Manor)

A 155 square-foot American yurt

Some of the most interesting lavish gifts are those that include trips. There are long (twenty-four days) journeys on the Trans-Siberian Railroad from Paris to Peking, arriving in Peking for a special banquet; there are short (three-hour) trips to an Alaskan glacier for a feast of grilled salmon in a green valley rimmed by mountains; there are luxury cruises to Pacific islands; there are culinary adventures with famous chefs in the French countryside.

One of my clients—a very wealthy couple who had recently retired—wanted to celebrate their thirty-fifth wedding anniversary in a special, unusual way. He wanted to find her a unique piece of jewelry or gem; she wanted to take him on a lengthy trip to places they had never before had time to visit. Their gift to each other was a trip that began near famous diamond mines, where they were entertained by the owners and selected a magnificent stone; then they went to the Netherlands to discuss the cutting of the stone with a well-known stone cutter; finally they went to Paris, where the setting was designed by a world-famous jeweler. It turned out to be the perfect extravagant gift in all respects. And the piece of jewelry is a constant reminder of an unforgettable gift.

PART TWO

AMERICAN GIFT GIVING HOLIDAYS

TRADITIONAL AMERICAN GIFT GIVING HOLIDAYS

Amerian holidays are a fascinating mixture of customs, traditions, festivals, and celebrations from all over the world. Some occasions are a combination of the religious and the pagan; some have deep meaning for the celebrants, while others are primarily social occasions. Many American holidays include special meals, festivities, and family, national, or ethnic traditions; several involve the giving or exchange of gifts.

Saint Valentine's Day—February 14
(not a legal holiday)

The day Americans celebrate as Valentine's Day was originally a Roman festival called Lupercalia. The festival was celebrated on February 14—the day on which birds were said to begin mating. It was a popular custom during the celebration for each young man to draw the name of a young woman from a box of names: these two would become "sweethearts" for the duration of Lupercalia.

Much later the name of the holiday was changed to honor two Christian saints, both of whom were named Valentine. One of the most popular of the Valentine legends is about the Christian martyr of the third century who was a champion of "true love." When the Roman emperor needed soldiers, he passed a law against marriage because he believed that matrimony kept men at home. Despite the law, Priest Valentine secretly married many couples. He was discovered, imprisoned, and condemned to death. Even in prison, young Valentine continued to demonstrate love and compassion for everyone he met. He performed many miracles, including the healing of his jailer's blind daughter. On February 14, just before his death, he wrote her a special message, which he signed simply "from your Valentine."

Modern Valentine's Day is a time when people express love to sweethearts, family, and friends. This is traditionally done with Valentines—printed or handmade cards containing an affectionate greeting. The message may be amorous, sentimental, or humorous. Many Valentine decorations still carry the ancient Roman symbol of love—the cupid with his bow and love arrows; and red hearts with lacy white trim are a time-honored custom. Many people exchange small gifts, the most popular of which are boxes of candy (often heart-shaped) and flowers that men give to women. Schoolchildren celebrate in their classrooms, usually by placing Valentines for their friends into a "Valentine Box," which is opened at the end of the school day—similar to the pagan Lupercalia custom of drawing names. Romantic dances and parties are popular with young people. Lovers who wish to remain anonymous sign their cards "from your Valentine." (For more special suggestions on Valentine giving, turn to page 44.)

Easter

An annual church celebration commemorating Christ's Resurrection, Easter is the first Sunday after the full moon on or next after the vernal equinox. If the full moon falls on Sunday, Easter is observed one week later. Thus, Easter may fall anytime between March 22 and April 25. Easter is the oldest and most significant Christian festival because it celebrates the supreme message of Christianity—the Resurrection of Jesus Christ. Christians, worldwide, renew their faith at this time.

For many Christians the season begins with Lent—the forty-day period prior to Easter, beginning with Ash Wednesday. Lent is a time of self-denial and self-examination, often accompanied by fasting.

Typical Easter gifts relate in some way to the concepts of rebirth or springtime: the egg, the chicken, the bunny, or rabbit. Flowers, especially the white Easter lily (Madonna lily), are symbols of the season.

Prior to Easter Sunday, children color and decorate eggs for their friends and family—some are hard-boiled; others are empty blown shells. On Easter morning children find Easter baskets at the foot of their beds. The busy Easter Bunny has filled them with candy eggs, chocolate bunnies, and tiny fuzzy stuffed chicks, all on a bed of paper grass. Special treats such as stuffed animals, dolls, or a model truck are sometimes included. The Easter Bunny has been known to hide eggs in homes or lawns for children to find. The annual White House Easter-egg-rolling event is often televised.

Easter is an occasion for giving flowers—potted plants, corsages, bouquets—to those you care for. Many churchgoers donate special flowers to their churches at this time. Confectioners tempt gift givers with elegantly decorated eggs of chocolate, spun sugar, and marzipan. Although children are the major recipients, adults often exchange greeting cards and small gifts.

Easter has traditionally been a time for gifts to children of live chicks, ducks, and bunny rabbits. Many of these animals are mishandled by children who are too young to care properly for them. Please consider before giving a surprise gift of a pet to anyone, as arrangements for post-Easter care must be made.

May Day—May 1

Although not a widely observed holiday, May Day is sometimes celebrated by children who dance around a maypole and crown the Queen of the May with garlands. Unfortunately, the custom of filling baskets with spring flowers and leaving them on the doorsteps of friends and neighbors—one of my fondest childhood memories—is rarely practiced today. The May basket is certainly one of the most delightful and felicitous holiday gifts, and a tradition that you may want to make your own as I have.

In Germany, Russia, and many other European countries May Day is observed as Labor Day.

Mother's Day—The Second Sunday in May

The ancient English custom known as "Mothering Sunday" at various times celebrated mothers from Mother Nature to Mother Church. The English rural custom today is to visit one's parents with an offering or gift on Mid-Lent Sunday.

Founded through the efforts of Anna Jarvis of Philadelphia, the day was designated for the honoring of motherhood in the United States by President Woodrow Wilson in 1914. Many churches hold special Mother's Day services; memorial wreaths and flowers are placed on mothers' graves. The American customs of celebrating this day have spread to countries all over the world—especially to those in Europe; however, it is celebrated at different times of the year.

On this day each year most people express their love for their mothers by some act of remembrance. Children, and sometimes grand-children, select appropriate cards and presents. Flowers, candy, and pretty, feminine gifts are most popular. Mother is usually treated to a special dinner on this day. Breakfast in bed is a wonderful luxury—if dishes and kitchen clean-up are included as part of the gift.

Mothers treasure especially anything that their children have made for them—no matter their ages. From my son's gift at age four of a brown clay elephant that resembles an anteater, to my daughter's professional "double image" photograph of an intricate grillwork design last year, most of the gifts I remember (and save) have been from my children.

Other especially thoughtful gifts could range from a home hairdresser's appointment or "day of beauty" to magazine subscriptions. If you live far from your mother and she complains about the infrequency of your calls and letters, you could arrange a gift certificate from the phone company for her to call you, or you could promise to call or write her on a regularly scheduled basis. If you live with her or nearby, coupons for chores or special outings are a welcome gift.

Father's Day—The Third
Sunday in June

President Woodrow Wilson officially balanced the days of recognition given to moms and dads by declaring Father's Day in 1916.

Many, many neckties, belts, and gallons of cologne ago, a widowed Civil War veteran named William Smart inspired his daughter to propose "Father's Day." Sonora Smart Dodd of Spokane, Washington, believed that her father had raised his six children with a devotion that would no doubt daze today's Mr. Mom. When suffragette Jane Addams heard Mrs. Dodd's idea for a national celebration equal to that of Mother's Day, she worked to have a day designated a national tribute to fathers.

Today, Father's Day is celebrated in more than twenty foreign countries with church services, cards, and gifts.

More than $1 billion annually is spent on the nation's 56 million favored fathers. However, little originality goes into the selecting of the 19 million neckties and 97 million cigars that American fathers receive each Father's Day. Most people say that gifts for their fathers are the most difficult they buy. Yet, there are many interesting and appropriate items that men will enjoy.

That first honored father probably would not have needed, at the turn of the century, a rowing machine or an underwater camera, but some of today's dads will love them. There are gifts for the workaholic dad—thermal carafe for his desk, membership to a nearby museum or health club, lighted magnifying glass, portable gym. For the father with a workshop—an encyclopedia of hardware, a course in woodworking, heavy-duty work gloves, or power tape measure. For the elderly—membership in AARP (1909 K. Street N.W., Washington, D.C. 20049), bathtub safety railing, large-print book or newspaper subscriptions, terrarium, or books on cassette tape.

Halloween (All Hallows' Eve)—The Evening of October 31

The most "be-witching" night of the year brings ghosts, goblins, spooks, pirates, visitors from other planets, and witches to our front doors.

In pre-Christian times the Celts celebrated the summer's end with a ceremony to thank and honor the sun. Their Druid priests also lit huge bonfires and performed magic rites to ward off the unfriendly witches, ghosts, and other spirits that were believed to be roaming the Earth. Later, the Roman Harvest Festival with its gifts of nuts and apples merged with the October 31 traditions of the Celts.

During the Middle Ages, animal costumes and frightening masks were worn to ward off the evil spirits of darkness on the evening preceding All Hallows' or All Saints' Day. This day was dedicated to all Christian martyrs and saints who had died.

Even though Christianity replaced the Druid and Roman religions, many of the early customs remained and are still practiced. Today it is with a sense of fun (and sometimes mischief) that children wear fantasy costumes and attend Halloween parties where paper witches, black cats, ghosts, and skeletons may decorate the walls. Often they bob for apples. Grinning or frightening jack-o'-

lanterns, carved from pumpkins and lit from the inside by candles, can be seen in windows and on doorsteps.

Children in the United States and Canada who dress in costumes are expected to ring their neighbors' doorbells with the customary threat "trick or treat." The neighbors, who may or may not be frightened by these strangely attired and masked creatures, have usually prepared gifts of candy, apples, cookies, or other treats, which the children collect in their bags. It is a newer tradition—for safety reasons—to offer fast-food restaurant or ice-cream coupons, small toys, rubber spiders and insects, or other nonfood items.

Thanksgiving Day—The Fourth Thursday in November

Thanksgiving is a gift giving holiday in three respects: most Americans give thanks to God for His bounty over the past year; we treat our families and friends to a traditional seasonal feast; and we give gifts of food to those who are hungry.

The first Thanksgiving was observed in 1621 by the remaining members of the Plymouth, Massachusetts, colony who had come from England on the *Mayflower*. The sixty who had survived the hard winter invited Chief Massasoit of the Wampanoag Indians (with whom they had negotiated a treaty) to share their first harvest. To their astonishment, he arrived with ninety brilliantly attired, hungry braves! Clearly, there was not enough food for everyone. So the Indians disappeared, soon returning with several deer and other provisions. The feast, consisting of wild turkeys, geese, ducks, oysters, clams, roasted corn, corncakes, cranberries, fruit, and apple cider, lasted for three days.

Thanksgiving has been regularly observed by most Americans since President Abraham Lincoln proclaimed it a national holiday in 1863. It is a time when families gather to give thanks and praise to God for the mercies and blessings of the year past. Both Americans and Canadians (in September) celebrate Thanksgiving with a feast that usually centers around a roasted turkey, duck, or goose stuffed with dressing. Other traditional foods are cranberries, oysters, apples, nuts, corn, and pies. Often guests who are far from home and family are invited, and food is donated to those who are less fortunate. Local agencies, schools, and churches collect food and distribute baskets to the needy of the community. Some businesses also give turkeys to employees or favored customers.

Christmas Eve and Day
(December 24 and 25)

Christmas, the most widely celebrated birthday in the Western World, recalls the birth of Christ in a stable at Bethlehem of Judaea in the days of Herod the King. Christians believe that Christ—God's only begotten Son—is God's supreme gift; and everyone who counts his days, months, and years by the Gregorian calendar is using Christ's birth as an historical starting point—A.D. (*anno Domini*—"in the year of our Lord") or, for events before his birth, B.C. ("before Christ").

Americans, with their many diverse heritages, celebrate this season in many different ways. Common ingredients are church services, family reunions, concerts, parties, greeting cards, hospitality, and gifts. Because sharing should come naturally to people who share Christ's love, Christians give to family, loved ones, friends, the hungry, and the homeless. They experience special joy in the act of giving at this holiday time. Often the Nativity scene is re-created (when the people and animals come to worship the baby Jesus). Some families open their gifts to one another on Christmas Eve; others wait until Christmas Day.

The season's spirit of giving is also represented in the mythical Santa Claus (or Father Christmas), who spends all year making toys for children in his workshop at the North Pole. On Christmas Eve he lands on housetops with his reindeer, slides down the chimneys, and leaves packages beneath decorated Christmas (pine) trees and small gifts in the children's stockings. In addition to Christmas trees, the season's decorations include evergreens, the colors red, green, gold, and silver, reindeer, holly wreaths, mistletoe, poinsettia plants, and snowmen. Traditional Christmas feasts feature turkey or goose, plum pudding, and fruit cake.

ROMANTIC
VALENTINE'S DAY
GIFTS

Probably the most distinctive gift offerings through the ages have been prompted by love—most of them from men to women. Husbands have sought rare jewels with which to adorn their wives; mistresses have been rewarded with everything from palaces to gilded bicycles; and some of the greatest masterworks have been created especially for a lady—a portrait by Goya for the Duchess of Alba, Keats's sonnets for his beloved Fanny Browne, Wagner's *Siegfried Idyll* for his wife.

A few other opulent examples:

Süleyman the Magnificent, ruler of the Ottoman Empire, first gave a beloved Russian slave her freedom as a love offering. Then he married her, making her empress. (I hope she cared for him.)

When Mark Antony expressed surprise at the opulence of a banquet Cleopatra had prepared for him, she dropped two pearls of great value into her wine. Drinking the concoction to his health, she insisted that her tribute to and feelings for him far surpassed the cost of the feast. Later, he presented her with Cyprus, Phoenicia, and parts of Arabia, Judea, and other areas—a grand gesture with more acreage than Texas and Alaska combined.

Elizabeth Barrett Browning gave her famous *Sonnets From The Portuguese* to her husband, Robert, after their son was born. These beautiful love poems were her most unique salute to their developing love and friendship.

In the early years of his marriage to his beautiful Creole wife Josephine, Napoleon lavished her with affection. Later, when he became emperor, he made up for his lack of interest by lavishing her with gifts (a not uncommon occurrence). One of the most magnificent of these was a tiara with 880 diamonds. (When he denounced her four years later, he allowed her to keep it.)

Gestures like these notwithstanding, how does one find a love gift that will be irresistible? If you truly care for someone, why is finding a gift to show it so difficult? And is it really true that "little gifts maintain friendship; great ones maintain love"?

Valentine's gifts are meant to be tokens of love, esteem, friendship, affection. As such, it seems inappropriate to give something entirely practical, such as a dish drainer and ironing board (don't laugh, it happened to me), or car wax. It is always more important to be romantic than clever.

Flowers are surely the most romantic gift of all. By nature, they are impractical and extravagant. The recipient cannot help but be flattered by their beauty and scent. And if you forgot, they can always be wired at almost the last minute (FTD has Valentine's sales of over $17 million per year). Although few lovers are aware of the ancient lore of flowers, almost every variety carries with it a special message: ferns signify sincerity; daisies mean "I'm thinking about you"; peach blossoms stand for love and beauty; purple flowers tell the recipient that you are her/his love slave or captive; and, of course, red roses mean passion. Flowering plants or the special gesture of a bush, tree, or garden that both of you can enjoy is especially intriguing if there is still snow on the ground. The gift of one beautiful, well-presented flower can be just as romantic and thoughtful as the quintessential "love-o-gram"—a New York firm (Pellicce Bascardi) provides an ankle-length Blackglama mink cape wrapped around an exotic floral arrangement. This unusual gift also includes a year's worth of weekly bouquets and a jar of beluga caviar in each pocket.

Emperor Montezuma wasn't the only one to use chocolate as an aphrodisiac. Most of the more than 570 million boxes of candy purchased for last Valentine's Day were bought as last-minute gifts on the afternoon or evening of February 14. Chocolate in itself connotes luxury, love—even sin. And one theory claims that one of its ingredients, phenylethylamine, does imitate the hormonal effects of being in love. (The average American devours ten pounds per year; I gobble about 30.) Chocolate choices are almost endless: hearts filled with chocolate creams, a milk-chocolate ring in a velvet box ($5.00 at E.A.T. Gifts, 1062 Madison Avenue, New York, N.Y.), chocolate cards inscribed with messages in their own gift crates (Kron–212–486–0265 in New York) your love's portrait etched in chocolate from a photograph—or how about a gift box of twenty-four gold-wrapped replicas of *your* face for him or her?—(Chocolate Portraits, 200 W. 57th St., Suite 1150, N.Y. 10019) chocolate-dipped strawberries, chocolate long-stemmed roses in dark, milk, or white chocolate (Rowe Manse Emporium, Route 3 & Bloomfield Ave., Clifton, N.J. (201–472–8170), or Kahlua truffles. The combining trick works well here, too. Give a hot chocolate set with two mugs or cups along with the chocolate and fixings or include a year's subscription to a chocolate newsletter with your candy.

An amusing gift of a favorite food (your lover's other love) is always a possibility. Many foods are available in heart shapes or can be made into or put into heart-shaped containers. For instance, does he or she adore fresh mozzarella? It's available or can be ordered in a heart shape. Place it on a lace doily and offer it with bottles of wine vinegar, extra-virgin olive oil, olives, and a mill full of peppercorns.

A fragrance is a romantic and sensual choice. The world of scentology tells us that we can convey almost any message through our choice of scent. If you are giving a cologne or perfume, it is best to select the recipient's favorite. Don't try something new unless there is a reason—he or she has expressed a desire for something else or you especially enjoy a particular scent. Remember that fragrances smell somewhat different on each person. Bath powders and oils, if appropriate, need not "match" the recipient's regular perfume. Potpourri, sachets, candles, and other scented items are sentimental and long-lasting remembrances. Entire baskets of luxurious bath items, including candles and white chocolate potato chips, can be ordered from companies such as Baskets Extraordinaire, (212–496–9510).

It is especially flattering to give a gift that you can enjoy together—a joint health club or other type of membership, a romantic trip together (to a botanical garden, a museum, an island), a picnic basket outfitted for two, a quiet candlelit dinner, a course or seminar. These gifts are well-suited to combining with, for instance, a desk calendar or agenda with a dinner date written in on the 14th.

Jewelry—especially gold (Cartier has an 18k gold bracelet which, once fastened shut, can only be removed with a special screwdriver)—champagne (hopefully with two crystal flutes) and caviar, designer Michael Katz's individually designed shawls with Valentine messages (available through Bergdorf Goodman, New York), and the hiring of a limo for a night on the town are other typical love gifts of the expensive variety. The budget-minded, enterprising giver can compete with beautiful, old-fashioned lace-trimmed Valentines, a special bottle of wine, an enormous bath towel emblazoned with monogrammed satin hearts, a special book of poetry, a selection of bulbs for planting, and even love ice—bright red plastic trays that produce heart-shaped ice cubes. However, breakfast in bed with a special rose and heart-shaped waffles or strawberry jam and croissant should prove irresistible to most romantics.

The most welcome gift of love, however, is probably a simple note to your beloved describing in delightful detail just how and why he or she is loved.

CHRISTMAS—
THE PLEASURES OF
GIVING

The ideal holiday season is one of both reflection and celebration—a time when giving should be as pleasurable as it is meaningful and at least as gratifying as receiving. A gift that is meant to please another and to foster the spirit of the season need not exhaust you or your checkbook. Thoughtfulness and imagination can enable you to find gifts that range from the fanciful to the near-frugal— all imparting the true meaning of Christmas.

Yes, I will point out that the well-organized giver is more efficient and that planning ahead (by finding appropriate items during summer sales or on vacation or business trips) is easier. You expected me to, didn't you? And right now you are thinking about Great-Aunt Ellen, who always superciliously finishes her Christmas shopping before August. How infuriating! I do agree that some of the Christmas spirit surely escapes between August and December and that Aunt Ellen may be missing some holiday atmosphere. But she *has* finished her shopping.

The best way to go about it—whenever you do it—is to make a categorized list: your family, your immediate family, your spouse's immediate family, business associates, friends, peripheral family, service personnel or those who deserve special tips, and any others. You may wish to designate a maximum sum for each gift so that you will be able to keep within your budget. It is also important to denote in some manner those persons to whom your gifts must be sent—

especially if overseas. I send so many gifts far from home that I usually must purchase them on my first shopping spree to ensure their arrival before Christmas. If you are shopping from a catalog, inquire to be certain that your gift is in stock and will arrive at its destination by Christmas. Personalized or mongrammed gifts from a catalog or store need extra time.

Christmas is *the* time to make your own presents. From a loaf of bread to a framed silhouette to a photograph of someone's child or house, this gift is from the heart as well as the hands and brings meaning, friendship, and love to the season. (See p. 15, "Easy Ways to Make Your Gift Giving Special.")

Many gifts are uniquely Christmas. Season's greetings and blessings are conveyed with certain gifts: Christmas candles—or candles of red, green, white, gold, or silver; Christmas music—recordings, discs, tapes, perhaps by a harpist or cellist from your local symphony, or a classical guitarist, tickets to *The Messiah* or *The Nutcracker*; for families, elegant editions of holiday books—*A Christmas Carol, A Visit From Saint Nicholas, A Children's Christmas In Wales* (Dylan Thomas) *A Christmas Memory* (Truman Capote), and others; Christmas motif platters, mugs, glasses, place settings; festive gifts decorated with gold or silver—picture frames, glass plates, a Christmas wall hanging, centerpiece, or bell pull, a crèche set, a calendar, desk planner, or diary for the coming year; gilt ornaments or decorative accessories, Advent calendar, individual Christmas stockings, card holder, or terra cotta cherubs or candle holders. There are a few unique items you can find, such as a box of designer apples with "Merry Christmas" or your choice of custom message on the skin of each apple—messages are placed on the apple while it reddens, thus leaving the message in apple white (Apple Attractions, Inc., P.O. Box V, 7 S.E. State St., Tonasket, WA 98855 or call (800) MY–APPLE, or in WA (800) 824–5836)! Traditionalists adore Christmas presents from Christmases past: antique tree ornaments, old baubles such as unusual perfume bottles or crystal decanters, or vintage glass pens and ink wells. The annual White House Christmas Ornament ($9.75 from the White House Historical Association, postage included) which hangs in a prominent place on the White House Christmas tree in the Blue Room each year, is always special and accompanied by an explanatory brochure.

Some Christmas gifts should appropriately arrive *before* Christmas for maximum enjoyment, making them particularly special and remembered—a Christmas tree, plain and undecorated, a box of Christmas greens, a small tree especially for a child's room, a seasonal arrangement or plant, a wreath, or a bouquet of mistletoe, perhaps with candles. A gift certificate from a florist or nursery for a choice of Christmas decorations is a wonderful idea. A gift certificate for a hair styling, day of beauty, massage, or foot reflexology will soothe the exhausted during the hectic season. How about a promise of garlands for the staircase whenever they want it, or a professional gift wrapper (or even you) who will go to the house one day or evening with papers, ribbons, cards, and tape to wrap all gifts (some even wrap and decorate packages to match the home's Christmas decor). Of course, some of these are also marvelous gifts to yourself.

We are all looking for something special for someone special. Amid all the rush and bustle of Christmas, it is particularly thoughtful to give a gift that will last throughout the year: a membership in a museum, radio or TV channel, symphony, opera, dance, health club, sports club, hobby association, garden or botanical club, or business group; a "something-of-the-month"— plant bulbs, pasta, fruit, chocolate, flowers, cheese, or dessert; or a year's subscription to an unusual magazine. This gift has the added advantage of renewal—*if* it has been a successful choice. It's also a good choice for matching present to personality.

Other ideas that will work for most people and are easy to find: elegant picture frames, a fluffy white down comforter, linen cocktail or dinner napkins, well-designed cooking equipment and utensils, crystal vase with fresh flowers, thick white thirsty towels or bath sheets, a lightweight afghan, special gloves, socks, slippers, or legwarmers (for those you know well), or a beautiful book.

You say it's December 23, and you're desperately flipping through this book looking for ideas—suggestions—anything. Help is *here*.

First, you must acknowledge that your real fear—and that of most last-minute shoppers—is not so much lack of time or money as it is lack of inspiration. Second, believe that last-minute gifts can be as special as those you found in the Souk on your last trip to Saudi Arabia. You can probably accomplish all with two stops—a general bookstore and a large drugstore. From one coffee-table book to a beribboned stack of paperbacks to a beautiful blank book to theme calendars, there are few ages, types, or needs that cannot be well met with appropriate reading/picture material. And art books of all kinds will satisfy the intellectual needs of many. For some people, a gift certificate from a bookstore is the ultimate gift. As for the drugstore, it's filled with surprising treasures—the latest electronic instruments, appliances, and gadgets, probably the smaller the more interesting; cosmetics, including sets of makeup brushes, lighted mirrors, traveling cosmetic cases, bath oils and scented soaps, pocket calculators, marbles, jumping jacks, sports equipment, dresser sets, playing cards, pocket flashlights, magnetic memo holders, small-size shampoo, hand lotion, etc., for travelers, aftershave lotions, bookmarks, photos of self taken in booth plus frame, notecards and stamps, perfumes and colognes, decorated toothbrushes, soap sculptures, cassette tapes, fancy shoelaces and hair ribbons, baskets to fill with collections, wrapping paper, ribbon, ornaments and cards, stocking stuffers, toys and stuffed animals, sweatsuits, loofahs, toy banks, and desk accessories. These items, and many more, can be quickly packaged or wrapped and presented beautifully: place bath oil, loofah, cologne, sponge, nail brush, and colorful shower cap or bath pillow in a lovely basket (maybe with a paperback book for bath lovers)—quick, easy, special, luxurious, and very last-minute.

Food and drink have always been excellent last-minute gifts— easy to order or obtain, enjoyed by most, and usually simple to send quickly. There are few people who do not like to receive gifts of food. Rather than the classic gifts of cheese, fruit, or smoked turkey, try fresh apple cider poured into a wonderful earthenware pitcher—maybe accompanied by a packet of herbs for mulled cider. One of my favorites is exotic herbs or spices beautifully packaged—I buy a supply of Hediard's combination of white, black, and gray peppercorns for friends whenever I'm in Paris. Other possibilities: your own creation of bread, cookies, candies, preserves, pickles; Christmas sweets such as a Christmas pudding with a bottle of port; a collection of ice cream toppings; olives and good olive oil; fresh pasta; a collection of cocktail tidbits or beluga with ivory spoons. You can also call Nationwide Gift Liquor to send a favorite brand of wine, liquor, or champagne to anyplace in the United States where it is legal (in a few states, for example, you cannot send hard liquor); Western Union will deliver regular or singing telegrams; balloon companies can send a colorful bouquet attached to a selected gift; Eastern Onion will provide an assortment of songs to be delivered by phone or by a costumed person. Consult your local phone directory for other quick message services.

Other last-minute inspirations that work wonderfully: a brunch or supper for friends the day *after* Christmas (when no one has any energy, spirit, or will to cook)—call on Christmas Eve or even on Christmas Day if you're that late; send a Christmas breakfast or brunch to your friends—croissants, jams, specially ground coffee or herbal teas, gorgeous fruit, possibly even a jar of fresh eggs and some black truffles; write a meaningful letter, poem, or limerick; invite guest(s) to join you for a Christmas Eve church service or family gathering; or give a gift certificate for Christmas or New Year's dinner for two or for a family, a gift certificate for a bush, tree, plant, or bulbs for the spring, or a pair of tickets to a holiday special event.

Finally, that holiday nightmare: you totally forgot someone. Don't send a reciprocal gift a few days later and pretend that you ordered it early but it arrived late. A classier approach is to send something special for New Year's Day—or even wait until Chinese New Year's or Groundhog Day for a memorable remembrance.

A SPECIAL NOTE: While Christmas shopping, treat yourself to a gift. You deserve it. I've always thought how lovely it would be to find in the middle of a large department store at Christmastime a soft, comfortable haven where I could take off my shoes and relax, surrounded by small luxuries that would pick up my spirits—fuzzy slippers, beautiful scarves, blankets of aromatic bath things, a wild pair of costume earrings, silk lingerie, an evening bag, wonderful gloves, silver trinkets and boxes, herbal teas, baskets of lavender and thyme, leather address books and agendas, a feather fan, patés. . . .

PART THREE

OCCASION GIFTS

BIRTHS
AND CHRISTENINGS

Gifts for a baby shower or birth are generally more practical or immediately useful than those given for a christening. Baby showers can take place before or after the birth and today may include men as well as women. Often, when the event is a social occasion for both men and women, the gifts are not opened at the party as is usual at more traditional showers. A shower after the baby is born allows the mother to introduce her baby and to see her friends during a period when she may not have much time for socializing.

Although baby shower and birth gifts are usually not expensive, friends or relatives may combine their resources to give major equipment that the parents will need, such as a playpen and pad, changing table, infant seat, high chair, car seat, or carriage (some convert to strollers). If you are buying an important gift or baby furniture, tell the parents or send or bring it immediately so that they will not duplicate your gift. Because babies wear little formal clothing for the first few months and because they grow so quickly, it is appropriate—often preferable—to give clothes for the baby's first or second year: one should usually double the age (for 6-month-old child, a "12-month" shirt).

Usually it is more difficult to come up with gift ideas for the second or third child—especially if they are of the same gender. However, this list should help you think of some new ideas:

Crib toys and mobiles
Crib blanket or comforter
Receiving blankets
Bath toys or puppet washcloths
Subscription to *American Baby* or *Parents*
Fitted crib sheets and pad
Crib gym
Baby bath towels and washcloths
Night light
Shoulder burp pad
Food mill or grinder
Baby's eating utensils, plate and mug, and weighted-base cup
Unbreakable mirror
Bunting
Baby clothes hangers
Vaporizer
Music box
Baby pillow and cases
Clothing
Bibs
Bottle warmer
Diaper bag
Snowsuit
Baby carrier such as backpack or Snugli sling
Small soft toys, rattle or teething ring
Feeding tray or dish

If you know the decor of the child's room, you could add a small nursery lamp, crib dust ruffle, decorative wall hanging, quilt or comforter, toy box, pictures, or a birth plaque.

Christening presents are expected from the baby's godparents, who traditionally give something in silver engraved with the child's name or initials and, sometimes, the date of the christening. This might be a silver cup, plate, porringer, or child-size spoon and fork. If you are invited to a christening and have already given the child a present, do not feel obligated to give another. If you have not yet given a gift, you may give it at this time. Usually only relatives and close friends are invited to a christening and their gifts are meant to be lasting. Classic jewelry that the child can wear when older (don't give jewelry so small that the child cannot wear it when old enough to appreciate it), a silver picture frame, antique cuff links or studs (especially if they have been handed down through the family), saint's medal for Catholics, an engraved silver jewelry box, sterling pacifier, or a savings bond purchased or account opened in the baby's name are all items to be saved for when the child is older and can appreciate the thoughtfulness and love of the giver. I like to search out antique silver bib clips or baby mugs and bowls with interesting old designs and inscriptions to give as christening gifts to dear friends.

Special gifts that parents will particularly enjoy include a Christmas stocking with the baby's name; baby book or book for baby's photographs and records; proof set of coins issued in the year of birth; a tree planted in the baby's name; a set of encyclopedias; a baby swing; antique children's chair or a miniature, handcrafted bergère caned-back Louis XV chair in antique finish with customized needlepoint cushion (available from Creative Resources, N.Y. (212) 974–1185); handmade quilt; helium balloons with a message sent to the hospital; cut crystal baby bottle with silver-plated nipple (a keepsake); personalized, hand-painted baby stool with layette items inside (Creative Resources); a child's classic book with an appropriate inscription; family genealogy; a spray of flowers to the hospital in a lovely cut glass or silver vase, perhaps with inscription to remember the occasion; rocking chair for child or parents; "good for" coupons for baby-sitting; books for parents; or—one of my favorites—a special bush or small tree for the yard to grow with the child.

Even the smallest baby gift becomes special with some thought. My friend gave me permission to share with you the legend on the following page that I included with her baby's gift last year. The gift itself was a very tactile small wooden spoon that I'd wrapped in a colorful, washable Marimekko bib.

CATHERINE'S SPECIAL SPOON

This high-bush blueberry wood spoon was made for Catherine by Dan Dustin—a Contoocook, New Hampshire, man who comes from a long line of men who split wood when they needed things: axe handles, plowshares, sleigh runners. The nature of his work comes from the process; he says that he suspends himself, bringing out what's there in the wood.

The native blueberry is so hard, so strong, and so tough to work with that it's seldom even thought of as wood. When Catherine holds her blueberry spoon, she will probably be holding the only thing she will ever see made out of this wood.

Catherine's spoon was entirely made in Dan's hand. The wood has never had any association with a flat surface, never been through a sawmill.

It was worked green and split with the grain, so that the grain runs through the length of the spoon. This makes your spoon wonderfully strong and flexible. After Dan split and hewed the spoon, he fired it out in molten beeswax and scrubbed and sanded it. Dan's firing process, which he developed at the inspiration of an old blacksmith friend of his grandfather's, "tempers" the wood. It drives out the water and fills the wood with wax, making it flexible yet hard of surface, yielding to the hand.

Catherine, you have been born and will be bred—appropriately—with silver spoons. Perhaps sometimes you will need something more down-to-earth, more intrinsic, thoroughbred in a different way. Then, you can reach for your special spoon.

SUGGESTED USES: This spoon may be used to feed dolls, taste lentil soup, suck on, serve jam for scones, find the last chocolate fudge in the jar, look at, eat caviar from the tin, hold pistachio nut shells or olive pits, stir witches' brews, or just to touch.

BIRTHDAY
GIFTS

Your birthday is the celebration of yourself—a remembrance that you are unique. As a child you probably even believed that your birthday was yours alone and were disappointed to discover that you shared it with others. (For me, discovering just a few years ago that I shared my birthday with Ronald Reagan was surprising, to say the least.)

In some countries, such as Germany, one's birthday is a time to celebrate and indulge the honoree. In many nations celebrants legally receive a half or a full day of vacation. And in other areas of the world one's name day or saint's day is more important than a birthday.

A thoughtful birthday gift should tell the recipient that to you, he or she really is special, exceptional, one-of-a-kind.

Selecting children's birthday presents can be glorious fun or a real burden. It is usually suitable for an adult to give a child a gift of money for his birthday—perhaps with a special use in mind. In communities where it is customary for each child to have a birthday party and where each guest is expected to bring a gift, parents often find the process both time-consuming and expensive. One solution is to include a two-dollar or five-dollar gift restriction on the invitation. This can encourage children to become less materialistic and also obviates the problem of the child who brings the too-lavish gift.

If you are giving the party, you may follow another community tradition, that of the party or loot bag. When leaving the party, each child is given a paper bag of gifts with his name on it. The bag usually contains an assortment of candies or sweets and sometimes inexpensive gifts adapted to the child's age—for toddlers, little soft animals; for primary-grade age, crayons, felt-tip pens, magnets, jacks, or marbles; for older children, playing cards, gift certificates for ice cream cones, or hair ribbons and plastic barrettes.

When an adult gives a birthday gift, he usually knows his recipient's interests. However, adults also find themselves looking for party gifts for mere acquaintances. Invitations to birthday parties for adults should explain the gift situation—for example, a request for no gifts or the statement that only inexpensive gag or humorous gifts are acceptable. Guests who do not follow these instructions are being inconsiderate to the host and to the other guests. Birthday gifts for adults are often inexpensive gestures that mark the occasion. Such gestures include the single flower, paperback books, a "good-for" promise, a special food treat such as home-baked cookies or the recipient's favorite dill pickles, or a beautiful card. Other suggestions can be found in the lists of gifts suitable for people with special interests and in the chapters "Easy Ways to Make Your Gift Giving Special" (p. 15), "Inexpensive Gifts" (p. 25), and "Books as Gifts" (p. 211).

Some gifts are especially suited for birthdays—birthday books such as *Winnie-the-Pooh*'s, special recordings, diaries and memory books, perpetual calendars, special candles, and, of course, the birthday cake. A present that relates to one's sign of the zodiac (for those interested) or that contains one's birthstone is a thoughtful gift. Birthstones—precious stones considered to symbolize the influences present during the month of one's birth—are: **January,** garnet; **February,** amethyst; **March,** bloodstone, jasper, or aquamarine; **April,** diamond or sapphire; **May,** emerald; **June,** pearl, moonstone, alexandrite, or oragate; **July,** ruby or turquoise; **August,** carnelian, peridot, or sardonyx; **September,** sapphire, chrysolite; **October,** tourmaline, opal, or beryl; **November,** topaz; **December,** lapis lazuli, ruby, turquoise, or zircon. Some months have more than one choice because of the availability of different stones throughout the world. Birthstones are also occasionally determined by the day of the week on which one was born: **Sunday,** topaz and diamond; **Monday,** pearl and quartz crystal; **Tuesday,** ruby and emerald; **Wednesday,** amethyst and lodestone; **Thursday,** sapphire and carnelian; **Friday,** emerald and cat's eye; **Saturday,** turquoise and diamond. Birthstones can be set into rings, pendants, cuff links, pins, tie clasps, bracelets, or earrings—or simply presented to be set at a later date or in a setting selected by the recipient.

A number of gifts can be individualized or customized for one's birthday celebration. An unusual present—and one of my favorites—is a fragrance formulated expressly for the individual. One of these is even tailored to one's specific pattern and vibratory level. This perfume, an individual cellular enhancer, is guaranteed to be exclusive to the user and can be ordered in lovely antique bottles. (Contact The House of Pharaohna, Dallas, TX.)

In our zeal to celebrate other people's birthdays, we sometimes forget that many people dislike surprises (such as parties), that some people prefer to celebrate the day but not the number, and that others are easily embarrassed by any attention.

Surprises are often more fun for the planners than for the shy honoree. Although a singing/dancing telegram type of gift is a good choice for an audience, sometimes the recipient is embarrassed, even humiliated. Even when you are certain that "good old Joe" would love it, check the wording of the verse or song to be used by the entertainers. You may discover—too late—that the words or language are offensive. And while the "Stripper-Gram" has become popular in some circles, please be sensitive when giving such an outrageous gift. Sometimes an office setting can be too acutely embarrassing for this "gag."

WEDDINGS

The 24 million couples getting married in this decade are starting a trend toward the large and very traditional wedding. The contemporary bride, however, is both practical and romantic—her gifts may reflect either, but the best gift will embody both.

I'm sure that as you read this book you are asking yourself, "What kinds of gifts does this gift authority and author give to her own friends?" That's certainly a valid question, and—even though I may find from now on that my gifts are no longer one-of-a-kind—I think this is a good place to answer that question. My favorite wedding gift for most American couples—whether a first, second, or third marriage—is a customized picnic basket for two. One can purchase all types of outfitted picnic baskets, from one filled with utilitarian plastic utensils to those that contain a full complement of crystal and silver accessories. It is also fun to put together your own picnic basket—especially for people you like and know well. I've outfitted baskets for couples who: enjoy camping on a Texas river, attend the elegant annual Bohemian Grove picnic near San Francisco, lunch on a speedboat in Ohio, listen to the summer evening concerts in Central Park and in Dallas, annually attend a turn-of-the-century formal picnic (replete with hoop skirts) near Philadelphia, regularly go to performances at Wolf Trap near Washington, D.C., and tailgate at football games in Nebraska. And each of these requires different utensils and accessories. I have assembled picnic baskets that include everything from wooden steak planks and checked cloths to utilitarian stainless steel camp utensils and Swiss army knives to ivory caviar spoons and linen and lace napkins. The response is unanimous—it's a great gift. Sometimes, if I know the couple well and can easily obtain baby or child portraits of them both, I present them—often restored and/or enlarged in matching frames. Or I send a special gift of crystal flutes and a bottle of champagne—perhaps with their family name on the label—to the honeymoon spot. And for some of my good friends I might add a romantic handmade photograph album with padded covers decorated with old silk, satin, lace, beads, and pearls.

Wedding Gifts

It is an excellent idea to send wedding gifts as soon as you receive the invitation or announcement. You have more choice—especially if you are using a gift registry—and you are probably more enthusiastic about the idea than you would be if you worried about it for two months. Besides, couples usually have more time to enjoy opening their early gifts. It also takes time to order special gifts or to get them engraved or monogrammed.

Although it is not necessary to send a gift for every invitation you receive, you are expected to send a gift if you accept the invitation. Usually, those who receive invitations would have warm feelings about the marriage and would want to send best wishes in the form of a gift or a letter even if they cannot attend the ceremony. Often gifts are given to the children of business acquaintances, even though you may not know the wedding couple.

If you know the couple or one of them well and/or are in the wedding party, you may wish to select something special—a gift that will also be a remembrance rather than one silver salad fork or four goblets. An exceptional gift need not be expensive. It could be something you have made or designed yourself. If you have a talent or ability that could provide a useful or beautiful addition to the wedding festivities—such as making lovely rice bags, selecting and arranging flowers or making centerpieces, repairing antique lace and veiling, making a wedding cake, or are an excellent photographer with the appropriate equipment—yours can be one of their most appreciated gifts. And there are other gifts you can make—a quilt, linens that you embroider or monogram, or a wedding plaque in needlework. Other inexpensive but individualized gifts could be an anniversary candle, a book filled with the names of relatives on both sides of the family with their birthdays and anniversaries; a meaningful photograph, framed; a family Bible; their first in a series of Christmas decorations—such as china or crystal; a frame for their wedding portrait; a tray or box in silver or crystal with their wedding invitation engraved on the cover; or a time capsule. Knowing the couple's tastes and lifestyle may inspire you to select special art objects, sports equipment, antique loving spoons, a tea set with a recording of "Tea for Two," a loveseat, or a copper espresso machine. Gifts such as antiques or family heirlooms have more meaning when the history or story of the present is included.

No wedding couple wants to receive an entire collection of unique gifts. The tradition of the wedding gift has long been to provide a new couple with the items needed to start a household. Yes, a gift registry is traditional, old-fashioned, and materialistic, but it is practical. As you will be one of many people trying to select a gift that the couple will need and want and that suits their lifestyle, you may wish to ask if the bride is using a bridal registry. This free service provided by many stores is a listing of the couple's choices of items such as china, crystal, silver, and linens. Many registries also include appliances, pottery, luggage, and kitchen items. The purchaser can either call the registry or go there to choose the wedding present. Some people resist buying from a registry list because the recipients will know the value of whatever gift they select. However, using the registry will ensure that you select something that the couple will like. Do not ever be embarrassed to send one plate or cup and saucer in their chosen pattern; your note and feelings are what make the gift important. The giver can also use the bride's registered choices as a guide to buying a present elsewhere or for making a gift that will be compatible with the couple's tastes.

Money is a popular gift, particularly from family. Checks, cash, stocks, bonds, and gift certificates are all acceptable wedding presents. Checks that are given before the wedding may be made out either to the bride or to the bride and/or groom. Checks that are given to the couple at the reception or after the wedding should be in the couple's married name (or names if the woman does not change her name).

If you are ordering gifts with monograms or names, such as linens, silver, or stationery, check with a member of the bride's or groom's family to be certain that you are using the proper initials or names. A gift of stationery engraved "Mrs. John Smith" to a woman who is keeping her name could prove embarrassing to both you and the recipient.

A shower is one of the most thoughtful wedding gifts one can give. It is a practical and delightful way for a bridesmaid or close friend to help a couple set up housekeeping. Generally, members of the bride's or groom's immediate family do not give showers, but the showers may be held in one of their homes. Joint showers for the couple with both men and women attending are popular. Refreshments usually are served; a shower for today's bride can be a potluck supper, an afternoon tea, a backyard picnic, a wine-and-cheese sampling, or a dessert party.

Some showers are specific—linen showers, kitchen showers, or lingerie showers. Others are open-ended. It is helpful if those sending the invitation specify the couple's colors or themes—few people appreciate rainbow kitchens or bathrooms—and if the shower is of the kind which permits the attendee to give an inexpensive item. Keep in mind that many of these same people will also be selecting wedding gifts and that those who are in the wedding party may have numerous other related expenses. Persons who receive a shower invitation but who do not attend the shower are not obligated to send a gift.

Shower gifts are usually more utilitarian than wedding gifts and are not as expensive. Imaginative shower givers may host paper showers or potluck showers (guests bring food to eat and leave the couple the recipe and the serving dish), or spice showers (guests bring favorite spice and recipe incorporating it). Sometimes friends attending a shower might decide to give a larger, collective gift such as a microwave oven, a sewing machine, or a food processor.

Here are a few suggestions for some of the more common types of wedding showers:

Kitchen shower. Pots and pans; matching towels, dishcloths, and hot pads; spice rack; crêpe pan; dispensers for paper towels or plastic wrap; space-saving equipment; recipe file and cards (maybe with some favorite recipes); cookie jar, food storage jars, or canisters; measuring cups and spoons; kitchen shears; cupboard organizers; cookbooks; shelf paper; juicer; teapot; cookie sheets; kitchen fire extinguisher; electric can opener; dish drainer and pad; kitchen clock and timer; mixing bowls; spaghetti pot; cutting board; colander. (For additional ideas, see "Entertaining Ideas for Hosts/Hostesses and Gourmet Cooks," p. 258.)

Linen shower. Be sure to check bed size, table size, and color preferences and have some idea of what the couple prefers before selecting most of these items—place mats; napkins; bed linens; aprons; table-cloths; face towels; mattress pad and cover; shower curtain; dust ruffle; electric blanket or sheet; down (or other) pillows; comforter; pillow covers; hot roll cover; kitchen linens; blanket; guest towels; afghan; duvet cover; bedrest(s).

Lingerie shower. Be sure to check on the bride's sizes and color preferences for most of these—the traditional garter (usually with blue); bedjacket; night shirt; summer robe; sachets or potpourri; lingerie cases; matching gown and peignoir; hose, with matching bra, panties, and half-slip; teddy; slippers; hostess gown; lounging outfit; lace-trimmed slip or camisole.

Encore Weddings

It is not necessary to send gifts for an "encore" (second or third or . . .) wedding unless you are especially fond of or close to one of the couple. A note of congratulations and/or a bouquet or plant can express your best wishes after you have received a wedding announcement. Brides (and often grooms) who have been married before, as well as couples who are marrying later in life or who have been living together for some time, will probably already have many of the necessary household goods including china, silver, and crystal patterns. If you know the couple well enough, you can certainly ask what they would like for a gift. Some suggestions that have proved successful—antique art book; monogrammed linens; collection of antique pewter or silver picture frames; additional old pieces of silver such as a berry spoon; leatherbound book of poetry; hammock for two; case of selected wines; breakfast-in-bed trays; silver chest; camera and film; silver cake knife or antique fish server with wedding date engraved (to be used for cutting the wedding cake); magazine subscription; badminton set; an offer to videotape the ceremony.

Receiving Wedding Gifts

Registering for wedding gifts makes it easier for people to select something you need and like, avoids the possibility of gift duplications, and, of course, provides you with things you can use. The bride who is unsure of her tastes and her needs will find a good bridal consultant to be of great help; however, do not allow the store to send out notices to your wedding guests that you are registered there.

When filling out the registration forms at specialty or department stores, don't hesitate to include nonconventional wedding items that you really want, such as pieces of luggage, an electric wok, athletic equipment for both of you, embroidered pillows, or a personal computer. Don't feel embarrassed to list expensive items, because often families, friends, or office mates may decide to purchase a joint gift. And don't be afraid to tell your family and friends what you want; you will be doing them a favor, as they would have had to ask you anyway.

Thank-you notes should be written and sent as soon as possible after the receipt of the gift. You will need a wedding-gift register and/or file to record your gifts. Entering a description of the gift, date of receipt, name and address of the giver, the store from which it came, and the date the thank-you was sent will not only ensure that you acknowledge each gift but will help you to return duplicates to the correct stores and will serve as a valuable reminder when you wish to thank people personally.

Although it was once customary to address wedding thank-yous to Mrs. Smith even though the gift was from Mr. and Mrs. Smith, modern thank-you notes should be addressed to whoever gave you the gift—if a couple signed the card, then both should receive the thank-you. Do not address a couple as "Dear Smiths." The signature should be only that of the person who wrote the note, although you might include your spouse's name and thank-you in the letter—"Bob and I both love the copper teapot." (Both the bride and the groom may write the thank-you notes—it is certainly a shared responsibility.) When a woman writes thank-you notes before her wedding, she uses her maiden name and her present address for the return address. Your notes should be as enthusiastic and as specific about the gift as possible; when thanking for a gift of money, it is thoughtful to mention how you plan to use the money—but do not mention the sum in the letter. If you have exchanged an item, thank the person for the item given, not for the item for which it was exchanged. Do *not* use pre-printed thank-you notes that you fill in with the name of the gift and your signature. Such an impersonal response can be insulting to your friends who have taken the time to select a gift for you.

If your list of guests is very large and your schedule is so full that you know you will not be able to properly thank everyone soon after the wedding, the bride or—more popular today—the bride and groom may send a formal acknowledgment when the gift is received. These cards, which may be engraved or printed, are intended only as confirmation that you have received the gift. Use them only if you really are unable to respond personally within a couple of months. You are still expected to write a personal thank-you as soon as possible. Thank-you notes are also sent after wedding showers, even though you have thanked the givers personally at the shower.

If you expect gifts to be brought to the wedding reception, a gift table should be set up and someone assigned to list the gifts in the bride's wedding registry. Gifts should not be opened at the reception.

If it is customary in your community to display the wedding gifts at home or at the reception, do not leave the gift cards attached. It is best not to display gifts of money, checks, or bonds, although some people do display them, with the signatures visible but the amounts concealed by a piece of paper.

Exchanging Wedding Gifts

Usually one should not exchange gifts from members of the immediate family or from very close friends as there is a likelihood that they will know whether you use and enjoy their gifts. Duplicate gifts and unsuitable gifts may be exchanged for something you want or need.

Returning Wedding Gifts

When a wedding does not take place, the gifts are returned to the giver with a brief note of explanation. Both the bride and groom are responsible for the return of their own friends' gifts. The same is true when an annulment takes place almost immediately after the wedding. If the prospective groom has died, the bride-to-be may accept certain sentimental gifts that the giver urges her to keep for herself. If a wedding is merely postponed for a short period of time, gifts are not returned.

Bridal Couple's Gifts to
Each Other

Often the bridal couple exchange personal gifts just before the wedding. These gifts usually have a permanent, sentimental value; traditional choices are a watch or heart with initials and the wedding date engraved, a piece of jewelry that has been passed down in the family, a strand of pearls, elegant cuff links, an engraved brush or dresser set, or a framed photo of you. This can also be an occasion for giving your spouse-to-be something special that he or she has always wanted—a musical instrument, a set of nature prints, or a special briefcase. One of the pair should not embarrass the other by giving much more lavishly.

Gifts for Wedding Attendants

The people who take the time to participate in your wedding deserve special mementos. The groom usually presents his ushers and best man with gifts at his bachelor dinner. The bride may give her gifts to her attendants at a luncheon or party or may give them individually at any convenient time before the wedding.

These gifts are often personalized and/or engraved with the initials of the bride and the groom and the wedding date. Usually the best man and the maid or matron of honor receive something a bit more elaborate than the other members of the wedding party. Traditional lasting tokens include gold or silver bracelets, cuff links, tie clasps or pendants; silver picture frames; silver compacts or pocket mirrors; key chains; silver bar accessories or monogrammed glasses; leather jewelry or stud boxes; silver or leather earring boxes with monogram; and belt buckles. More imaginative choices might include travel alarm clocks; elegant letter openers—perhaps with engraved, embossed, or printed stationery; silver or gold hair ornaments; antique silver serving spoons with date engraved in bowl; zodiac charm; or special recordings. Younger members of the wedding party should also receive gifts: for flower girls, a bracelet, locket, ring, hair ornament, or small engraved brush; for ring bearers, a watch, small folding telescope, or special sports equipment. It is especially thoughtful for the couple to send a small framed photograph of themselves or—even better—of the entire wedding party with a thank-you note after the wedding.

Gifts to Bride and Groom
from Wedding Party

In some sections of the country, especially in the case of formal weddings, it is customary for the wedding party to present the bride and groom with a gift to commemorate the occasion. These gifts, usually engraved with the wedding date and initials, can range from a set of silver goblets to matching his and hers wristwatches. A toasting goblet in crystal, pewter, or silver is a traditional choice; however, a mantelpiece clock with a brass plaque; a leather photo album or a special frame for the wedding photo; a crystal or silver vase, ice bucket, martini mixer, or cocktail shaker; a leather photo box or silver tray; or a bowl or tray with wedding invitation engraved are also appropriate selections for a collective gift. Wedding parties may prefer to select an item that would be especially significant to the couple, such as a recorded set of Beethoven sonatas or a print or sculpture by a favorite artist.

ANNIVERSARY GIFTS

The number of years the couple has been married, their lifestyle, the formality of the occasion, and your relationship to the couple are all factors to be considered when choosing an anniversary gift. Clearly some wedding anniversaries such as the twenty-fifth or fiftieth call for something special.

The early anniversaries are usually observed by the couple, perhaps their parents, and maybe some very close friends. Even though young couples often decide jointly to give a needed gift to themselves, it is thoughtful for each to add special flowers, candy, cologne, or some romantic token to mark the occasion. It is often appropriate for friends to bring humorous presents, especially to younger couples; generally, however, gifts for older people who have been married a long time need to be selected with thought and sentiment.

Joint gifts from family or friends are one answer for a major anniversary—vacations, home appliances, a Jacuzzi or large bathtub, matching recliners, a weekly or monthly service (from meals to gardening to cable TV to car service). Older couples also appreciate memorabilia—restored old family photos; a tray with their original wedding invitation painted or engraved; a copy of their hometown newspaper from their wedding day; a replica of their wedding cake and/or bouquet; an album filled with photos and messages from all their friends; a painting or photograph of a meaningful place such as the church in which they were married, a special street scene, or their first home; a family genealogy and/or a collection of written or taped experiences; special needlework; a conference call or special call to someone overseas; a gift of a second honeymoon—possibly in the same place as their first; jewelry or necktie with the grandchildren's and great-grandchildren's names.

Gifts for an older couple should be chosen so as not to add to the clutter of their home. Most persons who have been married long enough for an anniversary party are not interested in additional possessions—unless you know of something that they collect or have been looking for or unless it's something very special such as Steuben's pair of crystal geese or swans. Random bowls or vases are generally unwelcome. There are many gifts that will accomplish your purpose—giving best wishes and adding to their pleasant memories: potted plants; a basket of their favorite foods; an appropriate book; a bush, tree, bulbs, or plant for their garden; a gift certificate to a photography studio; a party or open house; a suitably engraved serving spoon, cake knife, or tray; original artwork; a subscription to a magazine of interest; tickets to a concert, the theater, or other program; luggage if they travel; an umbrella or bicycle for two; guest book for the anniversary party; or a movie or slide show of the highlights of their lives, complete with narration and music. (I did this for my parents' fiftieth wedding anniversary—the first shots were of their baby pictures.) They might also appreciate a contribution in their name to a favorite charity or community organization, altar flowers for their church, books given to the local library, or plantings for a church or park.

A younger couple might enjoy a double hammock; special gourmet foods; wines or champagne; books; a musical record or tape; a wonderful collection of paper plates and napkins; sporting equipment or clothing; matching furs; a snowmobile; a pair of exotic birds; special wine bottled with the family's personal label; a bouquet of flowers (perhaps similar to their wedding bouquet); monogrammed linens (if they have been married long enough to have worn out their wedding trousseau); something for the yard or grill; picnic or pool equipment or utensils; or a night on the town, complete with babysitting service.

For particular anniversaries, there are traditional gift customs as well as specific suggestions of minerals and gems:

1st	Clocks, paper
2nd	China
3rd	Crystal, glass

4th	Electrical appliances
5th	Silverware
6th	Wood (a tree is great!), iron
7th	Copper, bronze, or brass desk sets
8th	Linen, lace
9th	Leather
10th	Diamond jewelry, tin, aluminum
11th	Fashion jewelry, steel
12th	Colored gemstones, pearls
13th	Textiles, furs
14th	Ivory (bone), gold jewelry
15th	Crystal or quartz, watches
16th	Silver holloware
17th	Furniture
18th	Porcelain
19th	Bronze
20th	Platinum
25th	Silver jubilee
30th	Pearl or diamond
35th	Jade or coral
40th	Ruby
45th	Sapphire
50th	Golden jubilee
55th	Emerald
60th	Diamond jubilee

Please note how age enhances our value!

Of course, one does not have to consider these symbols in selecting an anniversary gift; and many people do not, except for the major celebrations such as the silver and gold jubilees. Nor do those occasions mean that your gift must be of real silver or gold—an elegant book with gold leaf trim, a tiny gold leaf frame, an afghan with some silver threads, a *Silver Palate* cookbook, or anything trimmed in gold or silver color would be appropriate.

If the invitation to an anniversary party specifies "no gifts," don't embarrass the host, honorees, and other guests by bringing a gift. If you feel you want to honor the couple with a gift for this occasion, send it or present it at another time.

HOUSEWARMING GIFTS

T raditionally, each guest or family brings a small gift to an official housewarming. Although a housewarming is usually given by the couple (or single person) in honor of their new home, it can be given by others as a welcome gift. If there is no party, it is thoughtful and customary to take a gift when you first visit your host's new house, apartment, or vacation retreat. Another type of gathering does not require a gift—the cocktail party, barbecue, or dinner that is given to "show off" a recently redecorated home or landscaped yard; however, you are expected to compliment the host and/or designer. (Do see p. 123 regarding appropriate Jewish gifts for a new home.)

Your gift selection, of course, will vary according to whether the move is to a larger or smaller home, a new or an old house or apartment, whether the owners have just moved to a new community, whether this is an easy-maintenance vacation home, whether this is a first house, and so on.

Most new homeowners can always use tasteful bookends; a gift certificate to a local hardware, gourmet food, or liquor store; stationery or return labels with new address; a plant or gift certificate for yard planting, seeds, or bulbs; notebooks, pencils, and magnetized pads for kitchen and telephones, with a list of reliable local tradesmen, repairmen, and so on; a gift certificate to beauty parlor; initialed soap; a first subscription to local newspaper or city or state magazine.

If you wish to be helpful to a person or family moving into your neighborhood, take them a picnic of sandwiches, fruit, and cold drinks; offer to entertain young children, get them a new mailbox, door knocker, house numbers or garbage can or garbage can caddy with garbage bags, or present them with a collection of necessary items such as picture hangers, light bulbs, paper towels, cleaning supplies, adhesives, wire, toilet paper, dust rags, shelf paper, and pen and paper, perhaps presented in a plastic garbage can.

Other suggestions: wine rack; plastic organizers of all kinds; knife sharpener; appropriate illustrated coffee-table book; candles (white unless you know their preference); guest book; neutral-color doormat; pool games or toys; umbrella stand; lawn furniture; closet organizers; set of scissors; smoke detector; automatic garage-door opener or light timer; fireplace equipment or logs; barbecue equipment and utensils; a collection of decorative paper plates, cups, napkins, etc., or of plastic glasses, lemonade pitcher, and glasses; outdoor bell; wind chimes; bathroom accessories; pillows; cookbook—especially one from the region; membership to local museum, club, or concert series; tickets to local event; personalized cocktail napkins; subscription to home improvement or decoration magazine if appropriate.

PARTY GIFTS

Creative hosts and hostesses sometimes include gifts for their guests. One of the most delightful aspects of planning a dinner, party, or benefit is that of selecting such gifts. These can add to the pleasure of the occasion without adding significantly to the cost. A garden flower, nosegay, or special sweet at each place can be inexpensive and enjoyable; individual masks or fortune cookies can be an amusing addition as well as provide an ice-breaker among table mates who are strangers.

Chairpersons for charity balls and benefits usually manage to find suitable donations from local merchants or producers. The most common benefit gift is the "goody bag"—a collection of small donated gifts in a presentation bag, also donated. The bag might include gift certificates, a trial magazine subscription, beauty and grooming items, small containers or packages of food, purse toilet water or cologne sprays, men's ties, coffee mug, key chain, picture frames, or various trinkets. Commemoration plates, trays, or decanters that list the event and date are also common but less useful mementos. "Goody bags" and larger items are often given to guests as they leave the event.

Some events furnish one gift per table. The centerpiece is selected by lots or by a number or sticker under one's chair. When seats have been preassigned, the recipient often turns out to be the host's best customer. The centerpiece might include a lantern, a piece of

Steuben crystal, a Western hat, candlesticks, a limited-edition sculpture, the model of a truck or plane, or simply a lovely basket of flowers.

The best party gifts are those that relate to the theme or the purpose of the event—a tiny treasure of a castle for a magical fairyland (Mr. Sandman, P.O. Box 1488, 1200 William Street, Buffalo, NY—(800)387-0303, minimum order $100.00); an actual souvenir of the Eiffel Tower for an Evening in Paris ball; a white china bell with anniversary dates in gold for a Christmas or fiftieth wedding anniversary; custom designed kaleidoscope covered with symphonic music for the symphony ball. (C. Bennett Scopes, Inc., 1001 East State Road, P.O. Box 721, Media, PA 19063, (215)565-3532)— minimum order $100.00, or Apres la Pluie, 14950 Beaumont en Auge, France, Tel. (33)31 64 87 12, shipped by Emery Air Freight, minimum order $250.) More innovative hostesses are banishing the usual perfume samples for more lively tokens: Carolyn Roehm, who chaired an annual spring gala at Lincoln Center for the New York City Ballet, gave tapes of Vladimir Horowitz's rendering of various Chopin works, many of which related to the evening's special program.

Corporate outings produce some real treasures—small silver, velvet-lined earring boxes, delicate sculptures, silver cache pot with silk plant (replaceable with real), or a contribution to a charity in your name.

With a little imagination the party gift shopper can shop almost anywhere. To go with an authentic chili supper, a beribboned jar of Texas hot salsa—from the grocery store; small, attractive acrylic desk accessories from the office-supply store for an office party; elegant notecards from the stationer's for a bridesmaids' luncheon. Small hand-formed terra cotta animals, decorative magnets, purse organizers, address books, scent bottles, key chain or cases, men's jewelry items, handsome blank book, decorative boxes, or Christmas-tree ornaments all make fine table gifts.

STOCKING
GIFTS

 Some stocking stuffers are quite practical: tubes of tooth-paste, dental floss, shampoo, nail-polish remover and other necessary items. Others are entirely frivolous.

I think that Santa meant our stockings to be at least partly whimsical and that he intended them for adults as well as children.

Some suggestions:

Cassettes
Notecards and stamps
Small sports-related items such as gold balls and trees, fishing
    flies, sailing gloves
Christmas ornaments
Seed packets or flower bulbs ready for planting
Candy and gum
Scented soap
Gift certificate
Magazine subscription
Small wind-up toys
Magic tricks
Puzzles
Bottle of champagne
Pocket calculator
Tiny travel alarm clock
Fireplace matches and colored pellets

THE ART AND ETIQUETTE OF GIFT GIVING

Batteries
Pen light
Colored marking pens
Packets of bubble bath, bath oil beads, shower cap
Swiss army or pocket knife
Change purse
Purse-size spray cologne
Bookmark
Handkerchief
Belt
Magnetic memo holders
Jewelry
Embroidery
Sachet
Favorite canned gourmet food, such as smoked oysters
Miniature hot sauce or mustard
Tiny picture frame
"Good-for" cards
Hotel-room samples
Overseas airline amenities kits
Mittens or gloves
Socks
Camera film
Pens/pencils, crayons, or finger paints
Shoe laces
Hair ribbons, barrettes, and combs
Candles
Coasters
Paperback book(s)
Fingernail clippers, cuticle scissors, files, and emery boards
Shoe polish
Cosmetics
Scarf
Necktie
Belt buckle
Cuff links
Bolo tie
Colored paperclips
Miniature stapler set
Scotch tape
Sewing kit
Magnifying glass

Clothes brush
Cat or dog collar or leash
Small stuffed animals
Wrapped candy canes
And, of course, an orange or tangerine for the toe of the stocking

INTERIM GIFTS

Well, what would you call them? In-between gifts, interval gifts, gift-bearing gifts?

There are those times when a special gift cannot be delivered or fulfilled until a later date—times when we want an appropriate or uncommon way of presenting a future gift now. Our reasons for such a need can vary from our desire for the recipient to select his own gift to simple forgetfulness of a birthday, anniversary, or other gift occasion. As for the message itself, in our family we call it a "good-for" card.

Occasions for interim gifts are diverse and unlimited:

- You promise to take them to Hawaii next fall.

- You managed to secure season's tickets to the ball park or opera.

- You promise to take your son to the local natural history museum.

- You've determined to wash your brother's car for the prom next month.

- You promise to photograph a significant family event.

- You are giving someone a particular magazine subscription.

- You promise someone part of your first tomato and corn crops.

- You will be sending something perishable such as steaks, lobsters, or turkey for someone's anniversary.

- You promise to build those closet shelves on the next rainy weekend.

- You pledge two weeks of tennis camp or lessons with the pro.

- You plan a romantic evening with a concert and dinner.

- You want your mother to know that you will keep your room clean all summer.

- You promise to pay tuition for a course in geology, flower arranging, or ballooning.

- You decide to take your love for a sleigh or horse and carriage ride.

- You guarantee to prepare and cook dinner for someone once a week.

- You promise to purchase and install the carpet if they will pick it out.

- You are giving someone a day of beauty, a makeup lesson, a health-club membership.

- You promise to let him pick out his own puppy as soon as the litter is born.

- You plan to go with her to select the new shoes you will buy for her.

Granted, a future gift can be described in a clever note at the bottom of a greeting card or announced at a party or dinner. However, it can also be presented with flair, fun, or elegance. Here are some of my favorite interim gift ideas—hopefully, enough to get your imagination started:

Appropriate frame (pewter, silver, leather, ceramic, crystal), holding relevant photo or message

Related miniature of future gift—toy, crystal, wood, china

Theme-related calendar marked with time for the present's arrival or day of trip or event

Monogrammed soap

Camera with which to take a picture of——

Doll or stuffed animal with card or message

Any type of trinket—small occasion box, jewelry, figurine

Champagne or favorite wine in silver or crystal chiller

Specially designed or selected chocolates

Leatherbound antique, or even paperback book relating to subject

Small map of significant area or marked atlas

Photograph of giver

Caviar and vodka; could also include glasses, server, condiments, and a waiter

For a trip to Italy, a wonderful basket of Italian delicacies and a guide book

Message delivered on elegant card/letter tray with opener

Calligraphed scroll or certificate, maybe delivered by costumed or liveried courier or placed in the middle of dessert or flower arrangement

On birthday in office, breakfast delivered and served with the note/card on the tray

Wine and roses, perhaps with musical tape or record

Small cachepot holding tiny plant

Placard holders or napkin rings with the message tucked into one

Small kaleidoscope with note or poem

Small robot—walking and talking—can hand card or small gift to recipient; some actually say "Happy Birthday."

PART FOUR

BUSINESS GIFTS AND OFFICE PRESENTS

SUCCESSFUL BUSINESS GIFTS—CLIENTS, CUSTOMERS, AND SPECIAL INDIVIDUALS

T he giving of business gifts is big business. The choice of a gift can convey power, sophistication, knowledge, and interest. It can enhance or harm a corporate image. Unfortunately, however, in most business gift giving any matching of the gift to the actual desires of the recipient is, at best, approximate. Glassware covered with huge logos, ten-pound ashtrays, shiny trays of unknown metals, and calendars that give you a different view of water tanks or cement trucks each month are difficult to accept with genuine pleasure.

From gifts for the chairman of the board to incentive and logo gifts, the selecting and giving of business gifts are often not comfortable activities for the executive. It's a task he or she readily delegates to others.

American corporations spend over $4 billion on business gifts each year! The most frequently purchased items—you may have guessed them—are pens, desk calendars, and small calculators that use the company's logo to advertise its products. Other top choices: clocks, liquor, diaries, watches, knives, glassware, fruit, jackets, and desk sets. By far the most popular executive presents are gifts for the office, followed by gifts for the home. Personal gifts are frequently exchanged, and food items are universally popular.

Apparently the majority of businessmen see the practice of executive gift giving as producing the intended results. A recent national survey of executives conducted by Frank N. Pierce, Ph.D., and published by the Specialty Advertising Association International, found that among firms giving business gifts, 47 percent of the respondents thought executive gift giving was either "effective" or "very effective," and another 39 percent thought it was at least "somewhat effective." Only 2 percent believed that the practice produced no appreciable results.

Why do companies give business gifts? According to the study, the most important reason for the giving of business gifts is to express appreciation (61 percent of respondents); the next-most-mentioned reason (54 percent) was to develop business by building goodwill. Half of the respondents gave gifts only at Christmas; nearly a third gave gifts on special occasions. I have noticed recently, however, that the more sophisticated businesses recognize that an ongoing gift program is a significant aspect of communication as well as an advertising and marketing tool.

Yes, there are ways to use gifts as a communications tool in your business. There are acceptable logo gifts that convey your company's image. There are exciting and useful gifts for members of your board of directors. There are gifts, other than plants and flowers, for the opening of a client's new office. In addition, there are solutions for internal-office-gift problems—the joint office gift and the perennial "what to get the boss" gift.

Successful corporate gifting in America is also the result of knowledge such as not spending more lavishly than the occasion calls for, designing only very tasteful logo gifts, and realizing that the entrepreneur may require a completely different approach from that of the entrenched corporate CEO.

Some large companies develop their own in-house promotional products catalog from which employees select gifts for premium and employee-incentive awards, promotional aids, mementos, and business gifts. Gifts in General Electric's catalog, for example, range from a $1.00 disposable pocket penlight to a nineteen-inch diagonal Vivicolor TV for $322.80.

Here are a few general guidelines for modern corporate gifts:

• Gifts are not a substitute for goodwill and good business practices.

• Some "blanket" gifts repeated annually may lose their effectiveness because they are taken for granted.

• When possible, give a gift that is useful or practical.

• Wrapping, presentation (preferably in person), and the thoughtful personal message on the enclosure card are of great importance.

- Use business gifts wisely and judiciously.

- The fact that the client is remembered is more important than the magnitude of the gift.

- Always try to select something that is both appropriate for the intended receiver and relevant to your company—perhaps a company product.

- The most appreciated business gift, like the personal gift, is as selective and individual as possible.

Gifts for Clients or Customers

The most popular and familiar category of business gift giving is often the most perplexing.

MULTIPLE GIFTS

High-volume gifts, such as multiple Christmas presents, must satisfy the needs of many different types of people. Some companies have managed to solve this in creative ways: the Boeing company, for example, sends clients large boxes of decorative holiday greens, candlesticks, and candles each Christmas—an eagerly awaited gift that is both practical and seasonal. Many public relations and advertising firms have created their own traditions: one of the most exciting is the Campbell-Mithun Christmas Angel. Each year since 1958 the company has commissioned an original Christmas angel from a famous artist or craftsman. According to the company, the angel embodies the Christmas spirit and is artful, creative, and original—typical of the agency and their business. Why an angel? An angel is a communicator, carrying a message, just as the advertising company is a communicator. Regular clients prize their collection of limited editions that range from Tyrolean musical carved wooden angels and Mexican silverplated lace figures to bronze trumpeters from Kyoto and a set of five joyous Capodimonte ceramic cherubs from East Germany.

If you are not yet ready to start a tradition, there are other interesting possibilities for a large number of gifts. Rather than a greeting card, you could choose a good-quality picture frame with a tasteful holiday greeting inside; coffee-table book—order two or three different ones to suit the interests of various clients and write a personal note to go with each; monogrammed leather passport cases, photo albums, or legal envelopes; smoked salmon in a carved wooden box; selection of ice cream sauces or preserves; Lamb International stuffed animals such as E.F. Mutton® *Executive Rams* or Ms. Mutton® (the female executive lamb) who come with *The Wool Street Journal* and preferred stock certificate (Lamb International, 78 Holten Street, Box 373, Danvers, MA 01923 (800) 336-LAMB, (617) 774-9001); or useful boxes, baskets, or containers filled with your product(s); steaks; a little portable desk complete with ministapler, ruler, Scotch tape, and scissors; reproduction sun or horizon dials; tailgate picnic service for four or eight; wine-tasting and -record book; dessert of the month for one, three, five, eight, or twelve months (vary with amount of business from client (address—page 23); customized design tins filled with candies, sewing kits, bath accessories, record tape care kit, shoeshine kit; fresh lobster package which includes lobster, cooking pot, seaweed, potholders, bibs, place mats, lobster cracker sets, wet naps, recipes, and lobster anecdotes, air-expressed (Great Maine Lobster Company (800) 222-5033 or (207) 772-0106); cutlery gift sets; executive travel pack rods and reels; monogrammed soap; or copies of business-related or resource books, such as the one you're reading now.

LOGO GIFTS

Most logo-bearing gifts are purchased for under four dollars; and although pens, pencils, key rings, letter openers, and calendars serve a purpose, there are alternatives. For a change, what about chocolate? Business cards, logo mints—Goodyear gives delicious chocolate blimps. Other common marketing tools include ponchos, radios, Frisbees, balloons, puzzles, bar glasses, thermos bottles, hats, and credit card cases. More expensive suggestions: scale model trucks in various sizes with your handscreened message; a tin box or bank shaped to look like your corporate headquarters; good quality, fashionable actionwear jackets. Many logo gifts are now selected to follow the trend for architecturally designed products.

No matter how insignificant, a logo gift must always be of the highest quality and in good taste. Any gift that bears your company name also conveys your corporate image—solid or fragile, serious or whimsical, powerful or ineffective, clever or ordinary, thoughtful or unconcerned, motivated or lazy, professional or careless.

Don't put your logo on just anything, and don't select a gift to put a logo on just because someone else did it with excellent results. Take a common logo gift, for example: gold cuff links—a handsome gift of the famous Clydesdale horses given by Augie Busch to his good friends and favorite customers, but a disaster in the form of sparkplugs to appease an eastern spark-plug mogul. The well-dressed executive is probably not going to wear his matching sparkplugs with pride.

BUSINESS-RELATED GIFTS

A gift that ties in with your business, product, or sponsored event is usually a most effective business present. Bantam Books has given Tiffany's crystal roosters (its corporate logo), sheet cakes decorated like bookcovers, specially designed gold and silver bookmarks, and presented one of its most famous authors with a quilt made up of the visual elements that appear in his books. A company like United Technologies Corporation, which has a symbol such as the eagle, can choose from an assortment of elegant, quality sculptures in various mediums, such as Steuben's in crystal. (They do not give their corporate symbol in China and Saudia Arabia, however, as there the eagle is considered a scavenger and bad omen.) Certain corporations commission well-known photographers, writers, or artists to create special books. One wonderful and amazing example was a Houston company that produced a beautiful coffee-table book of photographs of the city. Close examination revealed the company's corporate headquarters tower as the unifying feature of the book; it appeared, however minutely, in each shot.

Some corporations give successful gifts that tie in with events or exhibits they sponsor. Manufacturers Hanover, sponsor of the annual Westchester Classic Golf Tournament, gives signed limited-edition tournament posters by Leroy Neiman to guests; and as the only corporate sponsor of a Van Gogh exhibition, they hosted a series of pre-event parties at which they gave to eight hundred key customers the artist's painting *Oleanders* reproduced on a silk scarf. Firms that sponsor art exhibitions treat their customers to special opening galas as well as guides to or books about the collection—InterNorth's Maximilian collection; the Vatican exhibit, sponsored by several companies; United Technologies Corporation's Shaker Design exhibition, to name a very few.

Gifts for Special Individuals

Modern business people are finding new occasions for business gifts and more creative ways to show their thanks or pleasure. An early morning box of warm, tasty donuts can remind the marketing director that this is the last day he can accept your company's proposal; Financial Crunch Banker's Dozen, a box of molded chocolate coins in the form of a silver dollar with a bite taken out would be perfect for the executive doing next year's budget (Creative Resources, 212-974-1185); a flower in a small crystal vase or an attractive basket with a mug, infusion heater, and exotic teas lets your boss know she deserved the promotion and the new office; a basket filled with fresh cookies conveys your concern to a client whose wife is in the hospital; sterling chopsticks are an exciting symbolic gift for a peer who will be taking her first business trip to China; executive "briefcakes" (chocolate brownies in a simulated briefcase) are perfect for the salesman who eats on the run; a catered gourmet lunch sent to the desk of a busy lawyer thanks him for a special favor (but check first with his secretary). For Valentine's Day 1987, top executives from various companies throughout the world who had participated in the rollout of the Airbus Industries' A320 were sent bottles of champagne engraved with their names, the date, and two champagne flutes, with a special card that invited them to join in a toast at the appropriate hour.

Customers and clients especially appreciate any gift that reflects your interest in them as individuals. Examples include an appropriate membership or subscription; an antique map of their city, region, or country; something relating to their sports interest; an antique bank; tickets for a special event; a favorite food such as New York deli if they've recently moved from New York, or Cajun cooking if their home is New Orleans; or a desk footstool for the manager who keeps his feet on his desk.

Some occasions call for the unusual or exceptional gift, such as a custom designed handmade wooden footstool (President Reagan's is covered with the Presidential Seal, the legs are wearing boots; the legs on Vice-President Bush's sport a pair of Prince socks and tennis shoes; Zubin Mehta's birthday stool was distinguished by a baton, black tie, and his favorite Bally shoes—from Footstools Unlimited, John R. McDowell, 106 North Saginaw, Pontiac, MI 48058, (313) 335-9229; a large pasta crate with an unusual provincial Italian cookbook; a bowl or thyme basket overflowing with lovely sachets or aromatherapy candles for the "sweet smell of success" from Creative Resources, New York (see above); an ultimate basket (from The Ultimate Basket, New York, (212) 877-3291) filled with the trappings of success from champagne, a LIFE AT THE TOP T-shirt, and *The Millionaire's Diet* book, to desk accessories and a gold-wrapped chocolate brick for the executive who's "made it"; or, for the executive political activist, a *How to Cook Reagan's Goose* basket with a wonderful collection of recipes by famous Democrats, goose liver pâté, and jelly beans, not to mention Teflon scouring pads for cleaning up your act!

How about an individually designed ceramic Babble (replica of Scrabble board) or Metropoly game with your own permanent message or the recipient's life history clearly executed (personalized games from Nicholas Shapes Unlimited, 138 Elm Street, Glenview, IL 60025 (312) 998–9493); a solar briefcase—the owner sets his own combination and opens the case by entering his code number on a keyboard—battery is recharged by placing briefcase in natural or artificial light (The Price of His Toys, 9559 Santa Monica Blvd., Beverly Hills, CA 90210 (800) HIS–TOYS, in California (213) 274–9955); an English silver-plated desk set; a monogrammed leather executive repair case; a handcrafted designer desk (especially suited for the left-handed); transparent political globe (Farguhar Transparent Globes, Inc., 426 Sumpter Street, Charlotte, MI 48813 (517) 484–3874); a crate of caviar with all the trimmings; a voice-control alarm clock; a wooden attaché case; or a one-of-a-kind gift that incorporates the recipient's name and a series of complimentary adjectives in a calligrapher's original design called a "Personal Celebration."

Special gifts that I've recently arranged include a handsome briefcase equipped with three power sources—a cigarette lighter jack, an AC power adapter for extended use, and an internal Nicad battery pack—perfect for answering your ringing phone from the beach ($3000, from Oki, (800) 228-2028, ext. 65.); a private varnish (restored railroad car) with imported chef to serve a gourmet dinner for thirty clients traveling between two cities; and for the golfing chief executive of a major Japanese bank—a spot in a leading Pro-Am tournament and a set of handmade Pedersen clubs custom measured and made to his specifications (Pedersen, 312 Howard Avenue, Bridgeport, Connecticut (203) 367-1155).

TRIPS, CONFERENCES, AND OUTINGS

Gifts for clients and customers often take the form of special excursions. Corporations vie for tickets to the Olympics, the Super Bowl, and Hollywood galas; they buy out the openings of Broadway plays and scramble for space at the America's Cup. Firms create their own events by sponsoring art exhibits, ballets, or symphonies; they invite top clients on hunting trips in Spain, salmon fishing expeditions in Alaska, and skiing jaunts to the Alps. Lucky guests may receive many special related gifts—hunters may discover that their hunting apparel is waiting for them from hat to glove, in the correct size and monogrammed; Super Bowl fans might receive autographed footballs; Winter Olympics fans might be sent specially designed signed silver sculptures of winter animals, a limited-edition print, or First Day Olympic stamps; and Statue of Liberty Restoration or Tall Ships' participants have received a beautiful photographic record of their outing in a leather album. Some firms will on occasion make donations to worthy causes in their guests' names rather than give individual tokens; for example, American Express gave a card to each guest at a Statue of Liberty celebration indicating that a restoration donation had been made in that person's name.

TAXES ON BUSINESS GIFTS

The cost of business gifts to employees or to current or prospective clients or customers is deductible up to a maximum of twenty-five dollars per year per client/customer. A gift to the spouse or children of a business contact is considered a gift to that person. Amounts expended by employer for annual party, picnic, or entertainment for his employees are deductible. Items of nominal value are not taxable to one's employees.

However, the new tax bill makes business gift giving more costly for some individuals. For example, beginning in 1987, those in the 50 percent bracket who now receive the maximum tax benefit of twenty-five dollars on gifts of fifty dollars or more will be entitled to only a 38.5 percent maximum benefit, and even less may be deductible in 1988. The ruling that one's miscellaneous deductions will have to exceed at least 2 percent of adjusted gross income before one is entitled to make a deduction could also lessen the tax motivation for business gift giving.

Promotional items or logo gifts that cost four dollars or less each on which your name is clearly and permanently imprinted (such as pens, umbrellas, key chains) are not included in determining your deduction for gifts as these expenses are deductible as advertising.

GIFTS
FOR THE OPENING
OF A NEW OFFICE
OR BUSINESS

The traditional gesture for the opening of a new business is to send an arrangement of flowers for the opening party or day. This is a lovely custom, but other choices could prove more memorable as a business strategy.

For the new professional or entrepreneur the list is limitless: from subscriptions to trade or waiting-room magazines to luxurious desk and office accessories (desk name plates, electric pencil sharpeners, reference books, clock, bookends, jar of candy, picture frames, list finders) to magazine racks or memo pads printed with the name of the business.

An antique map or document pertaining to the area or business, a framed print, or a special rare book could become the treasure of a new professional office. And a leatherbound atlas or thesaurus imprinted with the firm's logo or name, a case of special wine, a leather telephone directory cover, an antique letter opener, an ink well, a container for pens and pencils, or an elegant silver water carafe can be unforgettable remembrances.

For a thoughtful but inexpensive gift, there are ways of wrapping or sending the congratulatory message itself. A friend once received a personal "good luck" message for the opening of her new boutique in a foot-long fortune cookie. These days one can even order a personalized salami with features designed to match the recipient's (black mustache or long blond hair) and outfitted for the appropriate profession or sport (order a salami-o-gram or a brownie-o-gram from Selectogram, 211 West 80th Street, N.Y., N.Y. 10024, (212) 874-0775.)

Even if this is strictly a business gesture and you do not personally know the owners but want to be remembered, you can be inventive. A card from a florist notifying the new business of a credit for flowers to be sent when truly wanted or needed would ensure that you are not merely part of the opening floral scene. If the firm is moving to a new locale—perhaps into your area or building—send a note with an invitation to a special luncheon at one of the best area restaurants or a gift certificate for lunch for four.

Your gift to a new business should be a communication of goodwill and good luck. If you also have in mind a specific business goal, such as initiating a new business relationship or reinforcing an ongoing one, remember that your gift selection itself is an important part of the strategy for accomplishing that objective.

JOINT OFFICE
GIFTS

In many businesses the ongoing solicitation of an entire office for various events in the lives of the employees has gotten out of hand, creating a strain on the time, energy, and resources of many employees. Three different policy suggestions: 1) that firms and/or employees have a small fund from which gifts are purchased for employees for designated occasions; 2) that firms allow an occasional solicitation for certain occasions if the maximum amount allowable is small; or 3) that company policy prohibit collections for gifts inside the office. Whatever the policy, it should be put in writing and observed by all employees in order to avoid hurt feelings.

Recently the disgruntled staff of the engineering department of a large corporation confided to me an annual problem. Every Christmas the chief engineer's longtime secretary and his wife decided on his office Christmas present. The original idea was to keep members of his staff from purchasing individual gifts and to guide them to an appropriate choice. Over the years, however, the concept had grown out of proportion. Last year the request was for an expensive shotgun that required a substantial contribution from each of his junior engineers, every one of whom had a much smaller salary and a young family.

Corporate office tradition there also mandated an annual small party that included the drawing of names for an exchange of gifts within each department. Even this had become expensive—and sometimes embarrassing—as no one had set any limit for these gifts. Last year I suggested that these young people agree to place a seven-dollar limit on these gifts. At first their reaction was disbelief, but—with very little help—they entered into the spirit, selecting delightful and imaginative gifts for their co-workers.

When finally opened on the afternoon of the Christmas party, the seven-dollar gifts were so charming and clever and well selected that they became the focus of the party. In such a setting the presentation of a shotgun to their boss was not only anticlimactic but appeared ludicrous. His bulletin board thank-you, dated January 5, requested that from now on he be included in their Christmas drawing rather than given a special gift.

Over the years "joint" or "group" office gifts have developed their own patterns and ruts—many of which seem to apply through-out most of the country. In many offices they have reached tradition status. For instance, many firms that have a gift fund automatically send plants for almost every occasion; or the employee who is confined with illness routinely receives fresh flowers and a humorous get-well card signed by everyone in the office. And of course, there is the "surprise" birthday cake required for each office birthday. Granted, these are nice and thoughtful gestures, but repetitive, dull, and—worst of all—anticipated by the recipient.

There are many, many ways to combat this sameness. Busi-nesses that have established guidelines and funds to take care of such occasions have a wide range of options beyond plants, flowers, and fruit baskets. Frankly, I feel that a plant is, or should be, a very individualized gift. Calling a florist to order an "attractive plant" or a "flowering plant" within a certain price range shows little concern for the recipient's preferences, decorating plans, space in home or office, time for its nurturing, ability to provide the appropriate environment (humidity, light), or even his or her interest in plants. Certainly, an expensive and beautiful but large foliage plant in any area where space is at a premium would be a disaster. Some of these same concerns apply to the nonpersonalized selection of cut flowers as the gift for anyone on any occasion.

Don't misunderstand: plants and flowers can be wonderful gifts, but they must be selected for the individual and appropriate to the occasion and environment.

There are options, however, that are just as easy to order by telephone as are plants, flowers, and fruit baskets. Interesting gour-met treats could include a selection of ice cream sauces, jams, and preserves (my favorites are from Sarabeth's Kitchen, New York,

212-580-8335); salad dressings and vinegars; gift-wrapped nuts or cheeses; a basket or other container of favorite foods or gourmet diet foods; a bottle of wine or champagne (especially with the recipient's name as a part of the label); a special cured meat or fowl or sausage, a smoked salmon; a wonderful quiche; or unusual coffees or teas in attractive packaging.

Nonfood gifts could be desk-dweller items, such as picture frames, chair cushions, small clock, nameplate, organizers, or a collection of small desk-size cosmetics or grooming aids.

As an alternative, some offices using the "fund" method designate someone who knows the recipient well to select the gift. This helps to ensure that the gift is personal and not an item that is routinely anticipated.

Small offices that permit the solicitation of limited amounts from individuals often find that they must work within quite small budgets. Imagination, thoughtfulness, and innovative packaging are required.

Books—even a selection of paperbacks—magazine subscriptions, tapes, records, tickets to a special event, or monogrammed stationery of good quality can be both personal and economical. Because office gifts are usually presented and opened with ceremony, the packaging can add significantly to the festivities. Wrap the gift in everyday office or mailroom papers, stickers, and stamps, attach a surprise to the package, or place one small gift inside another that is a useful container (flower pot, basket, bandana, dish towel, file box).

The most memorable joint office gift often is one that cannot be purchased. For a co-worker who is recuperating from an illness or injury, a rotating schedule of lunchtime, evening, or weekend visits that the patient looks forward to means far more than any one-time expensive purchase. In certain circumstances these visits might include bringing lunch or loaning a new selection of books.

If you are asked to contribute to an office gift and do not wish to—for whatever reason—do not hesitate to politely refuse. You might add that you are planning to visit your co-worker in the hospital or to write him or her a note.

GIFTS
FOR THE BOSS

I recently spoke to a large group of top international executive assistants and secretaries in Dallas, Texas. The organization consists of highly qualified professionals who must pass certain standards of certification and who—among their numerous other duties—are responsible for many different kinds of corporate and personal gift finding for their CEOs and board chairmen. As they registered for the evening, they were asked to fill out forms that included the question: "Within the last year, what has been your most difficult, either corporate or personal, gift-buying problem?"

As I read their answers during the reception, I discovered that about eighty percent listed as their most perplexing problem that of finding presents for their bosses. That's not surprising. Think of all the complexities of selecting a gift for the person for whom you work; it can't be too expensive or too inexpensive, too personal or too impersonal. It should show thoughtfulness and be appropriate. And it should appear to be more than a gesture.

Although it is unnecessary for staff members to give their bosses Christmas or birthday presents, certain relationships seem to require at least a token gift. If you decide to give one, many factors will relate to its selection: how directly you work for this person; how closely you work with this person; how long you've worked for this person; how involved you have become with his or her family on a personal level; and—very important—how you want to be perceived by this person as a result of this gift (more professional, clever, or thoughtful; less frivolous; sophisticated, competent, and so on).

Usually a gift to a close employer should have enough of a personal touch that it relates to an interest, need, or hobby of the recipient. Often the answer is obvious—she collects old cobalt glass; he has a new sailboat; she is a fitness buff; he thinks he's a gourmet cook. But what if you've found small pieces of cobalt for the last four occasions; his sailboat has just been appropriated by his kids; she gets shin splints; he has just returned from two weeks of special lessons with Chef Paul Bocuse and an assortment of pots, pans, and spices from France?

Then ask yourself how you want to appear.

Thoughtful and practical? A thermal carafe; a car vacuum; a folding snow shovel; something for the yard (bird house or feeder, rain gauge, harvest basket with seeds, markers, catalog); barbecue grill attachments or utensils; a collection of flower bulbs; a gift certificate for yard plantings of his or her choice; an X-ray proof film bag and prepaid film mailers; kitchen gadgets; a pasta crate (all the fixings for a special Italian dinner and recipes).

Knowledgeable and interested? Membership in a museum; a subscription to a travel magazine; tickets to a special event; language tapes; the perfect book for the office coffee table; an old map of the city or of an area significant to the recipient; membership in a society or tickets to an event that relate to his or her hobby or special interest—from antiques to polo.

Charming and humorous? A portrait in chocolate; a box of fortune cookies with fortunes related to a profession or sport (tennis, stockbroker, dentist, golf); a special gift for or related to a favorite pet (sweatshirt or tote bag with his or her golden retriever appliquéd on the front, or a blown-up framed photo of his or her Siamese cat); a desk footstool (if he or she habitually puts feet up on desk); a wittily presented large supply of favorite snack foods or drinks.

Clever and sophisticated? A liveried butler or maid for a special event; an executive puzzle; a gourmet breakfast or lunch delivered to the office for a particular occasion; a special bottle of wine, sherry, or champagne—perhaps with a personalized label; an elegant office place setting (a basket containing a colorful place mat and napkin, eating utensils, china plate, bowl, and cup); a new travel gadget or accessory, such as a money converter or a traveling gym that fits into a briefcase.

Remember that giving a gift to your boss—even at Christmas-time—is not necessary or expected, that it should not be an expensive gift, and that it must be in good taste. Some bosses would be embarrassed to receive a gift from an employee they have not known well or for a long period of time.

A spontaneous gesture such as freshly cut flowers for the desk, homemade cookies, or garden vegetables is always appropriate and often can be shared with others in the office.

GIFTS
FOR EMPLOYEES

M̲ost gifts for employees fall neatly into the categories of service awards, incentives, holiday, or retirement. Those that
do not fall into these categories usually require only your thoughtfulness and good judgment to be successful.

Service Awards

Beginning with the fifth year of employment, many companies—
especially large ones—recognize their employees' loyalty with small
gifts. A structured program service will continue to give awards
that increase in value every five or ten years. The successful
program gives awards that add to the employees' pride in themselves,
in their work, and in their employer; and the gift itself is something
they will value. *Typical five-year gifts:* leather or metal picture frame,
pocket calculator, leather desk agenda or calendar, wallet or address
book—many of these imprinted with a small company logo. *For the
tenth anniversary:* often something in gold or silver that can be
recognized by others, such as gold lapel pin with the company logo or
a desk clock. More important gifts should mark the fifteenth and
twentieth anniversaries; usually the twenty-fifth is of silver; the
thirty-fifth, of jade. Small, closely knit companies might prefer to
recognize significant anniversaries with individually selected gifts.

Incentive Gifts

The use of gifts to motivate employees, distributors, and dealers must be effective. Last year approximately 1.4 million companies in America developed an average of between 3.6 and 6.8 sales incentive programs. They bought more than $8.1 billion worth of products and services to give as productivity gifts. In addition, more than 850,000 U.S. businesses developed dealer/distributor incentive gift programs, purchasing about $6.5 billion worth of products and services.

Incentives range from tool sets complete with tape rules and a "how to" book, to logo duffle bags and passport cases announcing a trip to Spain. Companies such as State Farm Insurance reward their agents with an incentive gift program of well-planned travel to worldwide destinations based on volume and quality of sales. In turn, some of these agents design monthly incentives for their employees—a weekend sea-escape for two, or gift certificates from a beauty salon or a local department store. Employers who periodically take the time to creatively change the incentive gift feel that this makes the program more exciting and successful.

The current trend is to seek more unusual and sought-after incentive gifts. Tie-in programs such as participation in events, like the Statue of Liberty restoration, the America's Cup, or the Olympics, have been particularly successful; and the top salesmen and dealers for one automobile manufacturer have been motivated with the promise of family portraits by a well-known artist. Imprinted (with logo) goods usually are not good as incentive gifts. If they are imprinted, they should be of good quality, well designed, and with a small imprint—perhaps engraved on the back.

Holiday Gifts

Many businesses give holiday gifts to all employees; others prohibit gift giving. Although bonuses are usually received at year's end, they should not be considered a gift by either employer or employee, as a bonus is earned for one's job performance.

It is important to have a company policy on this subject in order to avoid misunderstandings and to maintain company morale at this time of year. Depending on the type of industry, local customs and preferences, and how well the company is doing, management may consider the annual company Christmas party or dinner as a gift (a much better gift if families are included); give employees a gift catalog from which they order an item of their choice (possibly one of the company's own product catalogs); give each employee the same gift (most often a company product, logo gift, or food such as a turkey, candy, or fruitcake); give money to charity or distribute gifts of food to the needy in the employees' names; or send a Christmas card signed by the CEO to each employee's family. Large businesses may also wish to have a policy to guide their individual offices or regions about holiday gifts and party protocol.

A boss's gift to his or her secretary or assistants should reflect the length of time the employee has worked for this boss, the amount of responsibility the employee has, whether the employee also does personal favors such as keeping the boss's checkbook, making personal appointments, and managing his or her weekly boat-crew list, and—to some extent—the boss's position or importance within the company. The cost of the gift can vary from twenty-five dollars to one hundred dollars, should not be too personal in nature, and should not decrease in value from one year to the next. A special check (not a bonus) is appropriate if you know that the employee has certain needs at this time; a gift certificate to a favorite store is another thoughtful gift. When managers share a secretary or an assistant, a group gift is the best solution.

Some executives prefer to give a small personal token to each employee in addition to the regular company gift. This is a thoughtful gesture that can make a significant impact on all employees, from elevator operators to cleaning persons; it is obviously something that the executive did not "have to do" and will be received with pride. A personal thank-you note to each employee for his or her contributions over the past year is also a special gift.

Retirement Gifts

An interviewer who was doing a story about corporate gift consultants once asked me what I thought was the perfect retirement gift for an employee who had worked most of his life for the same small company. I replied that there was no one gift that could satisfy such a question—that any employee who had spent a lifetime in one firm should be well known enough and well understood enough by his employers and friends to receive a gift selected especially for his interests. My response surprised her. Others had suggested everything from color TVs and Caribbean cruises to—yes—gold watches.

It is nice to have a lovely gift that retirees look forward to receiving—but it's even nicer to know that your friends realize that you've been looking forward to playing golf four times a week and thus present you with a set of high-quality clubs or a new golf bag. When the gift is traditional and anticipated, it should be personalized as much as possible—a warm, personal letter from the CEO or boss, or a scrapbook filled with the best wishes of co-workers and friends.

Recent, well-selected retirement gifts include: for a top executive at United Technologies, a radar set for his new boat; for the chairman of American Airlines, a wonderful party where everyone played a trivia game based on events in his and his wife's lives and where, among other gifts, they received a game table and, for her (an ardent needlepointer), a needlepoint copy of their own game; for the Chief Scout Executive of Boy Scouts of America, a fully equipped camper from his many national volunteers.

Special Occasion Gifts

Although Christmas is the usual time for gift rewards, it is good management policy to recognize hard work or an outstanding job on the part of an employee, group, or division. The now familiar TV ad where the returning executive enters his office, turns on his answering machine, and hears his boss praise his efforts, then suggest that he will find his reward in his desk drawer—airplane tickets for a well-deserved vacation—has universal appeal.

Not long ago, one of my clients was concerned because one section of his company had been working overtime for several months to complete a project. They were exhausted and their families had barely seen them for weeks. The solution was individually planned family excursions to New York City. Each family decided on either a family outing or just a husband-and-wife holiday. Employees were picked up at their homes by limousine and whisked into the city to see their choice of museum exhibits, musical events, and Broadway shows, and to eat at the city's premier restaurants. Even baby-sitting was arranged by the company. The gesture was a great gift that helped to restore family balance and let these employees know how much they were appreciated and understood.

Many companies look for ways to express appreciation to individuals who are instrumental in putting together a deal. Engraved leather mementos such as desk accessories, picture frames, or silver objects are common merger and acquisition gifts. It is customary for the head of the acquiring company to commemorate the new partnership with a token gift to the CEO of the other company. A Chicago company thanked each of the sixty-five persons who had participated in implementing a large stock offering for the American subsidiary of a company headquartered in Dublin, Ireland, with a music box that played "My Wild Irish Rose" when opened. Its cover, a brass plate in the shape of Ireland, was etched with a reproduction of the stock prospectus and personalized with the recipient's name.

PRODUCT
PROMOTIONS AND
PREMIUM
GIFTS

Almost all industries at one time or another use gifts to promote their products. My children were always more interested in the promises of wonderful gifts on cereal boxes than in the cereal they contained; as a child I always opened my Cracker Jacks® upside down, hoping to reach the gift first.

From inflatable pool toys that advertise that they can "inflate your sales," to Big League Chew® (shredded gum in a foil pouch like chewing tobacco), most sample and promotional gifts are clearly marked with the product or brand name or logo. When using the logo—even for small promotional items such as pens or calendars—be certain that it is tastefully done.

The competition for appealing promotional gifts has produced some interesting results for the consumer. Banks, which have long competed with promotions, have discovered that premium gifts that work in one branch or area may be unsuccessful in others. Saab-Scania of America, two weeks after delivery of a car, sent owners key rings and a key-registration form that guaranteed recovery if the keys were lost or stolen; twenty days after delivery, owners who also purchased tape decks were sent a tape-head-cleaning kit, and all owners were later sent a porcelain safety mug and a note of thanks from the company president. Computer companies are giving purchasers miniature TV sets and gift certificates for accessories; makers of toiletries offer customers the chance to win Chrysler convertibles, Renault

Alliance convertibles, and vacation trips, as well as a beach chair which they can purchase for $8.95 and three package wrappers. Some fur companies offer mink Teddy bears to customers along with their coats. Liquor companies have their own approach: during the holiday season, one company gave commuters in designated areas a free *New York Times*. Recipe books and calendars are other popular giveaways.

BUSINESS GIFTS:
SPECIALIZED APPLICATIONS

Certain gift situations and protocol questions seem not to fit into any business categories.

- Many companies that sponsor the arts should plan to reinforce that commitment with other gifts to staff and clients: memberships, tickets, or reduced rates for the museum, symphony, opera, or theater; client gifts from the organization's shop; or shop discounts for employees.

- Companies whose employees live in the area are usually expected to support community projects that include actual participation as well as gifts of money—activities such as Trees for Towns, local library drives, and the educational TV channel pledge campaigns. The additional donation of logo hats for campaigners or T-shirts for volunteers will help to enhance the corporate image.

- Certain important occasions in the lives of major clients or customers should be acknowledged with a tasteful gift. Although these goodwill gifts are sometimes made at the company's expense, they can be an excellent personal investment. The birth of a new baby, a client's marriage (or his or her child's), a hospitalized or convalescing customer, or a retiring friend all merit your thoughtful remembrance.

- If your company policy does not allow you to accept lavish gifts, don't be afraid to say so politely. Firms that have special guidelines or that do not permit employees to accept any business gifts, because the nature of their business might make the recipient feel indebted or obliged to the giver, should publicize this policy widely, especially at holiday time. Some companies have ethics programs; others have a conflict-of-interest agreement that includes gift policies.

• Any gift that is extravagant, too personal, or that has sexual or bribery connotations should be returned to the sender immediately. If you send a note with it, for your own protection keep a dated copy along with a description of the gift.

• Acknowledgment of employees' and customers' birthdays with cards or notes is a thoughtful gesture as well as savvy public relations. Physicians and dentists who have long used birthday cards as a subliminal reminder to their healthy patients set the precedent.

• The business person who accepts gifts with grace, responding quickly either with a sincere thank-you note or an appropriate gift for an unexpected favor or delightful dinner, displays both good manners and executive professionalism.

CORPORATE
GIFT CONSULTANTS/
SHOPPING SERVICES
AND HOW TO
USE THEM

Because time is money to busy executives, more and more corporations are hiring in-house personnel to be responsible for their gift programs, or are using outside consulting firms experienced in this area. They find that using professionals rather than overworked secretaries or purchasing agents is both more efficient and rewarding. And it makes up for their lack of time and knowledge of options.

A corporation's gift program might cover incentive gifts for employees; a retirement gift plan; gifts for officers and board of directors; rewards to faithful customers; mementos of special occasions such as the production of a new car or engine or a company anniversary; special employee awards for efficiency or service; gifts to announce a new product or account; congratulation gifts; merger gifts; appropriate presents for international business situations, both at home and abroad; gifts for the opening of new stores or offices; top management's peer business gifts; and even suggestions for premium gifts related to new product promotion.

Executive gift or image consultants can handle both the pragmatic side and the protocol of gift giving, a time-consuming but important aspect of doing business today almost everywhere in the world. Most outside services have great resources for seeking out gifts and arranging entertainment and are prepared to handle all the details.

How should you shop for a shopper? Some firms retain image consultants who become a part of their overall think-tank, acting as imager, packager, broker, protocol officer, and general information source. The best of these consultants offer companies many creative choices they didn't know they had; they also stress style and thoughtfulness. Many professional shopping services are limited to finding "what to buy for whom" and can do a good job of finding unusual and appropriate gifts that can be given to a large number of people—as at Christmastime. A few businesses provide international service—in the selection, presentation protocol, and, if necessary, shipping of the gift; it is important to have professional advice for international business gift exchange. Professional services follow up on your orders and monitor your transactions. All of them will meet with clients to assess their needs, review their budgets, and go over ideas; after exploring various suggestions and checking sources, the consultant usually returns to the client for the final buying decisions.

For the professional shopper, finding a gift that fits the image of the giver is just as important as finding the right gift for the recipient; and advising the client on how, when, and in what way a gift should be presented is an important aspect of the service. For special office gifts, the consultant will often have a dialogue with the recipient's assistant or secretary and may even sneak a look at the office.

Some professional shopping services buy in large quantities and act as retailers, not charging for finding the gifts; others charge an hourly fee with a set minimum. Most image and gift consultants who structure and execute corporate image, including special events and international gift protocol, prefer to work on a retainer basis.

Some of the better department stores—Neiman-Marcus, Bergdorf Goodman, Gump's—as well as specialty retailers—Tiffany's, Mark Cross, Steuben—have either personal shopping services or corporate buying departments to deal with executive-gift needs. Most of them, of course, are limited to their own range of products.

PART FIVE

INTERNATIONAL AND ETHNIC GIFTS

INTERNATIONAL
AND ETHNIC GIFT GIVING
AND RECEIVING

G iving and receiving foreign gifts is a plea-
sure and a subject of concern. Careful study of a people's gift culture
can reveal economic, social, and even political tenets, traditions,
attitudes, and conditions. Saudi desert hospitality, Chinese antimaterialism policy, and Japanese *giri*—the concept that debts and
obligations must be repaid in equal value—are inherent in the ways
they give and receive gifts. Whether the gifts are business or social,
an understanding of cultural differences is key to selecting a successful gift and avoiding embarrassment.

Appreciation of a different gift culture will expand your ability
to be effective in dealing with foreign business people and will help
you to avoid the "ugly American" syndrome. Thus, I attempt as often
as possible to discuss a country's gift giving in terms of its cultural
characteristics and provide interesting information on local customs
and traditions along with travelers' "dos and don'ts."

One of my choice international anecdotes and a favorite story of
James W. Symington, former U.S. Chief of Protocol, well illustrates
my point. During Thomas Jefferson's presidency, the American consul in Morocco was offered the gift of a handsome pair of lions for
the United States from the local viceroy, who represented the ruling
sultan. When the consul politely refused the gift because of prohibitions in the bylaws of the U.S. Constitution, the viceroy begged him
to reconsider. Accordingly, the consul sent a letter to Washington.

Sometime later the expected response confirming the rejection arrived. Upon receiving the news, the viceroy advised the American consul that it was regrettable for two reasons: first, there would be no further relationship between their two governments; second, he, the viceroy, would lose his head. The two lions lived out their old age in Virginia.

Very little has been researched or written about cultural gifts. Although most books concerned with techniques of doing business abroad or international protocol list gift exchange as an important form of communication, few give enough information to help the person who is actually responsible for selecting and presenting thirty or forty gifts for a business negotiation in Japan, for instance.

The most significant study of international business gift-giving customs to date is the excellent "The Protocol of Corporate Giving" by Dr. Kathleen Reardon, professor of communication sciences, University of Connecticut. Her work, which was based on a survey of American business persons who had done business abroad, indicated that they had several worries: (1) that the purpose of the gift might be misinterpreted; (2) that there was the possibility of incurring obligation or becoming obligated by return gifts; (3) that they might possibly embarrass the recipient; (4) that they might unwittingly commit a cultural faux pas; (5) that they were unsure how to determine what was appropriate given the nature of the relationship.

The primary characteristics of a good business gift were that it was American, utilitarian, and had importance as conversation value. Brand name, logo, and wrapping were also important considerations. In addition, Reardon's survey revealed strategic givers who admitted that obligation was their purpose and salesmen who described gift giving as "good salesmanship."

I felt it was important to compile several points of view in regard to foreign gift giving and receiving—those of business people and visitors with international gift experience and expertise; ambassadors, consuls, and representatives of foreign embassies and trade offices throughout the world; American ambassadors and State Department officials who have been stationed in various parts of the globe; business people, scholars, and visitors from various countries; people who have lived and worked in foreign countries; my own experiences and those of my clients. In the process I discovered that a foreigner's idea of the perfect gift or notions about giving customs were often inaccurate or outdated—and that sometimes acknowledging certain traditions (which they might still observe among themselves) could be construed as an insult in a rapidly changing environment.

For politicians ranging from heads of nations to minor government or state officials, knowledge, judgment, and good taste are the most crucial elements in selecting appropriate international gifts. According to Symington, the best gift is one that shows the respect that your society has for that of the other country—a flattering effort to communicate. Signature gifts are often selected to memorialize an important conference or major meeting.

President Lyndon Johnson's first trip to meet with the president of Mexico resulted in having his Secret Service men carry gift-wrapped watches in their pockets so that if he was ever again in the position of not having a reciprocal gift, he could inconspicuously receive a watch and present it to the gift giver. Even Letitia Baldrige, America's leading arbiter of manners and protocol, admits that she erred when, just before a visit, she sent multiple copies of President John Kennedy's photograph to key Indian officials: the dark blue frames embossed with the presidential seal were of calfskin. Needless to say, they were quickly replaced with something other than the sacred cow.

The variety of gifts given between countries is as extensive as their reasons for giving them. A sampling: George Washington's white battle steed was a gift from Spain's Charles III; two pandas, Ling-Ling and Hsing-Hsing, came to America as a gift from the Chinese government following former President Richard Nixon's first diplomatic visit to that country; the Philippines gave a quantity of high-yield rice seeds to the Vietnamese government; King Saud's gifts to everyone from President Eisenhower (a sword encased in a golden scabbard) to the wife of the deputy director of protocol for the State Department (an Oldsmobile) created many headaches; Secretary of State George P. Shultz gave Soviet Ambassador Anatoly Dobrynin a new chair like one that Dobrynin had admired in his office (Shultz purchased it with his own funds); and recently the Chinese government presented to Burma a theater with a seating capacity of one thousand people.

The official limit for gifts to the White House is $165. This is the gift's market value, including importation fees. Under the Foreign Gifts Act, larger gifts must be turned in to the General Services Administration within ninety days of receipt; however, officials may buy back those gifts. Thus, former Secretary of State Henry Kissinger paid $4,636 for a diamond necklace his wife received from Pakistan. Most gifts quickly find their way into the GSA vaults; their givers receive thank-you notes. A list of gifts received is published annually in the Federal Register, and nonpresidential gifts are publicly sold at auction after an appropriate waiting period. According to the White House Gift Unit, the Reagans will occasionally place some inexpensive gifts at the ranch, especially those that complement the rustic decor. They cannot accept the works of any living artist; he or she must be deceased for at least twenty years. This is to protect them from publicity-seeking artists who would advertise that their work has gone to the White House.

Recent exotic gifts include silver-encased ostrich eggs from Mexico; beer mugs from Japan; a diamond-studded pin from the wife of the former Israeli president; an organdy linen tablecloth with matching napkins from the wife of Lebanon's president; a silver jewelry box from the emperor and empress of Japan; a set of gold golf clubs from Japanese Prime Minister Yasuhiro Nakasone; mounted ivory tusks from the vice president of Nigeria; jade and gold cuff links from Korea's president; and an incense burner.

Mid-twentieth-century diplomacy disguises some financial dealings with giftlike names such as "foreign" or "economic aid." (I'll never forget my horror at discovering that the U.S. Food for Peace Program, which sends food to hungry nations, included tobacco; as a lobbyist I fought its inclusion—unsuccessfully.)

JEWISH
GIFT GIVING
CUSTOMS

J ewish tradition has many holidays and celebrations. This chapter is not meant to be a comprehensive explanation of Jewish customs and social practices, but a guide for gift giving situations that are unique to Jewish holidays and occasions. From bar/ bas mitzvahs and Rosh Hashanah to housewarmings and funerals, the traditions and etiquette of giving in a Jewish setting are an important and symbolic part of their enriching history.

The non-Jew, whether friend or business associate, can demonstrate both respect and thoughtfulness by using this gift giving knowledge to observe occasions properly.

Life Cycle Events

BABY GIFTS

Jewish tradition has special celebrations related to the birth of a baby. A close friend may be invited to a baby boy's brith (in Yiddish *bris*) milah ceremony, which usually takes place eight days after his birth. At this time the boy is circumcised, given his name, and given godparents. This ceremony usually takes place in a special room at the hospital or at the parents' home.

On the first Sabbath after they are born, girls receive their names in the synagogue; the ceremony includes the rabbi's special blessing. Close friends are also often invited to this service.

A small party or reception (a seudah, or feast, is often held in celebration of the brith) customarily follows each of these ceremonies and guests usually bring gifts for the new baby.

Whether attending one of these special events or receiving a birth announcement, one may wish to send or bring a gift. Note that there is a strong tradition of reluctance to prepare too much in advance before the birth of a Jewish child; thus most gifts are given after the child is born and his/her name announced.

The usual baby-christening type of gifts (see "Births and Christenings," page 55), as well as gifts of money—checks, cash, or bonds—are appropriate. In addition, in some Jewish communities it is customary to plant a tree to honor the birth of a child. Originally, the trees growing with the children were expected to supply the wood for the chuppah (wedding canopy) when he or she married. The traditional trees are cedar for a boy and cypress or pine for a girl. For apartment dwellers, you might choose an indoor tree or plant trees in Israel in the child's name.

THE BAR MITZVAH AND BAS MITZVAH

These ceremonies for Jewish thirteen-year-olds, which celebrate reaching the age of religious responsibility, are definitely gift giving occasions. Invitations to a bar or bas mitzvah are usually sent well in advance of the occasion. As with many invitations, only those who attend are expected to send or bring a gift; often, however, friends who cannot attend send gifts to the youth's home.

Because Orthodox Jews do not carry on the Sabbath, you should not bring a gift to a synagogue, unless you are certain that carrying is acceptable. Thus, if the celebration is held on the Sabbath (as most are), it is best to send your gift to the boy's or girl's home before or just after the ceremony. If the reception begins after the Sabbath or is held at another time, you may bring your gift then.

Most gifts that are appropriate for a thirteen-year-old's birthday apply here. Especially significant might be religious jewelry, a biography of a Jewish hero or heroine, stories, poems, or music by Jewish authors or composers, Israeli art objects or coins made into medallions, a donation to a charity in the youth's name, trees planted in Israel, or a subscription to a Jewish magazine. Also suitable are gifts of cash, checks, and savings bonds, books, records, sports equipment, jewelry such as initial rings and watches, and electronic gadgets. Lasting gifts are the most appropriate for this significant occasion.

JEWISH WEDDING GIFTS

As with most other weddings, people invited to a Jewish wedding need send a gift only if they accept the invitation; however, close friends and business associates often send gifts even when they are unable to attend the wedding.

A generous wedding gift is a Jewish custom, and a gift of money is always appropriate. This could be cash, a check, U.S. government or Israeli bonds, or a gift certificate to a favorite store or an establishment at which the bride has listed her silver, crystal, or china patterns. If one is mailing a gift certificate, check, or bond before the wedding, it should be made out to the bride-to-be and sent to her home. If presented at the wedding reception, it should be made out to both the bride and the groom.

Gifts should match your budget and relate to the couple's lifestyle. As with any other type of wedding, it is always correct to give something from the bridal registry. Friends or relatives may join together to give a place setting or serving piece. Practical gifts, special art objects, and items for entertaining are also welcome.

If you are attending an Orthodox Jewish wedding for the first time, it would be helpful to know that the bride and groom are often given certain traditional gifts from parents and grandparents. For example, you may notice that the groom is wearing an especially beautiful tallith, or prayer shawl. He probably received this fine tallith, made of silk or wool, from the bride or from her mother. Frequently the bride embroiders or has specially made a *tallith* bag as her gift to the groom. The bride's parents or grandparents may also have given him a silver kiddush cup. The bride's new mother-in-law traditionally presents her with Sabbath candlesticks; the grandparents with a special tray for the Sabbath challah bread or a fine cloth for Sabbath and holidays. Other heirloom ceremonial objects, such as a challah knife or Passover plate, are usually passed on through the family as wedding gifts.

HANUKKAT HABAYIT: DEDICATING A NEW HOUSE

A traditional Jewish housewarming has an element of dedication that centers around the hanging of a mezuzah (scroll). *Mezuzah,* which means "doorpost" in Hebrew, refers to the parchment hand-lettered scroll containing the texts of the Shema—parts of Deuteronomy—and its case, which is attached to the doorpost of a Jewish home. The Hebrew letter *shin*—the symbol of the Almighty—is arranged to be visible at all times through an opening in the container. A reception may follow the hanging of the mezuzah, where friends present good wishes and housewarming gifts.

Customarily, these gifts are small items such as plants, books, gourmet delicacies, utilitarian objects for new households, or wine. Often on moving day or before the family is fully settled in, friends or relatives may bring the traditional threshold gift of candles, bread, and salt to the new home; these symbolize light and joy and enough to eat in the house. For a housewarming, non-Jewish friends could provide an interesting variation on this theme—saltcellars or dishes, special candles or candlesticks, or books on breadmaking.

ANNIVERSARIES

There are no special gift giving customs associated with the celebration of Jewish wedding anniversaries. For young couples, gift certificates, money, or theater tickets are always correct. The usual themes—silver for the twenty-fifth anniversary—are observed, and the appropriate gifts apply.

EXPRESSIONS OF SYMPATHY

Jewish custom provides a formalized framework that helps friends to console the mourner. Attending the funeral and/or making a condolence call during the shivah, or mourning, period is the best expression of sympathy to a Jewish friend. Because a Jewish burial takes place a day or two after the death, you wouldn't call before the funeral service unless you were a very close friend.

Shivah means "seven" in Hebrew and is the length of the mourning period. Orthodox tradition does not allow family mourners to leave the house during these seven days; however, Conservative and Reform mourners may return to their own homes to sleep. Reform custom has shortened the shivah period for some to three days.

During the shivah period, the immediate family usually gathers in one house to mourn, remaining together and accepting condolences from relatives and friends. Friends or neighbors prepare a "meal of consolation" for the mourners upon their return. This simple meal is offered to the mourners as a gesture of sympathy and often includes hard-boiled eggs, as they are a life symbol. Thoughtful friends usually wait until at least the second day of the shivah to visit. Often the door is left unlocked in a house of mourning so that you may knock and then enter immediately. In a traditional house of mourning one does not greet the mourner. Often in Orthodox circles there is no attempt at conversation with the mourner unless the mourner initiates it.

Do not bring gifts, plants, or flowers to the home. Fruit baskets, candy, or prepared food for the mourners and their guests are always thoughtful and appropriate (observing kosher tradition if the family does).

Handwritten letters and cards of sympathy demonstrate that one cares. A memorial contribution to a charity may be made after you have checked with the family for a preference. Because the Hebrew number for eighteen (18) spells the word *chai*, meaning "life," memorial donations are often made in amounts that are multiples of eighteen.

One *never* sends flowers to an Orthodox Jewish funeral; generally they are not desired at a Conservative or Reform funeral, either. They are considered reminders of worldly pleasure or vanity.

Jewish Holidays

Because the Hebrew calendar varies so widely from the Gregorian and can differ greatly from year to year, months rather than specific dates are listed for each holiday.

ROSH HASHANAH/THE JEWISH NEW YEAR (SEPTEMBER)

It is thoughtful to remember Jewish friends, colleagues, or relatives at Rosh Hashanah by sending greeting cards. Although a text or design that includes the traditional "l'shanah tovah" (note: *l'shanah tovah tikatevu* means "May you be inscribed [in the Book of Life] for a good new year") is preferable, any card is made more personal with the addition of a special sentence or two. If the recipient is a business acquaintance, you may send the card to the office. Cards are usually sent out about ten days before Rosh Hashanah.

A holiday Rosh Hashanah guest might select a challah cloth, a special object from Israel, or the usual "hostess" gifts of fruit, flowers, books, wines, or sweets, observing the kosher tradition. Because the Hebrew letters of the word *nuts* can also form an acrostic spelling "sin," some avoid giving nuts for Jewish religious celebrations.

SUKKOTH (OCTOBER)

A joyful festival that begins five days after Yom Kippur (the Day of Atonement), Sukkoth commemorates the forty years of wandering in the desert wilderness after the Jews' Exodus from Egypt. It also celebrates the fall harvest and is a time for thanksgiving.

The sukkah itself is usually a temporary but richly decorated structure in the yard or patio with three free-standing walls and a roof (*skhakh*) that allows the stars to shine through at night. The building of a sukkah is a family project that is meant to symbolize the Jewish experience of living in temporary huts for those forty years.

Honey pastries are probably the most appropriate gift for a guest to bring to a Sukkoth party. Other delicacies such as liquors, wines, chocolates, fruit, and candies are suitable. Nonfood items might include attractive serving dishes for the sukkah.

HANUKKAH, THE FESTIVAL OF LIGHTS (DECEMBER)

The Festival of Lights commemorates the victory of the Maccabees over the tyrant Antiochus over two thousand years ago. The name *Hanukkah* means "dedication"—a remembrance of the rededication of the Temple to Jewish worship. The holiday celebrates the ideal of Jewish identity and distinctiveness.

Hanukkah is celebrated by the lighting of the special menorah (candelabrum) on each of the eight nights of the holiday.

In many American Jewish homes, Hanukkah gift giving has become quite lavish and at least as grand as Christmas giving. Children of the family customarily receive small gifts either on each night of the holiday or on the first and last nights. Often this is "Hanukkah gelt," money in the form of shiny new coins or gold-foil–wrapped chocolate ones—some stamped with symbols found on Israeli coins. Other small gifts that a guest could bring for a Jewish child are similar to the gifts that Santa Claus places in Christmas stockings.

A Hanukkah party guest may bring almost any "hostess" gift (foods should generally be kosher). Jewish items such as books, records, pictures, or ceremonial objects are especially appropriate. At Christmastime non-Jews sometimes send Hanukkah cards to their Jewish acquaintances. However courteous, this gesture is not a conventional Jewish observance and certainly not to be equated with the Christian observance of Christmas. It would be more meaningful to send Jewish friends a Rosh Hashanah card for the Jewish New Year, which falls in early autumn.

Sending a gift to a close Jewish friend or colleague at Christmastime without the Christmas wrapping paper and with a Hanukkah card often is appreciated.

PURIM, THE FEAST OF LOTS AND TIME
OF THE ADLOYADA (CARNIVAL)

Purim celebrates the triumph of Esther over the villain Haman. The name is derived from the word *pur*—a lottery—the method Haman used to select the date for his planned massacre of the Jews. It is a joyful carnival (*adloyada*) time. The celebration of Purim is largely historic in nature, and includes shalach monos—the sending of gifts and gladness to friends and the needy as set forth in the Book of Esther.

A thoroughly delightful tradition, Purim inspires Jews to send a gift of at least two kinds of fruit, cookies, or sweets to friends in the community. The costumed young messenger of the modest, attractively wrapped gift will be rewarded with a few coins and a return gift for the family who sent it. The tradition is that of charity: the more people you give to, the better.

If you receive an unexpected gift from your Jewish friends at this time, you certainly should not return it and should send some small token such as sweets in return. The young messenger will appreciate some small change.

PESACH/PASSOVER (MARCH–APRIL)

If you are fortunate enough to be invited to a seder, you will experience the home holiday most widely observed even by those who no longer participate formally in the other aspects of Jewish worship.

The keynote of Jewish identity, this festival of freedom is rich in symbolism and is family-centered. Most of the laws surrounding Passover pertain to "forbidden" and "permitted" foods. These foods are symbolic—each representing some aspect of the Passover story. During the seder each person usually receives a Haggadah (the Passover text) so that he can follow the service.

Because Pesach is the family holiday of Judaism, it is traditional to invite friends and those who are far from their homes (as well as those who have no family seder nearby) to one's seder.

The seder guest has several obligations: to be prompt, to eat some matzo, to partake of each of the four cups of wine at the seder, to follow the rituals, and to try to participate in the reading and singing. It is usual for the seder guest to bring a gift for the family.

If you wish to bring a liquor or food item, to avoid embarrassment it is best to observe tradition, as standards of observance differ from home to home. Select only those foods that have the kashruth labels. Popular food items such as candies, preserves, and wines must all carry a rabbinical seal and not merely the word *kosher* but *kosher for Passover*. Most breads and corn or wheat products are not acceptable. Fruits are appropriate and, of course, require no label. Grain alcohols are not kosher; plum brandy (slivovitz) and cherry liqueur (wishniak), which are properly certified, are appreciated.

With all these potential restrictions on food selections, the nonfood gift can be a simpler choice—especially for the non-Jew. If you particularly wish to honor the family and the occasion, you might select a hand-embroidered matzo cover or a lovely ceremonial serving piece. There is also a wide selection of books and records on Passover subjects (at Hebrew bookstores, large specialty stores, and the sisterhood gift shops usually found in synagogues). You may, of course, bring most of the typical "dinner" gifts, such as flowers.

THE SABBATH

The Sabbath is a traditional time for entertaining family and friends. Dinners, parties, and receptions can be elaborate or informal and your "hostess" gift should reflect the nature of the occasion. If you are bringing food or wine (kosher) to complement the meal, keep in mind that fish, a traditional Sabbath food, is often served.

Although it is unlikely that an Orthodox Jewish family would have a birthday party on a Saturday afternoon (they are not permitted to strike matches), if you are invited to one, remember to send birthday presents for Orthodox youngsters either ahead of or after the Sabbath.

CHRISTMAS

Surprised?

Jewish families and businesses are faced with various gift giving situations for Christian celebrations. In particular, Christmas, in many countries, is impossible to ignore.

It is proper to send Christmas greetings to Christian friends, neighbors, and colleagues; and the custom of sending cards to your Christian clients from your business is usually considered appropriate. However, holiday cards selected by a Jewish sender should not have a religious motif. Any other message—peace and goodwill, Happy New Year, season's greetings—is suitable.

Because the Christmas season has also traditionally become a time for thanking people, it is a time for giving tips or gifts to the service personnel or employees who have helped you throughout the year.

GIFT GIVING
CUSTOMS IN FRANCE

Individuality, elegance, and graciousness—all hall-
marks of the French character—are manifest in their attitude toward
the selection and bestowal of gifts. The appropriateness of the gift is
as significant as the occasion; the thought is usually of more importance than the value. Large or ostentatious gifts between business or
social acquaintances are considered gauche. Matters of detail, of
presentation, are carefully considered and observed, whether for one's
family, for a food package, for oneself, or for a small inexpensive gift.
However, this does not mean that the gift is wrapped elaborately, but
with proud care.

Holidays

The major gift giving holidays in France are Christmas Eve
(Noel) and New Year's Eve. On December 24th young children
place their shoes under the Christmas tree or near the chimney in
anticipation that they will be filled with confections and trinkets.
Throughout most of France, Santa Claus or Saint Nicholas is not a
familiar figure. Family members usually exchange gifts at this time.
Orchids, flowering azalea, cyclamen, and other flowering plants are
often given.

There is a more general exchange of gifts among family and

friends for New Year's Eve. Invited guests bring flowers, food, and perhaps other gifts to dinner; the hostess presents each guest with a small gift or token.

Of course, the romantic French celebrate Saint Valentine's Day. The usual gift is flowers—Valentine cards are seldom seen. Children often bring flowers to their mothers for Valentine's Day.

Mother's Day is also an important occasion for gift remembrance. Again, few French send cards, but do give gifts of flowers as well as perfume, scarves, and other feminine items. Although recognition of Father's Day is being promoted by certain commercial interests, such as the leather industry, this holiday has not yet become very popular among the French.

The first of May is traditionally welcomed with the giving of lily-of-the-valley to friends and acquaintances—a lovely gesture to spring.

Special Occasions

When a child is born, the mother receives flowers from both her husband and her father—especially if it is her first child. Friends and relatives bring or send gifts of clothing or toys for the new baby. If you are invited to a christening, you are not expected to bring a gift unless you are one of the child's godparents; then a special memento such as a silver cup or spoon is expected. The family will give small packages of candy-covered almonds (called dragée) to christening guests—blue for a boy; pink for a girl.

Until recently a Frenchman's name day (the feast day of the saint after whom he or she was named) was considered much more important than a birthday as a gift giving occasion. Now one finds that the urban and more sophisticated French are celebrating birthdays with gifts from family and friends. Special parties often mark the legal age of eighteen; sometimes the twenty-first, fortieth, fiftieth, and so on, birthdays are honored with a celebration. For many, name days have become more intimate, family-oriented occasions. Among the religious French families name days still take precedence. It is a particularly charming gesture to remember the name day of a Frenchman with a small gift or note—even if he no longer publicly celebrates it himself. Larger dictionaries as well as some date books, such as Cartier's, list all of the French name days.

Engagements are celebrated with an exchange of bouquets between the two families.

Wedding gifts are always addressed to the parents of the bride and are accompanied with a note congratulating them on their daughter's marriage. Wedding registries are popular even with those at the topmost rungs of society—many brides are registered at more than one store. It is quite proper to inquire; however, you will find that many Parisians are registered at Christofle, which carries china, crystal, and silver. It is also appropriate to send flowers to the bride at her home on the day of the wedding—especially if you cannot attend the festivities.

Major wedding anniversaries are celebrated among family and friends with parties and gifts. Husbands often give their wives a long-lasting rose tree or bush to mark the occasion and symbolize their continuing love.

One does not send flowers to a funeral unless one is a very good friend. More acceptable is a note or letter expressing one's condolences.

Business Gifts

Some of the current economic difficulties have resulted in a more conservative attitude toward the exchange of business gifts. Executives want to be certain not to give anything extravagant that might be mistaken as a bribe. It is important not to give a business gift that cannot be reciprocated, as one does not want the recipient to lose face. The French are usually very considerate in this regard. Corporate Christmas cards are seldom exchanged; however, it is perfectly acceptable to send small tokens for Christmas or New Year's. Few gifts with corporate logos are welcome; Europeans, and the French in particular, prefer gifts with a more personal touch. Enclose a handwritten note or card, not a business card, with your business gift.

Business entertaining is usually conducted in a restaurant; the visitor is expected to return the favor in a restaurant of comparable quality. Sometimes small favors are tucked into the napkin at each place setting.

Hostess and General Gifts

It is considerate to bring a small gift or to send flowers ahead of time if you are being entertained in someone's home. This is an especially important gesture if this is a first-time invitation and/or if one doesn't expect to be able to reciprocate in the near future.

Because the French—both men and women—have an unusual appreciation of flowers, they understand how to care for them, to make them last a long time, to dry them, and to use the petals in potpourri. The knowledgeable guest sends flowers the morning of the dinner party; it is thoughtful to match the home's decorating color scheme or to obtain the host or hostess's favorite flower. One can ask the hostess or use her regular florist. The French always send an uneven number of cut flowers—even numbers are considered gauche as well as more difficult to arrange artistically. (The number thirteen is to be avoided—you will find that a French hostess will have two separate dining tables rather than place thirteen persons at the same table.) If you know your hostess well, you may bring one very special flower—or three or five lovely blossoms. The French are fond of the more tropical and exotic blooms and appreciate those that will last a long time. Thus, three or five anthuriums or a few amaryllises are good choices for a French hostess. A more extravagant gift of flowers might include a lovely crystal vase. Do *not* give red roses. Yes, they do symbolize love and are given by lovers; however, they are also an unfashionable symbol of the Socialist party. Some Frenchmen believe that bouquets of six or twelve flowers—rather than being gauche— are reserved for lovers.

Plants are often given to older persons for special occasions or simply as a token when visiting.

Foodstuffs can be a pleasant gift. But remember that food is taken very seriously in France, and one should be careful not to bring beautifully packaged but inferior edibles. Smoked salmon or caviar should be of the highest quality, preferably from Petrossian; confections should have a proper pedigree; pastries are acceptable but breads are not. One should be careful not to insult the culinary standards of the host.

As a general rule, do not bring wine or liquor to the French. If you think they take their *food* seriously . . . ! They are truly careful about their spirits. The proper wines are planned along with the meal, so the gift of even a great bottle of wine—which carries with it the expectation that the wine should be served with the meal— might be awkward. You can always send it to your host the next day. Of course, if you know that your host enjoys some special wine, you can give it with the admonition to save it for his own special treat.

Other well-received gifts include scented candles, potpourri, or scent rings (for placement around light bulbs); books are always a fine choice, as are small crystal objects. If you are a houseguest and know your hosts' interests, bring games or sets of bridge cards, or perhaps decorative items relating to hunting or shooting. Perfume, including scents for men, is considered a personal gift. If you do not know your hosts well, select a high-quality item from a well-known establishment such as Hermès or a Dior boutique, which carry many items for home entertaining. An alternative is to send a gift after the visit; this may allow you to make a more appropriate selection.

There are many small, distinctive shops, especially in Paris, where the owner has a real passion for bed linens, flowers, antique lace, or fine papers. These are interesting places to find luxurious, elegant gifts that will express your appreciation to your host or hostess.

Hip French young people enjoy American fads as well as their own. Currently, Topsiders, university T-shirts, Swatch watches, anything with U.S. movie stars, especially Marilyn Monroe, on it, and clothing and accessories with the L.L. Bean label are popular items.

Americans who have developed friendships with Frenchmen might enjoy sending occasion cards—for Easter, Christmas, anniversaries—as the French have not commercialized holidays to this extent. Many visiting French spend several hours in our card shops selecting greeting cards—a lovely surprise for their friends.

GIFT GIVING CUSTOMS IN BRITAIN

Self-restraint and civility, reverence for tradition, and love of the English language are some of the admirable traits that the visitor will find reflected in British gift giving habits and preferences. English tradition decrees that if you can afford it, you should get the best, no matter what it is—then cherish it for your lifetime. For example, on Jermyn Street, shirttails of fine tailored shirts are made extra long so that when the collar wears out, the fabric at the bottom can be used to make a new one. However, gifts that give the most pleasure are those that demonstrate thoughtfulness and consideration.

Holidays

Most of us associate British gift giving with the Christmas season, conjuring up Dickensian images of huge log fires, roasting chestnuts, Christmas plum puddings, wassail bowls, and carolers in the snow (more likely rain—Dickens's snow was actually a meteorological freak). And correctly so, as this is traditionally their favorite holiday. Yuletide means Christmas cards, carolers, Christmas trees, gifts for family and friends, and a visit from Father Christmas to good children who leave their empty stockings on the mantel or at the foot of their beds to be filled with small gifts. The Royal Family as well as the rest of the British open or exchange gifts on Christmas Morning. Boxing Day, the first weekday after Christmas, is a legal holiday that originated in the custom of giving boxes of Christmas presents to one's servants, the mailman, and others the day after the family's Christmas.

Business acquaintances do exchange Christmas gifts, although the expensive business gift is more of an American tradition. Logo gifts—such as calendars and desk agendas, spirits (especially scotch and brandy), and chocolates are common gifts. Most British firms that do much business in the United States usually give something more serious to their American peers. For example, friends and clients of Rolls-Royce look forward to receiving crystal reproductions of English water jugs, wineglasses, or decanters at an elegant annual holiday luncheon each year.

Easter is celebrated with the giving of Easter eggs—often of chocolate or other candy—and flowers. Children often color eggs for their families and friends. A traditional pancake race, in which only women participate, is the highlight of Shrove Tuesday (the Tuesday before Lent). On the same day, friends treat one another to a feast of pancakes.

Valentine's Day, Mother's Day, and Father's Day are celebrated much the same as in the United States—but with less emphasis on size of gift and less commercialism. Valentines are seldom given to each child in one's class, but are reserved for very special friends and are usually unsigned; and remembrances for Mother and Father are likely to be carefully selected cards, flowers, or a thoughtful token. An English acquaintance was astonished recently to see a computer advertised as the perfect gift for Father's Day.

There is no Halloween trick-or-treating. However, on Guy Fawkes Day, various groups collect money to build effigies of poor Fawkes, which they burn in bonfires all over the country on November 5. Torchlight processions attest to their feelings about the fanatical Roman Catholic who conspired in 1604 to blow up both Houses on the day the King was to open Parliament. Fortunately, an anonymous letter to one of the lords alerted the King to the plan, which included the laborious digging of a tunnel from a nearby cellar.

Special Occasions

Birthdays are the other important gift giving occasion in England. Family gifts are most often presented on the birthday morning, and parties are popular, especially with the young. Although the British can now vote at age eighteen, they still usually celebrate the twenty-first birthday as the reaching of adulthood. Parties are generally dress-up affairs, and gifts from family and close friends are meant to be lasting mementos. For the Prince of Wales's twenty-first birthday, a friend sneaked a pair of his shoes out of Buckingham

Palace so that he could have custom-made in the correct size a pair of leather-soled velvet slippers embroidered with his crest of three feathers. Upon reaching eighty, ninety, or one hundred years of age, the celebrant receives a telegram from the Queen. Interestingly, all British celebrate the Queen's official birthday, which is scheduled each year for sometime in June and which has no relationship to her actual birthday.

Births and christenings are gift giving occasions. Those invited to the christening usually bring a gift; godparents give a traditional gift of a silver mug, plate, or spoon. Young people receive gifts from relatives and godparents for their confirmation; this is usually a gift of lasting value.

Showers are not given for anticipated births but are popular for weddings. Guidelines for wedding gifts are basically the same as in the United States. Sending gifts early is a good idea because some families enjoy displaying them for friends. Gifts should be sent to the bride.

Hostess and General Gifts

Hostess gifts are a thoughtful gesture. Often, if you do not know your hosts or their tastes well, it is better to send a well-chosen gift with your thank-you note than to bring something that may not be appropriate. Flowers, except for funereal white lilies, are a fine gesture. Arrangements should be natural—casual, but artful. One of London's leading florists—Pulbrook & Gould—ships its flowers and branches directly from country gardens, including Lady Pulbrook's. Curzon Lawrence Flowers in Knightsbridge has a profusion of potted roses and sweet peas to send to your favorite hostess. A gift of a lovely book is always admired and appreciated, especially if it concerns a topic of special interest to the recipient. If you must find a very special gift in London, Asprey can make small enamel gift boxes or engrave a coat of arms on a silver one; they also will bind someone's favorite book in leather. English Stilton cheese made in Melton Mowbray in Leicester and elegant stationery or gold-edged place cards from Smyths in Bond Street are considered special presents.

If you are invited to a country weekend that includes a hunt, remember to take some vintage port suitable for a saddle canteen for yourself and your host—or some of King's Ginger Liqueur, which is what members of the Royal Family are reputed to fortify themselves with while hunting. Other gifts for the person who is really serious about hunting—the latest dressage or rule books, quorn shirt from Turnbull and Asser, for a woman a sidesaddle apron or special breeches; stable blanket, antique flask, copy of the latest *Baily's Hunting Directory*, hunting hat or cap, or Beaufort hunting whip.

GIFT GIVING
CUSTOMS IN
JAPAN

T he Japanese have a ubiquitous sense of form. Tradition and ceremony place great emphasis upon harmony among persons—in both their business and their personal lives. Self-respect and respect for their fellow man seem to be bywords of Japanese life. Thus, gift giving is an institutionalized custom, an important part of business and social relationships.

The giving of gifts along with the bow is traditionally a part of Japanese greeting. Visitors to Japan, making more than casual acquaintances, should prepare to reciprocate in a similar manner.

Because the Japanese consider it vital to know the rank of those with whom they associate, the stylized exchange of business cards is as important to the Japanese as are the bowing and the exchange of actual gifts. This immediately indicates your status and the correct way to deal with you. Visitors should carry an ample supply of business cards (*meishi*), preferably with a Japanese translation on the back. This is an indication of your commitment to doing business with the Japanese as well as a gesture of courtesy. Many airlines provide this service for their customers; and some major hotels provide overnight service. If you have the time, it is probably better to have your cards printed by someone in your area. Most major cities have printers of Japanese business cards. (Unless you read Japanese, have the Japanese printed horizontally with the top of the Japanese side of the card the same as the English, German, French, or Spanish version on the reverse side, so that you can present your cards with the Japanese right-side up.) Carry a plentiful supply of cards with you at all times; to run out of business cards is considered inexcusable.

Basic Concepts

There are two Japanese concepts that the Westerner should attempt to understand in order to be successful in this unique gift giving culture. *Ningen kankei,* an incredibly complex sociological structure, in its simplest form translates to "human relation." *Ningen kankei* is the development of a rapport and the measure of the closeness and cooperation within a relationship. Because the Japanese achieves respect through the development of *ningen kankei,* his first meeting with a Westerner will be more important to him in terms of seeking to establish a long-term relationship of trust and mutual understanding than in terms of the immediate business.

Achieving *ningen kankei* requires patience and hard work, especially on the part of the *gaijin* ("outside person"). The astute business person can help to accomplish this by having thoroughly researched the Japanese company and the people with whom he will be meeting, by attempting to socialize with them as much as possible after work, by sharing the experience of a golf game—a very special ritual in Japan, and by performing acts of kindness such as giving a gift. (*Note:* A golf game is very expensive in Japan; there are few public courses. Some corporations hire female members of a "leisure partner club" to play golf or tennis with them and their guests.) What you may consider inordinate amounts of afterwork entertainment can be explained by the phrase *"Hito no kokoro wa yoru wakaru"*— "You get through to a man's soul at night." The more highly ranked in his company your host is, the better place he will choose for this drinking evening, and, of course, the higher the bill; but the purpose is always the same—to form bonds.

The second concept, *giri,* refers to debts and obligations that must be repaid in equal value. Although *giri* can be expressed in any number of ways, gift giving is probably the most tangible and immediate way for the Japanese to discharge *giri.* Thus, Japan is the most gift giving culture—in business and otherwise—in the world; and one from which you will not be able to escape the web of obligations thereby created.

The observant visitor will notice that the gift culture incorporates some of Japan's great passions—performing tasks with exactitude; paying attention to detail; and doing things en masse. These traits are manifest in their gift wrappings, their concern with ritual, their love of prestigious and "status" gifts, and in the seasonal gift giving customs when numerous gifts are sent from department stores directly to superiors at work or to customers to whom a person feels especially obliged.

Collective Business Gifts

It is not actually necessary for visitors to bring gifts on a first trip; however, it will help to build understanding and respect and strengthen the bond. At the outset of business negotiations a collective gift is always suitable. It should be presented to the senior ranking person with whom you deal. Ideally, this group gift would reflect your company or the region of the country that you represent. Gifts made in America or Europe are most appreciated. The Japanese, noted Francophiles, have a special fondness for French exports. Gifts should *not* be produced anywhere else in East Asia, as that could be considered an insult.

Collective gifts that American corporations have recently given include a lovely leatherbound book of photographs about the history of a corporation, a sterling silver bowl engraved with the recipient company's logo, a meticulously crafted scale model of a commercial airliner, and a crystal Steuben animal (a corporate symbol/logo). In each of these instances the gifts in some way represented the corporation or were made especially for their hosts.

Individual Business and Social Gifts

Before presenting individual gifts, Westerners must fully understand the executive hierarchy within Japanese corporations. Gifts must be selected and graded according to rank. Usually gifts are given to the top four or five people with whom you will be associated, the ranking executive perhaps receiving something in the one-hundred-to-two-hundred-dollar range. Do not be concerned that your Japanese counterpart has presented you with a more expensive gift. Ideally, of course, your gift should be equal in value. However, it is always preferable to give the Japanese a lesser gift than you are given. You are better able to tolerate the *giri*.

The Japanese love status gifts. Anything from a prestigious store is especially appreciated. With a name like Gucci, Tiffany's, Hermès, or Vuitton, often the thought counts more than the content. Part of the significance of the event is discovering where the gift was purchased. You will find that sometimes the gift is rewrapped so that the recipient can show others how it was presented from the store.

Designer-made items—umbrellas, leather goods, key chains, scarves and ties, or pens—are especially significant to the Japanese recipient. Also, celebrity and/or name-brand items, such as Jack Nicklaus polo shirts or Pierre Cardin scarves, help the Japanese to "be" with the crowd.

Edible gifts are enjoyed by the Japanese. Even duty-free shops around the world can be used for last-minute shopping for items such as European chocolates, candies, and cakes; boxes of frozen beef, Danish hams, and tasty sausages. Foods that are unusual to the Japanese—pecans, maple syrup from Vermont, smoked salmon from Seattle—are gratefully received. American Indian turquoise jewelry is a current fad. Grapes and melons are an excellent house gift as they are quite expensive in Japan. Although they do have domestic scotch, they prefer universally known name brands (Chivas, Johnnie Walker Black Label, Courvoisier) for their scotch and brandies. Imported liquor is a greatly treasured gift. Chivas, for example, costs about forty-five dollars a fifth in Tokyo.

The Japanese love books and music. How could they not with Mozart concertos playing over the loud-speakers in the railroad station? Tapes, records, and books of photographs are good selections.

A high-quality item typical of your home region is an acceptable gift in Japan as in most other areas of the world. A pewter reproduction of George Washington's cup from Mount Vernon, a Western bronze or painting, a Navaho rug, a Western hat, a one-of-a-kind crafted country basket—all would be considered thoughtful and personal by the Japanese.

Gift Giving Holidays

In addition to the unique gift giving that is an everyday part of Japanese business and social relations, there are certain holidays when it is important to reinforce your business relationships with the giving of gifts.

OCHUGEN AND OSEIBO

There are two major gift giving seasons: Ochugen and Oseibo. Fortunately, biannual bonuses coincide with these traditional midsummer and year-end gift giving occasions, so that gift etiquette may be observed by all.

The peak of Ochugen, the summer season, is reached on July 15, Midyear's Day on the Japanese calendar. Originally it was a consolation for the families of those who had died in the first half of the year, and traditionally a fish was given. In the Tokyo area, the major celebrating takes place in mid-July; however, in the Kyūshū area, it is in mid-August. Fortunately, there is no one day on which to send or present gifts; anytime during July or August is fine. Sometimes called "Christmas in July" by foreigners, Ochugen is the occasion when the Japanese celebrate their good fortune by exchanging "summer gifts."

The Japanese, who enjoy a reputation for being as generous as they are affluent, each summer spend $10–$12 billion in the nation's retail stores, especially the large department stores. Airports, billboards, and subways are crowded with ads proffering prepackaged gift sets—usually food or drink. Entire floors of stores—some approaching a city block in size—are devoted entirely to Ochugen gift sets, costing an average of five thousand yen but with some as high as thirty thousand yen. Typical and popular gifts are imported beers, coffees and teas, boxes of assorted concentrated fruit drinks, canned fruits, towels, dishes, soy sauce, and cooking oil. Current status items include smoked salmon and salmon roe sets from ten thousand yen up, imported liquors, and California grapefruit—four for five thousand yen. Hand towels are a very common gift, so they are not a recommended gift to bring from a foreign country. Even some newspaper companies present their customers with small hand towels each month when they pay the bill!

For the Japanese, Ochugen involves giving gifts to "superiors" at home and at work. The average wage earner spends at least fifty thousand yen on ten to twelve summer gifts for his parents, elders, supervisors, former teachers, or company brass.

Oseibo is the most important of the Japanese gift giving holidays. It takes place during December, before the New Year's celebration called Oshogatsu. These year-end presents to family, friends, and colleagues are to thank them for having put up with the giver for another year. The gifts at this time are usually a bit more expensive and more important than those given for Ochugen. Again, there is no particular day for gift presentation.

Any foreign corporation maintaining Japanese business relationships must remember its associates with a gift on both of these holidays. It should be recognized that gifts there are usually given as a form of repayment or to express gratitude. The Japanese always send gifts to their "superiors" during these seasons; they do not give gifts to colleagues of equal or lower rank unless that person has helped them in some extraordinary, private way. Mid-year and end-year bonuses, to reward workers for their diligence, are timed to coincide with these two gift giving occasions. Gifts are usually either sent to the home by the department store or taken in person to the recipient's office. Money is not given for either of these two occasions, although a gift certificate is acceptable. It is customary to thank the giver as soon as possible either in person or by phone; thank-you notes are not commonly exchanged except over long distances.

NEW YEAR

The New Year (Shogatsu, January 1) is a special time for all Japanese—a family time much like the Western Christmas celebrations. They enjoy holidays over *osechi-ryori*, the special dishes for the New Year, sake, and *mochi*, a rice cake. Many families (about 70 percent) go on *hatsu-mode*, the visit to a Buddhist temple or a Shinto shrine on New Year's Eve or during the first days of the new year to pray for happiness and longevity. There is no general gift giving for Shogatsu; however, New Year's greeting cards are exchanged (much like Christmas cards).

Last year the Japanese delivered nearly 3.5 billion New Year's cards—an average of 29 cards for each Japanese, including those too young to read or write. Many families receive many hundreds of cards—the number is a guide to their social status as well as a determination of credit rating. It is assumed that those who receive many *nengajo* must be people of substance. And the finance companies that use this as criteria even go so far as to evaluate the type of card. Senders are judged on a point system of 1 to 5, and handwritten messages are considered worth more than the preprinted varieties. Because for many Japanese it would not be New Year's without the cards, the post office delivers all of these cards on New Year's Day! Anyone who delivers cards to local post offices before December 28 is assured that the greetings will be distributed at that time. Postal authorities put regular workers on extra shifts and hire 2.7 million part-timers. The cards themselves range from individually designed prints to preprinted cards provided by the government for about twenty cents apiece.

For New Year's, children or young people who have not yet entered the work force receive money gifts. *Otoshidama* are usually presented on January 1 or within the holiday time that follows. The newly printed money (one thousand to five thousand yen, average) is put into a small envelope for each child. It is preferable to use the gaily decorated envelopes that are made for this purpose. If you visit a Japanese home at this time, it is thoughtful to remember the children in this way. Do not be surprised if, before you leave, the hosts check the envelopes to be certain to give the identical amount to your children.

CHRISTMAS

As less than 1 percent of the population professes to being Christian, it is somewhat surprising to foreigners that Christmas has entered Japanese custom as a festive occasion. The Japanese have a love of festivals; and historians trace the origin of their adoption of Christmas merrymaking to what took place on Tokyo's Ginza on the evening of December 24, 1955. On this date a government white paper solemnly proclaimed that the postwar period of shortages and privation had come to an end. An estimated 1.5 million people, mostly males, thronged the famous thoroughfare in a giant explosion of revelry. Following this, for a number of years, Christmas Eve in most Japanese cities became an occasion for libation, exclusively by the male segment of the population. The inevitable consequence was a slowdown in business activity as office workers, many of them nursing hangovers, trudged to work the following morning. This period, referred to as the "men's Christmas" phase, became a great source of revenue for bars and nightclubs. In the 1960s this was gradually replaced by the "family Christmas" period. Instead of heading to their favorite bar after work on Christmas Eve, fathers began stopping at confectioners' to buy cakes to take home. Today, factories of major bakers each churn out an estimated 2 million Christmas cakes. In addition, independent confectioners, numbering 30,000 nationwide, each sell an average of 100 such cakes. The dairy industry followed the yuletide trend, offering special Christmas ice cream desserts, and the department stores exerted their influence on the Japanese to persuade them to accept Christmas as a festival. They decorated their outlets with yuletide symbols and programmed their Muzak systems with Christmas music. Nowadays, year-end shopping has two distinct phases. Oseibo sales peak on the first weekend in December, when shoppers' pocketbooks are bulging with new bonuses. The following weekends, particularly the one before Christmas, a second phase of more individual-oriented purchases reaches its climax. This is the time when parents buy toys for their children and young men and women select gifts for their lovers. Mainly a day for children, the Japanese celebration includes the legend of Santa Claus but seldom recognizes that Christ's birthday is the original reason for joy. Japanese business acquaintances do not exchange gifts for Christmas.

Other Holidays and Gift Giving Occasions

Both Mother's Day and Father's Day are gift giving days for Japanese children; and on Valentine's Day the girl gives her lover a gift. A woman who gives a man a necktie is "choking" or "cutting off" the relationship.

BIRTHDAYS

The Japanese seldom give gifts for birthdays; occasionally, however, there will be a birthday cake. Special birthdays—sixtieth, seventieth, seventy-ninth, eighty-eighth, and ninety-ninth—rate gifts and congratulatory messages.

HOSPITALITY GIFTS

Unless you know your hosts well or have already established *ningen kankei* with someone, you probably will not be invited to a Japanese home. As the Japanese do most of their entertaining in restaurants, clubs, and bars, to go to someone's home is considered a great honor. If you are so honored, a small hospitality gift is expected— fruit, sweets, wine, or fresh flowers. The flowers should be an uneven number and not arranged, as arranged flowers are a recent introduction and are used primarily at formal receptions, weddings, and such. Also, many Japanese women enjoy practicing the art of ikebana.

WEDDINGS

Traditionally, the bride and groom receive gifts of money; however, today the usual gifts of silver, china, crystal, and such are also appropriate—especially from foreign friends and acquaintances. Gifts other than money should be delivered to the house from which the invitation came at least two days before the wedding. Special envelopes stamped with gold and silver cords are usually used for money gifts; these may be purchased at any Japanese stationery store. The person giving the gift writes his or her name below the cord. If you are attending the wedding, you will find a table set up at the entrance to the wedding hall where someone will take your envelope of money.

CONGRATULATORY GIFTS

The Japanese mark many occasions with gift giving. Business openings, births, new homes, graduations, and promotions are all reasons for presents and celebrations. Although fresh or dried fish was the traditional congratulatory gift, your recognition of these occasions with appropriately chosen gifts will be greatly appreciated. Those attending such occasions will receive gifts and mementos to take home with them.

GET-WELL GIFTS

Fruit, flowers, money, and books are taken or sent to someone who is ill. Presents are also sent when one recovers from a long convalescence.

FUNERALS

The major gift is money. However, fruit, incense, or flowers may be brought on a sympathy call. Black and white or black and purple are best for funeral wrappings. The gift envelope is called *bushugibukuro*. Condolence notes and cards are always appropriate.

RETURN GIFTS

Foreigners are often shocked—after a wedding or a funeral or any gift giving occasion except Oseibo or Ochugen—to receive a return gift usually of about one-third to one-half the value of their original gift. Newlyweds will often purchase some of their return gifts *(o-miyage)* while on their honeymoon. A return gift for an expression of sympathy is sometimes tea, as tea is given as a gift only in times of sorrow. These gifts are usually sent directly from the stores and are to be expected as part of the *giri* system.

GIFTS OF MONEY

Cash gifts, including large tips, are normally presented in special gift envelopes called *Shugibukuro*, which are available at stationery stores in hundreds of sizes, colors, and designs. Furthermore, each occasion has it's own message and colors, so be certain that you don't select a funeral envelope for your translator's tip. The wrong envelope—like the wrapping on a gift—is a serious breach of etiquette and may sometimes even be interpreted as an ill omen.

Unless the Japanese is your guest or your gift is a reciprocal one, always let the Japanese initiate the gift giving. Unless you are a guest at someone's home, the host presents the gifts.

Present the gift when others are not present unless you have gifts for them also. Do not present a gift in any way that could be misinterpreted as a bribe—even from a distance. The Japanese are very sensitive about this issue.

Do not expect the recipient to accept the gift as soon as it's offered. In Japan, overeagerness is bad manners, so continue to offer your gift in the quietest manner possible. Remember to present the gift with both hands.

It would be very presumptuous for a foreigner to try to act Japanese. You are not expected to follow the custom of refusing a gift several times. Simply accept the gift with humility, reservation, and quiet pleasure. Japanese men are not receptive to displays of emotion. After accepting, it is polite to ask if your host would like you to open your gift.

The worst offense is to refuse a gift. A gift that seems inappropriately lavish to us is to the Japanese simply part of a long tradition of liberal gift giving. Most modern Japanese companies understand that their American counterparts—for legal reasons—often cannot compete with the Japanese practice of showering business friends with expensive presents.

Do not be surprised or offended if a Japanese does not open his gift at the time of presentation. Greeting gifts, in particular, are seldom opened at the time of greeting

Although it may appear that the *giri* gift giving, both in business and among friends and acquaintances, becomes a sort of competition, it is important that you not "outgift" the Japanese. Let them fully enjoy their custom by not being obligated to you and thereby losing "face." Your gift need not represent 100 percent reciprocity. Thoughtfulness is more important.

The Japanese Visitor in a Foreign Land

Japanese visitors expect to be treated with the same formal hospitality and gifting that they accord to their visitors.

A serious effort to make the Japanese feel welcome is a wonderful way to repay *giri* to them. If you are entertaining them and seeing to their needs in a foreign city, the welcoming gift itself need only be a token. If the visitor is an important celebrity or executive, arranging special tours of museums or meetings with key officials can repay *giri* and develop *ningen kankei*. They are especially honored to be invited to your home. This shows your respect and your desire to know them personally. You should have a small gift ready to give them in exchange for the probably lavish gift they will bring to your home.

Gift Wrapping

The wrapping of a Japanese gift is of great importance. Giving unwrapped money is considered bad manners, and traditional Japanese wrappings are preferred to the Western style.

When purchasing a gift in Japan, the most important thing to remember is that gifts are not wrapped at home by the giver; rather, the shop wraps it for you and usually also delivers it. This means you do not have to learn to wrap Japanese-style, although it is fun to watch them wrap, folding from corner to corner. Packages are crisp and clean; wrinkling is avoided and folding is precise. Boxed items may be left open-ended to demonstrate "gentle concealment." On top of the gift the store places a piece of paper on which is printed a tied string design called *noshigami*. The colors of the strings indicate the type of occasion—red, gold, or white for happy events; black and white or black and purple for unhappy events. The name of the sender is written below the strings. Then the store wraps the gift with its own signature wrapping. This is especially significant for foreigners to know about because there is a definite hierarchy among the stores in every city. It is important to buy the gift from the top department store even if you can purchase the identical gift for less somewhere else.

Gifts are usually wrapped in lovely papers—often rice paper. The Japanese select papers for their design, elegance, and significance.

If you are either desperate or determined, however, this is how to properly and elegantly wrap a gift for a happy occasion: Wrap with high quality—preferably white, handmade—paper. Tie with gold and silver or red and white cords made of rolled paper *(mizuhiki)*. For unhappy occasions and tie with black and white cords.

Avoid bows, which the Japanese consider ugly, and remember that different colors of ribbon convey various meanings to the recipient.

Gifts of money, which are placed in specially designed envelopes, are printed with red and white cords for happy occasions, such as births and graduations, gold and silver cords for weddings.

The Japanese are very appreciative of lovely wrapping, so, when unwrapping their gifts, take great pains not to tear the gift paper. You will often find them undoing a package with care in order to preserve the paper.

Gift Rules

- Gifts that consist of a lesser number of items than ten should be given in odd numbers (for example, place settings and tea cups are sold in sets of five).
- Do not expect a Japanese to open his gift in front of you.
- Do not make a ceremony of a gift to a Japanese. It should not seem a source of pride to the giver.
- Present the gift with both hands and a slight bow.
- Do not give a much better gift than they give you.
- Allow the Japanese to initiate the gift giving.
- If possible, do not wrap the gift yourself. If you must, do not use bows, and do use high-quality paper.
- Always bring a gift when visiting a Japanese home.
- Avoid the numbers four and nine, as they have homonyms that mean death and suffering—you may notice that some Japanese hospitals still do not have a fourth or ninth floor.
- *Do not refuse a gift.*

Record Keeping

The continual exchange of gifts with the Japanese—especially after a few years—can be very hard on the memory. Because a gift should *never* be repeated (with the exception of liquor or something you've been asked to repeat), it is helpful to keep a record of all gifts given to your Japanese friends and associates. Western business people often put their records on computer to avoid the sin of duplication.

Sometimes, of course, the "duty" aspect of gift giving can degenerate into a mere formality just as it does in the rest of the world. Interestingly, gifts that have no conceivable use for the recipient are sometimes passed on to another just to meet the obligation of giving and returning (often unopened). The practice of *taraimawashi,* which in Japan is accepted social practice and insurance, is not unlike your giving the green gargoyle vase that Great-Aunt Emma sent to you last Christmas to a distant nephew for his second wedding.

If you truly wish to develop *ningen kankei* with your Japanese friends, select gifts that are thoughtful and well presented, not ones that will become a part of their *taraimawashi* tradition.

THE ART AND ETIQUETTE OF GIFT GIVING

GIFT GIVING CUSTOMS IN CHINA

China, with more history and heritage than any other nation on earth, is experiencing a transformation that has few parallels in the contemporary world. The post-Mao period (since 1977) has seen both cultural and political changes and has been marked by initiatives toward economic, technological, and cultural exchanges with the Western world. The Chinese are proud of their many contributions to civilization and enthusiastic about their recent economic and social accomplishments. Visitors from the West would be well advised to study China's history and culture before departure as well as to view their trip as a learning experience. Most visitors—even those with a tour group—will find themselves from time to time in the role of international emissary.

Business people intending to deal with the Chinese should consult with experts before making any overtures. Americans can receive assistance from government organizations such as the U.S. Department of Commerce's Industry and Trade Administration or from private organizations like the National Council for U.S.–China Trade (also in Washington, D.C.). Chinese expertise can also be found within many U.S. corporations, the United Nations, and in recent publications such as the "Chinese Checkers" chapter in Neil Chesanow's book *The World-Class Executive* (Bantam Books, New York).

Before exchanging gifts with the Chinese, the foreigner must recognize that there is quite a differentiation between some of the local traditions and the more modern trends, and that the gift culture—along with the economic and social aspects—is undergoing rapid changes. Expect diversity throughout China. Understanding of the following characteristics is basic.

- *The concept of "face" (mian zi)—for the more traditional Chinese.* The Chinese are extraordinarily sensitive to the opinions of their peers and associates in all social and business relations. For example, traditionally one gives money only to subordinates or employees; thus, tipping—in most places in China—is considered an insult or is not understood at all. (And of course, many are not allowed to accept tips.) Several times I have left a small tip on the table as a token of appreciation for especially good service, only to have the restaurant personnel come chasing up the street after me waving the money I'd "forgotten."

  Because of their concern with "face," gift selection is a serious matter. They carefully choose gifts based on what they know or believe to be the recipient's preferences and expect others to do the same. (After expressing a preference for the color dark blue, I received several gifts in this color.)

  They work hard to please their friends and take special pleasure in giving things that are useful or helpful. One of their gifts that I most needed and enjoyed was a paper bag filled with warm breakfast pastries from a famous bakery on Nanging Road. It was presented to me at five-thirty in the morning on my way to the Shanghai airport to fly to Tokyo and New York—a really thoughtful gesture.

- *The antimaterial party policy.* The Chinese, who have been taught to shun materialism and avoid private ownership and are constantly guided by such maxims as "Human pride is human weakness"—a motto prevalently displayed throughout work places and academic institutions—are concerned that by accepting a gift they will appear greedy and self-centered. Members of my class of international journalists at the Shanghai University of International Studies initially refused my class gift of slices of American fruitcake by stating emphatically that they did not want to appear greedy. I had to convince them that it was a necessary part of their understanding of Western Christmas customs, which we had just discussed.

  Local custom often discourages the acceptance of anything other than token gifts by individuals; group gifts, such as business to business or to a school library rather than to the dean, are preferred. Government officials cannot accept expensive gifts; even a small calculator—when given in front of others—has to be accepted on behalf of the work group. Remember that all the Chinese are under scrutiny and can be informed on by their fellow countrymen. The solution is to give gifts that are inexpensive and useful and/or that have some value that the recipients can cite to justify their acceptance. Small imprinted logo items such as pens or calendars are appreciated by individuals. If you do give something of real value to an individual, by no means let others know, if you want to continue to have good relations.

Visitors will discover that the Chinese are very interested in the prices of Western goods and have had little opportunity to learn the value of things outside of China. Do not be surprised to be asked the price of anything, from your gift to them to the shoes you are wearing.

- *Chinese protocol.* As a result of centuries of crowded living, the Chinese are very sensitive to the feelings of others. They are exceedingly courteous and—to some Westerners—quite formal. Rooms are entered in order of rank, with the highest-ranking person entering first. One never interrupts in conversation, especially with a superior or a visitor. That they are delightful and generous hosts does not mean that they agree with your proposal or that they will negotiate quickly and satisfactorily.

Westerners find ungracious if not insulting the Chinese first refusal of a gift with the phrase, "I don't need this; I already have one." For the Chinese, this has been the traditional way of demonstrating their lack of greed or covetousness and should be understood as such by the giver. In contrast, the Chinese may consider grasping and crass the Westerner who exclaims, "This is exactly what I'd hoped for," or, "I've always wanted one of these."

Traditional Chinese Symbolism

As in all cultures, concern with traditional superstitions and symbols is more common in the rural and more remote regions than in urban areas.

ANIMAL SYMBOLS

The dragon, originally the emperor's emblem, denotes power; the phoenix, the empress's sign, signifies both beauty and power; the tiger is also used to symbolize power. Pigs can convey laziness, but fat pigs can express bounty or plenitude. The symbolic use of a mouse often indicates that something has been stolen.

COLORS

Red means happiness and good luck. Yellow, the color associated with emperors, is not a good choice. Gray and drab green remind some people of the Cultural Revolution. Purple denotes a barbarian. Black and very dark colors means misfortune and death. White symbolizes purity.

MISCELLANEOUS

The number thirteen is bad luck; even numbers are good luck, especially for weddings. Writing with red ink means that you are cutting off your friendship (does not apply to cards or characters already printed in red). In some provinces, a white embroidered handkerchief sent to a young man indicates that the young woman is interested in his attentions. Giving a gift with the year's symbol, such as a calendar with a rabbit, for the year of the rabbit, is a gesture of good luck.

Traditional Gift Occasions and Gifts

BIRTHS

Family and friends bring gifts to the newly born baby and for his "full-month" (thirty days) birthday. Parents often give a special dinner on this occasion. Another gift giving celebration is held when the child is one hundred days old. Traditionally, the child's photograph is taken on each of these occasions.

BIRTHDAYS

Most birthdays are noted with small gifts from family and close friends and are often marked by the more sophisticated or "Westernized" Chinese with a cake. The traditional serving of long noodles at a birthday dinner forecasts long life for the celebrant. Upon reaching the age of thirty, the Chinese are considered adults; thus, there is usually a festive celebration for this occasion. For men the sixtieth birthday is of particular significance and is usually combined with retirement, although men not engaged in factory work or physical labor may continue to work to the age of sixty-five. For women, reaching the age of fifty is an important milestone. Chinese who reach the ages of seventy-nine and eighty often receive a particular liquor that is rumored to promote longevity and that portrays on its label a very old man and the ginseng root. Their great respect for the elderly is evident in their celebrations of these occasions.

EDUCATION

At the age of six, the Chinese child is sent off to school with good wishes and gifts from his family and friends. Pencil boxes, new clothing, and book bags are typical presents. Sometimes when a teacher visits her student's home, he or she will bring a small book or dictionary intended to encourage the student to study harder. The student who passes his university examinations always presents his teacher with a small gift as a token of his appreciation. Often the class will give a group gift.

WEDDINGS

Most Chinese give money for wedding gifts. It is considered the most practical way to help young couples start a new home. Other gifts are more likely to be useful than beautiful. Prior to the wedding, the groom usually gives his bride a watch or a special jewel; his mother gives her a piece of jewelry. The young people's working unit presents them with government publications that describe how to live together harmoniously and prescribe birth control measures. The Chinese symbol for double happiness is used on wedding cards and wrapping paper.

CHINESE NEW YEAR

Usually celebrated in January or February, the New Year's festival is a major three-day holiday. Families and children visit the elderly as a token of respect and to wish them good health and fortune for the new year. Traditional fireworks and exotic lanterns illuminate the streets, and small gifts are presented to friends and family. Family household help receive gifts or money; and fortunate children are given red paper bags filled with money. Each region and city has its own customs: Chengdu, for example, is noted for its ancient tradition of creating marvelous lanterns in the shapes of swans, lotus blossoms, and animals.

China has four official public holidays: January 1, New Year; May 1, Labor Day; October 1–2, Anniversary of the Founding of the People's Republic of China; the Spring and Autumn Lunar (Moon) festivals, observed according to dates on the Chinese lunar calendar. March 8, International Women's Day, is celebrated with a half-day holiday and women are given free film tickets for their enjoyment (each work unit has a Women's Federation). Gifts are sometimes given to young people for Youth Day, May 4. The Autumn Moon festival each October is celebrated with the wide distribution of the traditional sweet known as "moon cake" to one's friends. This holiday celebrates the harvest and the day of the "roundest" moon. It is a time for family get-togethers and for feasting.

Western Gifts

The correct presentation of gifts to the Chinese requires knowledge, good judgment, and common sense. Become familiar with the legal implications of expensive gifts. When you enter the country, you will be asked to list watches, radios, cameras, bicycles, and similar items on your customs declaration; you may be asked to show that you still have these objects in your possession when you leave. (Don't lose your copy of the declaration form!)

Wrapping gifts shows that you planned ahead—that these are not last-minute purchases, bribes, charity, or makeshift gifts. Red paper is preferred; plain white wrapping is considered funereal.

When presenting a formal gift it is courteous to say something like, "This is only a token of what I wanted to bring." Always present individual gifts in private, and do not expect the Chinese recipient to open the gift in front of you. Remember that the Chinese can be extremely sensitive to the acceptance of business and social gifts.

BUSINESS GIFTS

Western business executives working in China will probably receive many small gifts. The gifts will be commensurate with the importance of their firm, the size of its business proposal, and their rank within its corporate structure. Objects carved of semiprecious stone and ivory, double-sided silk embroidery, small tapestries, and objects of cloisonné are typical gifts. When you have gotten to know someone well, he or she may give you small souvenir-type gifts for your children. The Chinese enjoy hearing about foreigners' families and lifestyles. The limiting of families to one child in this family-oriented society has made children even more precious. My Chinese business associates and students have selected delightful gifts for my children—most recently, a miniature gold panda pin for my daughter.

Upon first meeting in a business situation, small gifts are often exchanged. Unless you are giving a collective gift, each member of the Chinese team or delegation should receive a gift, otherwise the nonrecipients lose face—a very poor beginning for a new relationship.

Logo gifts are acceptable, and a gift associated with your state, country, or region will be appreciated. Subscriptions to American publications, such as *Reader's Digest* (which has an official agreement with China), are very desirable; specialty trade journals or technical and/or scientific publications in the recipient's field of interest are especially welcome. Many Chinese enjoy news magazines such as *Time* and *Newsweek;* however, you would have to know the recipient well enough to be certain that political and social issues that conflict with Communist ideology would not offend him. Books about U.S. nature, geography, or history (especially with photography), personally engraved pens, cognac, classical records and tapes, English and Chinese–English dictionaries, appropriate technical materials, and name plaques are all successful business gifts.

SOCIAL GIFTS

The one element of Western culture that's universally desired is the ability to speak and read English. For almost any occasion an English book or periodical is a treasured present.

The Chinese really appreciate small mementos. They enjoy photos of you and your family; and token gifts for their children will quickly win you popularity. Other inexpensive reminders of your friendship could be stamps (the Chinese are avid international stamp collectors), calendars, or memo pads. Tapes, records, and T-shirts from the United States or Europe are great gifts for young people, although some Chinese have had to have their English-reading friends point out the true meaning of the messages they were proudly wearing. One shy young lady was shocked to discover that she was wearing a shirt that read KISS ME. Service personnel whom you would ordinarily tip for performing personal services for you will usually accept small wrapped gifts, such as pens, key rings, tiny flashlights, or pins.

Once on a business flight from Hong Kong to Beijing, the purser collected all the small orchids that had been served with the luncheon trays and presented them to me. (I assume this was because I was the only woman in the cabin.) His spontaneous gift to me turned out to be one of the most marvelous presents I've ever given! Winter in Beijing is cold and barren—a bitter wind, not a blade of grass. Greenhouse plants are a rarity; tropical flowers almost nonexistent. (The hotels for foreigners do have beautiful indoor plants, but nothing that the average Chinese would ever have the opportunity to see.) From the hotel's concierge (who sported it in his buttonhole until it wilted) to a business friend (who wanted to know everything about orchids) to a five-year-old girl sitting behind me at the Chinese opera (who kept slipping me caramel candy), my flowers were an astonishing success. I think a part of that success was due to the contrast between the exotic tropical flowers and the dreariness of Beijing's winter, and that between the totally impractical and short-lived nature of this gift and the Chinese insistence on utility and durability.

When visiting schools, factories, and communes, it is nice to bring general gifts for all to enjoy—posters, children's records, picture books, novelty toys, Frisbees, or sports equipment such as a bat and ball or a basketball. Ping-Pong, the national sport, and badminton are both very popular throughout the People's Republic of China. Football, basketball, and volleyball are becoming favorites.

If you are visiting China as part of a special interest group—farmers or teachers—you might take related movies, books, or rock and shell specimens.

An invitation to a Chinese home requires the usual "hostess" gift. Candies, egg cakes, fresh fruits, fruit juices, and other local favorites are appreciated. If you know your host or hostess fairly well, you might ask about foods (particularly candies) and kitchen gadgets that are not available to them but that are readily available to you at the Friendship Stores and hotels for foreigners. Surprisingly, there is a variety of American ginseng tea (especially light and therapeutic) that is highly coveted by the Chinese.

When giving food as a gift, keep in mind that most Chinese have not acquired Western tastes any more than you crave their delectable black eels on your rice. Chinese food preferences vary markedly from region to region and range from the sweet-sour dishes of the southern provinces to the hot, spicy cuisine of Szechwan and Hunan. Ignoring my own advice, on my most recent trip I took small bags of shelled pecans (a common American nut), wrapped in traditional pecan recipes for pralines, pecan pie, brownies, and so on. I also had a few unshelled pecans, a nutcracker, and a pick to demonstrate whence the nuts came. Fortunately, the recipients were delighted and really enjoyed the pecans.

So many things were stolen from China by looting foreigners over the years that the ultimate gesture of friendship and support for the current policy of openness to foreigners is the returning of a relic—preferably one with historic value. The British once returned a sword that had belonged to one of the Taiping rulers. It now resides in a Taiping museum. Old photos of foreigners in China and significant old documents are potential treasures. Write first to the Bureau of Historical Relics in Beijing and to the museum in the city relevant to the relics you wish to give, asking if they would be interested in receiving the relic as a gift.

All Chinese respond favorably to having their photographs taken. Color photos of themselves or their children—especially those taken with a Polaroid—are wonderful gifts. (However, use of a Polaroid has created many a traffic jam in China over the last few years.) Be selective, or you may find yourself taking—and mailing—many more photos to strangers than you ever intended.

If you expect to be writing to Chinese workers or students after you return home, purchase some Chinese stamps before you leave the country. Mailing to the West is an expensive luxury for the ordinary Chinese. He will save face if you enclose the stamps with your letter and state that you did not use them while in China and now have no use for them.

GIFT TABOOS

Avoid giving clocks to older, more traditional Chinese; the English word *clock* is a homonym for the Chinese word *funeral*.

In some regions, do not bring apples to someone who is ill or in the hospital. In some local dialects, the pronunciation of the Chinese words for *apple* and *death* are the same.

Do not give expensive or lavish gifts or those that are considered ostentatious, such as obvious luxuries or gifts of gold or silver. Try not to display any signs of materialistic vanity.

The Chinese are not allowed to accept any foreign currency. Even commemorative coins and medals should be avoided as they could be mistaken for money. (The availability of Chinese currency is carefully controlled. There are two types of currency in use in China: renminbi, or RMBs, and foreign exchange certificates (FECs). RMBs (not traded on the international market), or people's money, is issued by the Bank of China. FECs, or tourist money, have been issued in China for use by overseas tourists, diplomats, and overseas Chinese. Most visitors will have little occasion to use RMBs but will find that the Chinese like to accept and swap their RMBs for FECs so that they can buy imported goods in the Friendship Stores.) Foreign currency must be carefully registered if you intend to bring it into China. They prefer that you change it to FECs.

BANQUETS

The accepted way to return hospitality or to show gratitude for a favor is by giving a banquet. Sometimes the first round of business negotiations is begun with a dinner. Traditionally, the Chinese host a lavish banquet at the conclusion of a foreigner's successful business visit. This is meant to be a symbolic sealing of the deal. In such situations, the top executive of your firm is expected to be present—the Chinese will invite their own top official. Often they will also give a welcoming dinner in honor of visiting business partners or delegations. Depending on the protocol required, the dinner can be an elaborate banquet—complete with formal invitations and a detailed seating plan—or a simple, informal meal.

Collective gifts are usually exchanged at banquets. The host makes a brief speech, then presents the package to the group as a gift for everyone, even though it will be handed to the group's leader, who will acknowledge it and present their gift in turn.

A banquet is considered a gift, and, if possible, the visitor should reciprocate by hosting a banquet of his own for colleagues and people who have been particularly helpful. You might invite your guide and interpreters as well as business associates. Always make clear whether spouses are invited.

One should familiarize himself with the banquet ritual before attending or hosting a banquet. Your importance is indicated by the type of banquet you are given, so you should host a banquet in the same price category as that which you were given; this could range from twenty-five to one hundred dollars per person. Former hosts would lose face if you were to host a considerably less or more expensive meal. An interpreter, a guide, or the restaurant manager can help you to assess this situation and select the proper menu. For his help he should be given a small thank-you gift—usually better received than a tip.

It is best to order the entire banquet ahead of time. Elaborate dishes must be ordered at least twenty-four hours in advance. It is usually a good idea to let the chef select the menu; let him know your favorites, but let him tell you what is in season, such as fresh crab in late autumn.

If you are hosting a banquet, be certain to be the first to arrive. Upon arrival your guests, who will be on time, gather in an anteroom where they sit and drink tea before entering the banquet room.

Consider language problems as well as tradition when you make your seating plan. Place cards are a very helpful tool. The guest of honor usually faces the door and sits to the right of the head of the host group. Round Chinese banquet tables usually seat ten or twelve with a lazy Susan in the middle of the table. At the occasional rectangular table, the place of honor is at the center of the long side of the table—again facing the door. (In the event of attack by enemy assailants, the guest of honor can escape first—historically.) Unless you are with an official government delegation, don't worry overmuch about formal protocol in the seating arrangement.

A banquet can last for three or four hours and consist of as many as ten or fifteen courses; each of the eight regions of China has its own specialties. As host, you should serve your guest of honor from the lazy Susan first, then serve the other guests who are within reach. When the Chinese host the banquet, often the host continues to add things to your dish, keeping it full. (Careful observation of the host's role at their banquet for you will prove most helpful later.)

Guests are expected to eat at least some of each helping. Do not take the last portion of food from any of the communal dishes, as that would be taken as a sign that there was not enough food. Always leave some food on your plate when you are finished or you may automatically be given more. The meal is over after soup has been served and hot towels distributed. Occasionally for a large banquet fruit will be served after the soup. The guest of honor is expected to leave the banquet with members of his party before the host leaves.

Toasting at banquets is a complicated art, but foreigners are not expected to know all the finer points. Your place setting will probably have a water glass for bottled water, beer, or *qi shui* (a ubiquitous orange-flavored soft drink), a wineglass, and a small shot or cordial glass for the mao-tai (a 120-proof liquor made from sorghum and wheat yeast, aged five to six years, and always served at official state dinners) or one of the "eight most famous spirits." Do not drink the mao-tai or spirits until the toasting, which the chief host (or you as the host) initiates. The host will rise and toast to the friendship and unity of the people of your country and those of China as well as to the health of all friends and comrades present. Subsequent toasts—

and there could be very many—could be on their sadness upon seeing you leave their country, and such. One does not have to continue toasting with mao-tai or spirits, but may change beverages after the first toast, which is usually downed in one gulp. You will discover that even some of the Chinese put tea in their shot glasses after a while! Foreign and Chinese women need not drink the mao-tai at all if they wish not to, but they should join in the toasting.

A lunch is often a substitute for a banquet if there is not enough time and/or if you feel the expense is too much. For a lunch you may invite only the chief negotiator in the business deal.

Receiving Gifts

The Westerner receiving a gift is not expected initially to refuse the gift or to make self-deprecatory remarks about being unworthy, as the Chinese often do. Accept your gift with gratitude and humility. If the Chinese do not open their gifts in front of you, do not open yours unless they insist. A thank-you note is always appropriate.

In addition to the visitors' usual business and social situations in China, I had the good fortune to get to know university teachers and students on a more personal basis. Because I was teaching Chinese journalists and graduate foreign-affairs students about Western protocol and customs, I acted as "Western" as possible in my acceptance of their gifts. At first taken aback by my obvious delight in opening their presents, they soon took pleasure in watching me exclaim, "This bamboo brush holder is really beautiful and will be perfect for the pens on my desk. As a matter of fact, I really need it—my current holder is top heavy and spills my pencils and pens out all over the desktop."

On my final evening in Shanghai the chairman and vice chairman of the department and my interpreter and guide took me to a marvelous acrobatics performance. At intermission they surprised me with a wonderful array of gifts—a Chinese calendar, jewelry, a cloisonné brush-and-comb set—and insisted that I open them then and there. Despite their antimaterialistic beliefs, the more sophisticated Chinese do enjoy our Western pleasure in receiving their gifts.

GIFT GIVING
CUSTOMS IN WEST GERMANY

F oreign visitors to Germany—particularly Americans—often comment on the "formality" of the Germans with whom they come in contact. However, their gift giving customs, along with other aspects of the German culture, have been changing more and more to resemble the lifestyles of other Western industrial societies. Even the long-standing traditions still practiced in rural Germany have become more relaxed. Nonetheless, there are some basic differences; and understanding social gift courtesies can make your visit and subsequent relations much easier.

Gift Giving Holidays

CHRISTMAS

The Christmas season is their time for giving gifts. It begins (especially for Catholics) with the Advent ("coming"), a period of pre-Christmas preparation that begins on the fourth Sunday before Christmas Day, when the Advent wreath (fir branches and red ribbons with four candles) is placed on a table or suspended from a central chandelier. Then, on each Sunday before Christmas, the family gathers to light one of the four candles. For German children, December 6—Saint Nicholas's Day—is eagerly awaited. While they are sleeping, *Nikolaus* (Saint Nick) comes on a sled drawn by a donkey. He generously fills the polished shoes or boots (which they have placed on their window sills) with small gifts, fruits, and sweets. Some adults also exchange gifts on this occasion.

Most Christmas gifts are purchased at town Christmas markets (*Weihnachtsmärkte*) in the weeks before Christmas. They are always exchanged around the Christmas tree (usually with real candles) on Christmas Eve rather than Christmas Day. The traditional gift bringer is *Weihnachtsmann,* or "Christmas man." *Christkind* (Kris Kringle) still plays "Santa Claus" in some southern German regions.

GOOD FRIDAY AND EASTER MONDAY

These are both legal holidays in Germany. Popular Easter customs include Easter rides, bonfires, fire wheels rolled down hills, the coloring of Easter eggs, and Easter-egg hunts. Chocolate eggs and bunnies in baskets are given to children, and grownups sometimes exchange small gifts.

MOTHER'S DAY

Mother's Day (the second Sunday in May) is celebrated with small gifts, flowers, and family gatherings.

LABOR DAY (*TAG DER ARBEIT*), OR MAY DAY

This is celebrated on May 1 with maypoles in many towns and villages. Often a young man will place birch twigs or branches on or in front of his girlfriend's door.

Special Occasion Gifts

FESTIVALS

Each year many folk festivals take place throughout Germany. From the world-famous Oktoberfest in Munich to Rose Monday in Cologne to regional wine festivals, these traditional celebrations center around eating and drinking. However, none of these includes any special or formal gift exchange. A visitor attending a German folk festival for the first time should understand that there is little "treating." Each participant expects to order and pay for his own food. If a German does offer to treat you, accept with thanks, but reciprocate as soon as the opportunity arises. It is generally considered rude to "grab for the check" during a festival.

BIRTHDAYS

The Germans take birthdays seriously. Celebrations take place in offices and homes, and some Germans receive the gift of a half-day vacation. Children usually wake up to a special table of flowers and gifts on their birthdays. Flowers and wine are common gifts among friends.

WEDDINGS, BIRTHS, CHRISTENINGS, AND OTHER OCCASIONS

Although there are no bridal showers in Germany, the custom of *Polterabend* is very popular. Friends of the couple go to the bride's house on the eve of the wedding and smash dishes and pottery (to break glass is considered unlucky) at the door or under her window. The loud noise scares away bad luck; and, if the bride sweeps up all the broken pieces herself, she will assure future married bliss. Wedding presents of household goods are sent to the bride's home before or during the church ceremony or are taken to the wedding. It is considered bad luck to give anything pointed, such as knives, scissors, or even umbrellas. It is considered rude to send a wedding gift sometime after the event if you have had sufficient time to obtain one beforehand. There are no gift registries in Germany, and money is not considered a suitable gift (unless from family, of course).

The Germans enjoy giving gifts for many occasions: when receiving an engagement, wedding, or birth announcement, they send a bouquet of flowers along with their congratulations. Engagement presents and christening presents are often exchanged. Even if you are not invited to the christening but are asked to come to see the baby, you should bring flowers and a small gift. Flowers or fruit are appropriate gifts for sick friends. Church confirmations or Communions and anniversaries are also occasions for congratulatory gifts. Whenever a new building is erected, a *Richtfest* is held when the roof's framework is raised. Traditionally a pine wreath decorated with ribbons or decorated bush is placed atop the roof. After the head carpenter climbs up to deliver a joyful, poetic speech and ask God's blessing on the building, all participants are treated to food and drinks. An especially charming custom is that of giving youngsters huge, colorful cardboard cones filled with sweets and small toys for their first day of school; this is meant as a consolation.

If you are formally invited to a German's home, consider this a special gesture of friendship. Guests are expected to bring small gifts to their host or hostess. A flower bouquet should consist of an uneven number of flowers (definitely not a dozen as Germans are familiar with the American saying "cheaper by the dozen"), and the wrapping should always be removed before presentation. Red roses are usually offered by a young man to his sweetheart, so do not make the mistake of giving them to your host's wife unless you have amorous plans. Many white and yellow flowers, particularly some types of chrysanthemums, are used almost exclusively for funerals. It is thoughtful to send flowers before or after an enjoyable occasion.

Because most Germans take pride in their front-window decorations, you will see many potted plants and flowers. (A recent survey showed that each German family has an average of twelve potted plants!) Thus, sending or bringing a lovely or unusual plant is always a welcome gesture.

If you are invited as a houseguest, your hosts will expect you to bring a little *Mitbringsel* (gift), perhaps something from your region or country. If you know that your host plays or is a fan of soccer (*Fussball*) or nine-pin bowling (*Kegeln*), you might bring a related gift. Gifts for the children of the family, such as T-shirts or tape cassettes, are appreciated.

Business Gifts

Business travelers will probably be entertained by their German associates in a German restaurant. Remember that at a German dinner no one drinks before the host has done so. Usually he tests the wine for temperature, then fills the glasses of his guests, his own last. Customarily, he raises his glass to the woman on his right, then toasts the health of the group. (Visitors are expected to do the same when they host a reciprocal dinner.) In formal toasting, an old German custom, the person of higher rank initiates the toast toward his inferior, who is expected later to return the toast. A man always makes the overture to a woman. Germans clink their glasses only when wishing each other luck or when celebrating a special occasion, such as a birthday. Glasses filled with wine or champagne—and sometimes beer (in Bavaria)—may be clinked, but usually not brandy or after-dinner liqueurs.

Gifts may be exchanged between business associates at Christmastime as well as at the conclusion of a business deal or negotiation.

THE ART AND ETIQUETTE OF GIFT GIVING

Gifts are not essential for these occasions and should not be overly expensive or extravagant. Quality and appropriateness are important elements of any gift for your German associates. Often the best gift is an American version of something the recipient enjoys—musical tapes or records, tobacco, a book, or art objects. An interesting photo book from your area or one relating to the business; unusual foods such as packaged pecans or macadamia nuts, maple syrup, gourmet coffee beans, or special teas; Western art (especially Remington and Russell); tasteful logo gifts and calendars; your host's favorite liquor—all of these are good choices. Smoked turkey breast is considered a special treat. Germans are quite serious about their wines; and because they often drink beer or wine with their meals, many of them are wine experts. Unless you are certain of your choice—whether French, German, or American—wine is probably not a good gift idea.

Do not be insulted if your German friends do not write thank-you notes after a party, dinner, or weekend. A verbal thank-you is considered adequate. Foreigners sometimes become irritated by this behavior and feel that their guests either did not enjoy the function or are behaving rudely.

Gift Tips

- Always bring a gift and/or flowers to your host or hostess.

- Gifts of flowers should be in bouquets of uneven numbers, and must be unwrapped when presented; avoid giving red roses and most formal white and yellow flowers, such as chrysanthemums.

- Always deliver wedding presents before—or on the day of—the wedding rather than after the ceremony.

- Do not give wine unless you are certain both of the wine and of your German friend's tastes.

- Do not give sharp or pointed objects; they may be thought to bring bad luck.

GIFT GIVING
CUSTOMS IN ITALY

Italians are taught the arts of giving and receiving as young children. If your good friend admires your book, presenting it to him is a gracious gesture that he will truly appreciate. Italians usually put a great deal of thought into the selection of a gift and feel it is importnat to present *Bella Figura*—a beautiful image.

Gift Giving Holidays

NEW YEAR'S

The giving begins after church on the first day of the year. At this time the children visit all family friends—particularly the elderly—to wish them Happy New Year. In return, these youthful family ambassadors usually receive gifts of money. Many families also exchange New Year's greeting cards.

EPIPHANY

Epiphany (in the Western Church a commemoration of the coming of the gift-bearing Magi as the occasion of the first manifestation of Christ to the Gentiles) is a major gift giving holiday. Well-behaved children who hang their stockings receive small gifts and sweets from Befana, a "good" witch who arrives, of course, on a broomstick. Bad children find their stockings filled with coal.

THE ART AND ETIQUETTE OF GIFT GIVING

VALENTINE'S DAY, MOTHER'S DAY, AND FATHER'S DAY

These holidays are relatively recent phenomena for Italians. The inevitable commercialization makes them more popular each year. They are celebrated with cards, flowers, and small gifts.

CARNEVALE

Candy and other sweets are exchanged during Carnevale (before Lent) when children are dressed in costume. Easter, however, brings special gifts and sweets, all in the form of eggs or hidden inside eggs. Both children and adults participate in Easter giving; there is no mythical Easter Bunny to bring baskets. Easter cards are popular.

CHRISTMAS

Italian children believe that their Christmas presents are gifts from the Christ Child. Within a family the gifts are always well hidden and cannot appear until after midnight on December 24th— the time of Christ's birth. Thus, they are opened on Christmas Morning. Gift exchange among adults is usually a private affair often observed at the family Christmas dinner.

Special Occasion Gifts

NAME DAY

One's *onomastico,* or name day (the day on which the patron saint after whom one is named became a saint of the Roman Catholic Church), is much more celebrated than his or her birthday. Special cards, gifts, and parties from friends and relatives are a tradition; however, both the party and the gift presentation always take place on the evening preceding the actual *onomastico.*

HOSPITALITY

The thoughtful guest in Italy will not bring a gift to someone's home, but will send it to the host or hostess the following day—or even sometime later. This demonstrates consideration for the host's tastes in flowers, decor, food, and wines, and affords the guest an opportunity to select something appropriate. Even when being taken to a restaurant meal, the guest is expected to send a gift later. Cut flowers, potted plants, special sweets or wines, or other small gifts are welcome tokens.

WEDDINGS AND ANNIVERSARIES

Weddings and anniversaries are celebrated with gift giving traditional in other Western countries. Silver, crystal, china, and other home accessories are usual gifts; a gift of money is not considered in good taste. Wedding presents are usually sent to the bride's home. Knives and scissors are not considered bad luck.

FUNERALS

One would send flowers (usually chrysanthemums) to an Italian funeral. This should be followed by a condolence card or note. Food and other gifts are entirely inappropriate.

Business and Social Gifts

Business gift giving is a part of Italian tradition. Gifts are exchanged at the conclusion of a meeting, conference, or negotiation, not at the beginning or during. Quality logo gifts are appreciated, as are souvenirs from one's country or region. In recent years Americans who gave gifts from the U.S. Bicentennial celebration or the Statue of Liberty renovation were especially pleased with the response. A beautifully well-chosen book is always appreciated. Foreigners should be careful about giving regional foods—few Italians have shown a fondness for maple syrup or Tex-Mex chili; and don't care for smoked foods such as fish or meats. A very special gift, however, is a large, fresh turkey—a rare treat for Italians, who seldom see poultry of this size. Most jams, jellies, marmalades, and candies are usually safe.

A gift of liquor or wine is not a good idea unless you know well your recipient's taste. Their local wines are a source of great pride, and most Italians have definite preferences. Few Italians drink scotch, and most still prefer an aperitif wine to a cocktail. Good cognac is an exception. French champagne is a treat. Remember that only the finest wines and liquors are acceptable gifts.

One would never give anything at all personal as a business gift. For example, even the gift of a scarf for a woman would be considered bad manners. A pen, however, would be acceptable.

The latest electronic gadgets are usually a successful choice—from digital watches in pens to special calculators. Certain American products have become status symbols. Some are trends, such as brand-name jeans and Ray-Ban sunglasses. The American traveler would be well advised to discover the latest American fad in Italy before shopping for small gifts.

At another level of corporate giving, precious gifts of art native to the giver—contemporary or antique, from crystal to sculpture—are well understood by the Italians.

Certain local gifts are appreciated as well. The quality goods of world-renowned Italian establishments such as Gucci, Valentino, Armani, and Pucci are especially enjoyed by the Italians. And Italy has wonderful craftsmen who produce a variety of lovely things. Each town has its own beautifully packaged confections and specialty foods. Even cookbooks and sketches from different areas make charming gifts. Intricately embroidered handkerchiefs are a lovely gift, but are considered bad luck unless the recipient "pays" you for them—usually with a token coin.

Although gifts are usually opened in front of the giver, thank-you notes are also expected.

Gift Rules

- Do not give chrysanthemums, except for funerals, as they are the flowers of mourning.

- Avoid giving flowers or gifts in the color purple as it is a symbol of death. However, it is certainly acceptable to give a bouquet of violets to a good friend who loves them or a scarf with some purple in it because it matches her coat.

- Flowers are always given in uneven numbers.

- The number thirteen is the luckiest—for flowers as well as for overall good fortune; many Italians wear jewelry in the shape of this number.

- Red roses symbolize love and passion.

- Do not send a gift of money for a wedding.

- Always bring—or preferably send later—a hospitality gift to your host or hostess.

GIFT GIVING
CUSTOMS IN THE
ARAB WORLD

T he Arab world is both intriguing and confusing to the Westerner who recognizes that the gift exchange process is not to be taken lightly.

Basically, an Arab is a person who speaks Arabic and who thinks of himself as an Arab. Most Arabs worship Allah, the one God, and believe in the teachings of Islam. The Koran, the Islamic holy book, records the direct word of Allah and together with the Shari'a (legal code) and the Hadith (customs, sayings, and actions of the prophet) is the Muslim ethical and civil code. For most Muslims, Islam is an entire way of life—a reason for human existence. Thus, Islam influences most areas of Arab life: loyalties, business hours and conduct, legal system, treatment of women by men, personal conduct, and social customs. Nonetheless, in many respects the Arab world is not one world anymore, as each country has developed somewhat different customs. What is acceptable in one place is probably less so in another.

Although what we call the Arab world encompasses most of the Middle East and Northern Africa, the American business person (usually a man) does most of his business with the Arab (Persian) Gulf countries that have substantial oil production and reserves.

These rapidly developing countries—often sophisticated in business, industry, and government—continue to behave in traditional ways that often result in cultural compromises. Consequently, the visitor to an Arab country needs to understand the impacts of Western education and technology on the Muslim Arab as well as the Arab's traditional culture. Most of the suggestions and guidelines in this chapter refer more to Saudi Arabia than to any of the other Arab countries.

Camel caravans tracking their way across the hot desert sands are largely a thing of the past. But the traditions, values, and culture of the desert still permeate modern Arab societies from the simple farmer to the Western-educated city dweller. Even the bedouin, who long ago established themselves in the cities and villages, remain proud of their desert roots. The most outstanding characteristics of this heritage remain bravery, hospitality, generosity, and pride—an important quality that can cause a lot of trouble. Equally noteworthy is that even an enemy is assured three days' hospitality and protection in a bedouin's tent. His sense of obligation to passing strangers far outweighs the importance of material possessions. Accordingly, the bedouin may well slaughter his last goat to provide a meal for guests. With this fundamental tradition, it is no wonder that the nomadic bedouin retain a prominent place in the national psyche despite their decreasing numbers, and that Arab society in general adopted these values centuries ago. Modernization has done little to dilute them at any level, particularly in Saudi society.

The hajj, the annual pilgrimage to Mecca, is one of the five acts central to the Muslim faith. Each Muslim must make the journey to the Holy City at least once in his lifetime if he is physically and financially able. Saudi Arabia feels that it is a holy privilege to offer hospitality to pilgrims, and the country provides every commodity for them during their stay in the kingdom. Special wide roads, bridges, tunnels, potable water pipes, and bathrooms have been built for the convenience of the pilgrims. Even special cities have been constructed to take in pilgrims, providing lodging, food, and various services. Free medical care and medicines are available at hospitals and clinics.

Both the bedouin traditions of generosity and the Arabs' sacred obligation to ensure the safety and comfort of all pilgrims are manifest in the hospitality that they extend to friends and visitors today. However, we must recognize that Arab hospitality is based on reciprocity. They are generous and appreciate magnanimity in others. Thus, the giving and receiving of gifts is not to be taken lightly.

The visitor—especially the business person—who wishes to become comfortable with the gift exchange in most Arab countries should understand that the Arabs believe their public image is greatly enhanced by such actions as giving lavishly; that they judge their actions by what people will say; and that they are aware that their gift selection will be judged by many. The giver who pays tribute to the Arab's honor and enhances his self-esteem will have presented a successful gift.

Special Occasion and Holiday Gifts

BUSINESS GIFTS

The gift exchange process is important to successful business relations.

'ID AL-FITR
"THE FEAST OF THE BREAKING OF THE FAST"

During Ramadan (the ninth month of the Muslim—lunar—calendar year, which shifts every year as their year is ten days shorter than ours) Muslims fast from sunrise to sunset for thirty days. 'Id al-Fitr, which is marked by many parties and banquets, lasts from three to five days. At this time Arabs give small gifts and "sweets" to one another and often exchange business gifts as well. Although the 'Id al-Fitr is not well known outside the Arab world, it is a sign of respect for Americans and other foreigners who conduct business with the Muslims to acknowledge this holiday with a card or a small gift. This would be especially important for companies with permanent establishments in the Mideast.

NEW YEAR'S DAY

Family and friends typically exchange gifts; the lavishness of these gifts differs among the various Arab countries.

HOSPITALITY

Candy and flowers are always well-chosen house gifts.

WEDDINGS

There are no bridal showers in most Arab countries. Proper bridal gifts are the traditional crystal, china, and silver, but do not include utilitarian household items such as toasters. Members of the family often give jewels to the couple. Gifts are usually sent to the couple *after* the wedding; however, it is wise to make discreet local inquiries as to where the gift is to be sent—to parents of bride or groom or to the couple, as there are some variations.

FUNERALS

It is appropriate to send either a card or a telegram of condolence, but no flowers or gifts, to the grieving party. There is no tradition of donating to the deceased's favorite charity. It is acceptable to acknowledge a businessman's wife's death.

Gifts are not usually given for birthdays, births, or anniversaries.

Presentation of Gifts

Generally, gifts should be presented in front of others but not in a public place—unless you know the recipient well. It is an insult to offer your gift (or anything else) with your left hand. If for some reason you must offer or hold something or must write with your left hand (i.e., if you're left-handed), apologize for being forced to use it so that the Arab is assured that no insult is intended. Do not expose the soles of your shoes or feet—even if you are seated on a floor cushion. It is considered offensive to make a public display of the feet, as they are the lowest part of the body and have touched the ground.

Gift Guidelines

The wide cultural gap between the Arab and the Western worlds emphasizes the importance of the numerous taboos associated with gift giving in the Arab culture.

DON'T give any alcoholic beverage as a gift, no matter what you may have seen an Arab drink in another country. However, if one knows an Arab well and knows for sure that he drinks, it can be not only appropriate but desirable to send him—discreetly and legally, of course—a bottle or even a case of whiskey. Of course, the giver has to be very sure where the whiskey is being sent. In the home of the Western person the Arab visitor often likes to know where he can find a drink and enjoy it discreetly; this could be a separate room or any other place that seems suitably private. In Beirut, Amman, Masqat, and Bahrain, one can drink quite openly in public places; in Saudi Arabia, however, it is strictly forbidden, and severe penalties, including prison terms, await those who are caught. Of course, diplomatic premises are exceptions.

DON'T bring a gift for your host's wife (or wives). Don't even inquire about his wife or ask how she is feeling unless you know her personally. If the Western visitor was with his own wife when he met the wife of the Arab, it is perfectly proper to ask about her health. You may bring gifts for children.

DON'T bring or distribute logo gifts unless they are especially significant or elegant. Logo gifts in general are regarded as distasteful and "hard sell."

DON'T feel you must bring a business gift on your first trip or when you first meet someone; if you meet with someone several times during the same trip, you may wish to give a small gift as a gesture of goodwill. It is always appropriate to send a thank-you gift to your host after you have returned home.

DON'T give food. This may offend an Arab's sense of hospitality, in which an abundance of food as a show of generosity is stressed. You would be implying that he is not an adequate host. An exception is fine chocolate—Swiss and dark, if possible.

DON'T give a gift that is too expensive; government officials are especially outraged at expensive gifts that they might perceive as a bribe.

DON'T give sculpture depicting an animal or human form. These are considered graven images and may give offense. They may also be confiscated at the airport on your arrival.

DON'T bring books or magazines that contain paintings or photos of nude or "improperly dressed" persons. This might include persons in bathing suits as well as Greek statues.

DON'T expect the Arabs to write acknowledgments or thank-you notes, although those who are more Westernized may do so. It is well for the Westerner to send thank-you notes, however, as many Arabs are aware that it is a Western custom.

Arabs recognize quality and appreciate the thought and effort that go into the selection of a gift. They consider American, German, French, and Swiss merchandise to be of good value.

Quick acceptance of gifts or hospitality may be considered ungracious—even impolite. On the other hand, after accepting the traditional ceremonial small cups of aromatic coffee offered in several Arab countries, the small glasses of sweet tea that automatically follow *must* be accepted. No hesitation is needed in accepting it. It does not matter that you do not drink coffee and/or tea: courtesy dictates that you must accept them. After one or two cups of coffee, the recipient should turn his cup slightly with his hand, swiveling from the wrist. This is a signal to the server that he has had enough. If coffee and tea are served by the host rather than a servant, one could indicate this verbally to the host. Both the offer and its acceptance are symbolic. A refusal to accept anything that your host offers is considered a rejection of the host and his family or his business.

Under circumstances of traditional Arab hospitality, if a guest particularly admires something, the host will feel some compulsion to give it to him as a gift. In such cases, awkwardness may arise, because to refuse the gift may be insulting. Not all Arabs feel this, since many understand the cultural differences between East and West. Nonetheless, the Westerner should be careful not to praise too extravagantly any of the host's possessions, particularly if it is something he really does not want.

Business Cards

Be certain to bring translated business cards. Both sides should be of equally high-quality print. If your firm's name is unfamiliar and/or hard to pronounce—or if your name is difficult to pronounce—have a phonetic transliteration as well. Present your card to the receptionist and to your host as soon as you meet.

Special Gifts and Suggestions

The best gifts are those that help to open new and broader channels of communication and foster better understanding between your country and the Arab countries.

The gift of a DC-3 from President Franklin Delano Roosevelt to King Iben Saud (Abdul Azie bin Abdul Rahman Al-Saud), the founder of modern Saudi Arabia, is still a cornerstone of U.S.-Saudi friendship. The plane became the beginning of the Saudi national airline—Saudia.

The head of a major U.S. corporation, who is obviously of Scottish descent, commissioned a Steuben crystal sculpture of a thistle to present to some Arabs. The occasion was to express appreciation at the successful conclusion of a mutually satisfactory business arrangement. A Saudi minister was so pleased with the gift that he insisted that a photograph be taken of himself and the giver with the gift—a most unusual request from an Arab.

To most Arab leaders, a trained falcon is a truly splendid gift. Of course, the recipient must be a sportsman. Remember, however, that the export of falcons from the United States is illegal and covered by serious penalties.

Have you ever seen an oryx? This antelope is believed to be the origin of the legendary unicorn of the Middle Ages. The oryx had its home in the Arabian desert, but had become nearly extinct when some American organizations, with the help of Aramco, helped to rescue the last living ones and set up a breeding station in Arizona. Now that the oryx is back in Saudi Arabia, it is an unusual and significant gift for an American to give to an Arab. It represents an understanding and caring between the two nations.

Non-Arabs are often understandably confused about the escalation of gift value in their reciprocations. However, it is not necessary to purchase lavish and extravagant gifts. One of my clients, upon his return from a business trip to Riyadh, was concerned that he could find no gift suitable for his wealthy and eminent host. His present of a custom-made mail box (complete with his personal seal) for the sheikh's newly acquired western ranch was received with great delight.

Folios of photographs, paintings, or prints, as well as coffee-table books or albums depicting the key features, history, or culture of the giver's country or region, with an appropriate handwritten dedication, are well received.

Ancient cartography of the recipient's homeland or any evidence of their early exploration, navigation, science, or mathematics shows great respect and thoughtfulness.

For good friends, the latest modern household gadgetry is welcome. There should be no bar gifts even if there is a bar in the Arab's home.

Western women may exchange personal gifts with Arab women who are good friends.

Remember that some Arabs are more internationalized than others; and that even though they may adopt Western dress and manners in other parts of the world, you will find them wearing their traditional robes and shunning alcohol at home. Your task is to treat them as internationally sophisticated businessmen while at the same time observing and practicing basic Arab manners and customs.

GIFT GIVING
CUSTOMS IN SCANDINAVIA

T he Scandinavians have a practical, relaxed approach to gift giving and receiving. Their giving is certainly not ritualistic and centers around the Christmas season and individual birthdays.

Gift Giving Holidays

CHRISTMAS

The major gift giving holiday in all Scandinavian countries is Christmas; the gifts are exchanged on Christmas Eve. Sweden begins its Christmas celebrations with Santa Lucia's Day, December 13. On this date Swedish cities, offices, and schools choose their own "Lucia Brides"; and the eldest daughter in the family, wearing a white dress and a seven-candle crown of evergreens, serves a gift of coffee and special Lucia cakes to the family. (The legend is that many years ago during a great Swedish famine Santa Lucia, surrounded by a halo of light, miraculously appeared to provide the country with food.) Then, on December 24, Father Christmas or his elf brings gifts to Swedish homes. In Norway, Father Christmas brings the children's gifts after a family dinner of typically Norwegian dishes and returns later to place small gifts in their stockings. Danish gifts are presented after the family dances around the Christmas tree, and the children put out a portion of porridge for Julemand (Santa Claus). The Finnish Joulupukki places the gifts under the tree, then leaves in his sleigh.

EASTER

Often small gifts are exchanged for Easter, and children receive chocolate eggs, sometimes in nests or baskets.

MOTHER'S AND FATHER'S DAYS

All the Scandinavian countries celebrate Mother's Day each spring with flowers, chocolates, and small gifts. The Finns like to prepare coffee and cake for their mothers' breakfasts and give special potted roses. Father's Day is celebrated with small gifts.

VALENTINE'S DAY

Occasionally this is celebrated in all Scandinavian countries. Norwegians customarily give red roses to their lovers to celebrate the anniversary of a relationship—one rose for the first year, two for the second, and so on.

Special Occasion Gifts

HOSPITALITY

It is very important to bring a house gift, especially if you are visiting someone's home for the first time. Fresh flowers (except for funereal white lilies) and chocolates are always correct; flowers may be sent in advance. If you are a houseguest and do not know your hosts well, you may wish to bring a token gift, then send something more significant later with your thank-you note.

BIRTHDAYS

Birthdays are important occasions, celebrated with cakes, candles, gifts—and in some Scandinavian countries an official half-day vacation. The Danish family sets a festive breakfast-gift table for the honoree on the morning of his birthday. Children's parties are frequent. Name-day celebrations—for those who observe them—are usually less formal.

THE ART AND ETIQUETTE OF GIFT GIVING

WEDDINGS, BIRTHS, AND CHRISTENINGS

Wedding customs concerning gifts of money differ somewhat throughout Scandinavia. In Norway, money is seldom an acceptable gift, whereas in Finland both money and checks are acceptable. Some banks in Finland have a wedding registry for the bridal couple: the bank collects money from their friends, then presents the couple with a new bank account and list of contributors. Scandinavians enjoy practical gifts such as useful household items as well as silver, crystal, and china. Gift certificates are appreciated. Most gifts are sent to the home of the bride or, if it is a less formal affair, brought to the wedding.

Major wedding anniversaries are gift occasions. Denmark has the unusual tradition of celebrating the 12½ anniversary with gifts of copper. (Why 12½? It's halfway to 25!)

Births and christenings are observed with gifts for the child; silver spoons or cups are traditionally given by the godparents.

FUNERALS

Expressions of sympathy can be notes of condolence or—often in these countries—a charitable contribution in memory of the deceased. Unless instructed otherwise, flowers and wreaths are appropriate—usually white. In Denmark, white carnations are associated with death; in Finland, calla lilies and special large condolence cards called *addressi* are sent or brought to the funeral.

Business Gifts

Business travelers will find that they are not expected to exchange gifts with their Scandinavian associates, nor are they expected to have their business cards (if in English) translated. Business cards can be exchanged at the beginning or conclusion of a meeting. Of course, it is always thoughtful to bring a token typical of your region, but nothing extravagant. The Scandinavians, who are very considerate people, may host you at a restaurant or at their homes. It is not necessary for you to reciprocate at that time. Christmas gifts are often exchanged between business acquaintances, and often employees receive gifts of food or wine from their employers. Although wine drinkers generally prefer red wines from France and white wines from Germany, they are interested in trying new American wines as well. For many, American wine is a curiosity. Liquors are very expensive in the Scandinavian countries. If you happen to know that your host enjoys cognac or scotch, the gift will be appreciated. In some areas, vodka is not considered an appropriate gift item.

Thought and quality are more significant than the amount of money spent. Imported items are especially appreciated—chocolates, pictorial coffee-table books, leather goods, small prints or paintings, and electronic gadgets (if compatible with current and plugs). If you need to purchase a gift over there, a bottle of aquavit, classic china or crystal, smoked and dried lamb, excellent local chocolates, and—of course—smoked salmon are all excellent choices. Anything with a religious symbol or motif should be avoided, as most Scandinavians do not openly express their religious feelings.

Thank-you notes are customary among friends and acquaintances. After a large birthday or anniversary celebration, the Finns sometimes place their thank-you message in the local newspaper.

Rules

- Give high-quality but not extravagant gifts.

- White flowers are usually best left for mourning occasions.

- Do not give anything bearing a religious symbol.

- Always bring your hostess a gift—fresh flowers are fine.

- Translation of English-language business cards could be taken as an insult.

GIFT GIVING
CUSTOMS IN KOREA

As a newly industrialized country of great potential (predicted to emerge as the fifteenth largest economy and the tenth largest trading nation in the world by the year 2000), Korea has been giving priority to export expansion so that it can pay for the raw materials and capital goods necessary to sustain this rapid growth. As a result, Korean society is changing with great speed. However, beneath this transformation there remain centuries-old traditions and customs that—while modified to fit a new society—still have influence and meaning. Thus, the foreigner bearing gifts will immediately realize—particularly at the business level—that Western philosophical concepts, customs, clothing, and goods predominate. For example, many leading Western manufacturers have turned to Korea for manufacturing, making top designer labels and quality available in Korean department stores at a fraction of their U.S. prices. On the other hand, it can be important to know just how traditional your recipient is in order to avoid embarrassment or misunderstanding.

When addressing a Korean in writing or in person, ascertain which of his names is the family name or surname. Traditionally, Koreans have three names: first, the family name (only a few family names cover the vast majority of all Koreans); then, a name identifying the generation (usually the same for all male members of a clan); then, either the given or personal name or the generation name—the order alternates between second and third place with each generation.

When writing their names in the roman alphabet, or on Western business cards, Koreans will often invert the word order, placing the family name last.

No special formalities or customs are observed in the receiving of gifts. Expect the usual protestations—"you shouldn't have bothered" —and an appropriate thank-you. Thank-you notes are not commonly sent except for wedding gifts; then, guests are also thanked for attending the wedding.

Red is the preferred color wrapping paper for most happy occasions; gifts may be store-wrapped or wrapped by the giver.

Host/Hostess Gifts

If you come to know a Korean very well over a period of time, he may invite you to his home. Although Koreans usually bring to one another gifts of food that are expected to be shared with the group or party, this would be too informal a gesture for a foreigner to make. Traditionally flowers have been used for funerals, so they are seldom gifts, except among the most Westernized of Koreans. Foreigners' most appreciated gifts would be something from their own part of the world or some useful Western gadget or utensil.

Gift Giving Holidays

The three major gift giving holidays are Chusok, New Year's Day, and Christmas.

CHUSOK (HARVEST MOON FESTIVAL DAY)

In some ways this holiday is comparable to the American Thanksgiving. On this day (the fifteenth day of the eighth month of the lunar calendar—usually in September) a feast is prepared and the new rice and fruit harvests are celebrated. Because the day itself is a national holiday, workers usually receive a three-to-four-day leave; they return to their family home to hold memorial services at the family grave site. Gift giving of one's crops or fishing catch is a significant aspect of celebration—among family, friends, and business acquaintances. Viewing the full moon is a feature of the evening.

NEW YEAR'S DAY

Although the first three days of the new year (January 1–3) are generally celebrated, the major celebration—Lunar New Year's Day—is on the first day of the first month on the lunar calendar (the same day as the Chinese New Year). This occasion, a national holiday, has also been designated National Folklore Day. It is observed with family rituals honoring ancestors, special food, traditional games, and gift exchange among family and friends. During this period, people give money to those more powerful or influential than they, in the hope that they will receive favors during the coming year as a result. It is common practice to "buy" connections, referrals, and recommendations. Foreigners will find that this system will work for them, too. As a delightful Korean woman explained it, "You go fishing, but the gift is the bait, not the fish. You hope to land a big fish by casting the bait."

CHRISTMAS

Korea today is a melting pot of world religions, with the three most predominant being Buddhism, Protestantism, and Catholicism. Both Christians and other citizens celebrate Christmas as in the West. Christmas gifts are given among adults; and children anticipate Santa Claus's visit on December 24.

Other gift giving holidays include Children's Day, May 5 (a national holiday) and Parents' Day, May 8. Children's Day is celebrated with various events for children, who are usually taken to special programs and meals by their parents. They also receive gifts from parents and other adult family members. Parents' Day is an occasion for honoring one's parents with small gifts. As in Western cultures, the carnation has become a symbolic gift for mothers. Valentine's Day is becoming a popular gift/card-giving occasion among young Koreans.

Special Occasion Gifts

BIRTHDAYS

In the life of a Korean, the two most important birthdays are the one-hundredth day, and the sixtieth year. At the former party, the child is dressed in a colorful, traditional costume and receives his gifts amid piles of cookies, fruits, and rice cakes. The sixtieth birthday is an occasion for festivity because it is considered an important landmark in life. (Originally, it was celebrated as the end of the active life cycle.) A magnificent banquet with rich food, many gifts, and wishes for longevity is traditional.

WEDDINGS

There are two kinds of Korean weddings: traditional and Western-style. Unfortunately, the old-fashioned ceremonies with the beautiful traditional costumes are rare. At the far end of the spectrum, many weddings now take place in an urban wedding hall, where music, flowers, bridal gowns, dress suits, and photographers can be rented. Most Koreans give money as a wedding gift. Wedding guests leave their envelopes at a table or desk at the entrance to the wedding hall. Close friends who know the couple's needs and tastes might bring a special gift. Foreigners who will not be attending the wedding and who would be uncomfortable sending money may send gifts of silver, crystal, appliances, or utensils to the home of either the bride or the groom. Most couples receive at least one pair of traditional wooden mandarin ducks—one red (female) and one blue (male) for good luck. Wedding gifts or greetings are usually wrapped or decorated with gold and/or silver.

CONVALESCENCE

If someone is ill, flowers or suitable fruits are common gifts.

FUNERALS

Funeral attendees are expected to leave envelopes of money at the door. The sending or bringing of flowers—especially white or yellow chrysanthemums—is traditional. Other gifts or gifts of food are not acceptable. A note of condolence is always appropriate.

Business Gifts

Business gifts are usually presented at the beginning of formal negotiations. Foreigners will find that the Koreans—still a bit uncomfortable about gift giving—are inclined to equate expense with appropriateness, and therefore may give needlessly expensive items, especially if they are not the hosts. The most appropriate and appreciated gifts are those special products from your country or region. Anything French—and almost anything Italian—indicates status; YSL and Leonard are the current designers of choice. The Koreans are also very conscious of well-known designer labels and stores, so even small items such as Gucci pens, Mark Cross address books, or Tiffany desk accessories are very well received. Koreans are not flattered when presented with gifts made in China.

The remembrance of Korean business friends and associates for Chusok is an especially thoughtful gesture. The greeting on an accompanying card for this occasion would read "Happy Chusok." Christmas cards and gifts are also exchanged.

Business cards are always exchanged during initial business introductions. It is thoughtful for the foreign business person to have his printed in Korean—on the reverse side or separately.

Entertaining is a common form of business gift. There are no formal procedures or protocol to be observed such as at a Chinese banquet, and the recipient (visitor) is not necessarily expected to return the favor with a meal, but he is expected to respond by presenting a gift to his hosts during the meal. Lunches, dinners, and geisha evenings are all common forms of business entertaining.

Taboos

• As few Koreans drink red wine and only the more sophisticated drink white, a gift of wine may not be appropriate.

• The number four is considered unlucky—so don't give a set of four items.

• Snakes, black cats, and crows are considered to represent bad luck.

• Knives and scissors are not given as gifts because they signify the "cutting off" of a relationship.

• One does not give shoes to a friend, as it implies that the giver wishes to kick him.

• White and yellow chrysanthemums are not given on any occasions except for a death; they are the traditional Korean funeral flower.

General Gift Information

Quality Western-made goods are particularly successful gifts. Some current brand preferences among the more sophisticated Koreans include Lancôme cosmetics, Gucci handbags and luggage, and the traditional Burberry clothing.

Gifts of liquor are generally appropriate—especially on the three major gift giving occasions. Chusok, Lunar New Year's, and Christmas are all times for celebrating with feasting and drinking. Koreans drink scotch (preferably well-known brands). Bourbons, brandies, gin, vodka, sherry, and afterdinner drinks are not familiar to most

Koreans. The familiar sake is always appreciated; however, the traditional *soju*, made from sweet potatoes, is too common to present in a formal gift setting. White wines—foreign or domestic—are appropriate for the Westernized Korean.

Koreans are very involved in athletic development and pursue their sports—as both participants and spectators—with great vigor. They are proud that many of the events of the 1988 Olympics will be held in the Seoul Sports Complex. Although soccer and baseball are the most popular sports, it would be thoughtful to discover the sports interests of your recipient so that you could give a sports-related gift. Most youths enjoy competitive kite flying in the spring.

Remember that family and group ties are still very strong. Patriotism and filial piety are virtues taught to all children. Gifts for groups and family gifts as well as gifts that demonstrate your appreciation of their history, values, and education are especially appreciated.

GIFT GIVING
CUSTOMS IN THE
SOVIET UNION

Russia is a very large and diverse country with many different traditions among its various republics. Outside the major cities, many of the people still adhere to old customs; however, most foreigners who exchange business or social gifts probably communicate with the more sophisticated city dwellers.

Although gift giving is an important aspect of Russian relationships, the actual value of a gift is not nearly as important as its selection. Their gift giving is neither extravagant nor formal and is usually observed between relatives and close friends. Small, thoughtful tokens or souvenirs are greatly appreciated.

Gift Giving Holidays

NEW YEAR'S DAY

This is the USSR's major gift giving holiday. Fir trees are decorated and families gather to feast and toast. Grandfather Frost, dressed in red and with a long white beard (and looking much like the Saint Nicholas of Western legend), brings the children's gifts in his horse-drawn sleigh. Adults who are related or well acquainted customarily exchange gifts; and this is the one time of year for the giving of business gifts.

INTERNATIONAL WOMEN'S DAY

This, my favorite Russian holiday, is recognized annually with a national holiday on March 8. On this occasion women are extolled, feted, and given gifts from children, friends, relatives, spouses, and employers. Early spring flowers, such as daffodils, are an especially popular offering. As Mother's Day is not observed, children of all ages honor their mothers at this time. Cards are sent to the women one most admires.

SPRING AND NATIONAL WORKERS' DAY

This celebration occurs on May 1. The Russians usually wear and give flowers as a part of their holiday celebrations. Because the revolutionaries wore red carnations in their lapels, the red carnation is the most traditional, patriotic flower for these occasions. Roses and asters are also popular gifts and decorations. Greeting cards are given to friends.

THE ANNIVERSARY OF THE GREAT OCTOBER REVOLUTION

This holiday, which is celebrated each November 7, is similar to France's Bastille Day or America's Fourth of July. Red carnations are given and worn, and many greeting cards are exchanged.

Special Occasion Gifts

WEDDINGS

Weddings are usually big celebrations; gifts are generally brought to the wedding. Gifts from persons not attending can be delivered to either the bride's or the groom's home. Customary gifts are for the home—the usual linens, china, and so on. Beautifully crafted decorative items such as music boxes are also appreciated. The giving of knives and scissors is considered bad luck. Major anniversaries, such as the twenty-fifth and fiftieth, are celebrated with gifts and family and community festivities. Roses are the romantic flower.

FUNERALS

Foreigners wishing to offer condolences may send flowers to the funeral—calla lilies are traditional. It is important to send an even number of flowers. A note or letter is always appropriate. As philanthropy is nonexistent, there are no organizations to make memorial donations to. Ten days after the funeral there is a remembrance ceremony. Participants speak about the deceased and have a meal together. Attendees bring gifts of food.

BIRTHDAYS

Birthdays are celebrated with large parties of family and friends and many gifts. The sixteenth birthday is especially significant, as the young Russian achieves full political and social rights—he can make the decision to leave his family, marry, and such. The eighteenth and twenty-fifth birthdays are also important milestones.

Among Russians, gifts are usually opened in front of the giver so that thank-yous are immediate. Thank-you notes are an infrequent form of communication.

Business Gifts

Foreign business travelers are more likely to be entertained in a restaurant than in a home. Dinner is usually accompanied by a great deal of toasting. The visitor is expected to reciprocate if time allows. If you are invited to someone's home for dinner or a party, a token gift of flowers, sweets, or a souvenir is customary. Because of the Russians' changing attitudes toward alcohol, many of them no longer welcome gifts of liquor. If you know the recipient's preferences, sometimes wine is acceptable.

Because the nobility always had calling cards, they are now exchanged only in official government and business relationships, seldom among the majority of Russian citizens.

Any exchange of business gifts must come at the close of negotiations and must not be extravagant. Foods such as candies, cakes, or nuts and regional souvenirs or books are good choices. Logo gifts are acceptable. Customs regulations prohibit bringing in coffee or tea unless it is canned; and all canned meats are prohibited. The Russians treasure ancient crafts from different regions of their country— wonderful painted miniatures on wood from Paalekh; elaborate wooden dinnerware and vases from Khokhloma; china from one of the best porcelain factories in the world in Dudyee; whalebone carvings from the ArcAngel region; blue and white ceramics from Gzhel; intricate scenes and toys from Dymkoev.

Travelers to Russia may discover a special rapport symbolized in a gift exchange. On a recent trip to Moscow, my brother gave a young student the book *A Day in the Life of America* in return for help in reading signs and maps. The next day the student took him to the movies, interpreted for him, then gave him a pair of 80-year-old sandals from his grandfather's village in Siberia—a gift he will treasure forever.

GIFT GIVING
CUSTOMS IN AUSTRALIA

The Australians—a friendly, outgoing people who enjoy meeting foreigners—have an open and informal lifestyle. This is reflected in both their social and business relationships. Telephone calls usually take the place of thank-you notes, and gift wrapping is casual.

However, Australians can easily be overwhelmed—even embarrassed—by the extent and lavishness of gift giving demonstrated by the Japanese and Americans. Thus, foreigners need to be careful not to overdo in either number or extravagance of gifts. A small token of good quality is always more appropriate than a large gesture; and neither the store or the designer/brand name is of undue significance. An Australian will probably not open his gift in front of the giver and will not expect a recipient to open his.

Gift Giving Holidays and Special Occasions

The Australians observe many of the same holidays as the Americans. Their gift giving on these occasions, however, is on a smaller and less commercial scale. Christmas brings the remembrance of the birth of Christ and the presents from Father Christmas. Because of the intense summer heat, most of the celebration takes place outdoors, so there is little need for indoor decoration. On

Mother's Day, usually in May—their fall season—chrysanthemum plants are traditionally given to mothers (mums for mums) along with a special dinner. Father's Day may be recognized with a card or a flower for his buttonhole; and Valentine's Day is sometimes observed by romantic lovers. Easter eggs and chocolates are standard gifts for young children; but, as Easter is in the fall season, the holiday does not have the same spring symbolism as it does in the Northern Hemisphere. They do not celebrate Halloween.

Among Australians, birthdays are recognized with a card or a small gift—the eighteenth and twenty-first birthdays commanding more attention and gifts of more lasting value. Graduation, wedding, and anniversary gifts are similar to those of most Western countries, including the celebration of silver and golden anniversaries. Knives and scissors are considered bad luck. An eagerly anticipated part of the Australian wedding reception is the reading of congratulatory telegrams from distant relatives and friends. They are especially delighted with messages from abroad. Wedding gifts are usually brought to the reception. Those who cannot attend send telegrams and/or gifts to the bride's home prior to the wedding. The usual flowers and condolence notes, as well as charitable donations when requested, are appropriate responses to a death.

A small selection such as food, wine, or a plant is a good "hostess" gift. Many particularly enjoy imported beers and wines as well as good port. Don't make the mistake of bringing gladioli. Australia's very popular comedian, Barry Humphries dressed as Dame Edna, wears a quilted pink robe with a gigantic three-dimensional bouquet of "glads" embroidered in the middle of her back. He/she has made this flower the symbol of the Australian working class—an obvious insult to receive as a gift. Rosemary is used for remembrance—to friends as well as for their veterans' Remembrance and Anzac days.

Business Gifts

The exchange of gifts is not an important aspect of everyday Australian business. Logo gifts, scotch, and beautiful books are appropriate for Christmas as well as to mark certain business arrangements. Local gifts—Australian leather goods, pewter, brassware, glassware, and wood products, and, for special occasions, opals are well received.

Quarantine Laws

A protected place, Australia has very strict quarantine laws of which potential gift givers should be aware. All meats—even canned—straw articles, certain "origin"-related wood products, feathers, egg products, and dairy products including cheese are banned. Some goods such as wooden articles, nuts, bamboo and cane articles, baby food, and furred skins may be taken into Australia, but must be shown to quarantine officers on arrival.

GIFT GIVING
CUSTOMS IN
THE NETHERLANDS

Y ou'll find hundreds of windmills, plenty of wooden shoes, miles of bright tulips, and many barrel organs—but only one Saint Nicholas. His birthday, the most important birthday in all the Netherlands, is celebrated each December with parades, feasting, and an imaginative exchange of gifts. Saint Nick (Sinterklaas, as man and festival are both called), the compassionate Bishop of Myra, travels to Holland from Spain each year by steamboat in order to distribute these gifts.

During most of the year, Sinterklaas records the behavior of Dutch children in his large red book, while his servant Peter (Piet) stocks up on presents for the December trip. After he arrives and is formally welcomed by the Queen and her family, who receive his first gifts, he leads a magnificent parade while his servants throw ginger nuts and other traditional sweets to the crowds.

According to Dutch tradition, all presents must be camouflaged in an imaginative fashion and accompanied by a rhyme or poem written for the recipient. The packages themselves are not expected to be pretty, but rather disguised, hard to locate, or difficult to open. On December 5, Sinterklaas Eve, the Dutch sit around a table laden with sweets and bakery goods, their places marked with large chocolate initials, and begin to open their Sinterklaas gifts. Recipients often have to work for their gifts, following a sort of treasure hunt around the house or digging through a glove filled with wet sand. The rhymes which accompany them are expected to be humorous and to cause the good-natured embarrassment of the recipient. (Those who cannot write clever verse will find that many stores will provide a selection or a versifier for you.) All poems are signed by Sinterklaas and recipients shout a loud "Thank you, Sinterklaas." Gifts among both family and friends are traditionally exchanged in this way.

Later that night Sinterklaas returns on his white horse to fill the shoes of good children with small gifts (especially those who have left hay or carrots for his horse) and to leave Piet to administer the birch rod or even bundle into his large bag those who have misbehaved during the year.

With most of festivities and gift giving over, the Dutch Christmas is a season of peace and goodwill. The tree, which is first lit on Christmas Eve, should disappear before January 6—when the Magi arrive. Although gifts are again often exchanged among family, friends, and business acquaintances, the gaiety belongs to Sinterklaas.

There is a long-standing tradition that one must receive something new for the new year. Thus still on New Year's Day small presents such as handkerchiefs are exchanged to ensure good luck for the coming year.

Special Occasion Gifts

BIRTHDAYS

Birthdays are celebrated with parties, gifts, and the traditional cake and candles. Family presents are often arrayed at the breakfast table, and children take sweets or snacks to school to distribute to their friends. The twenty-first birthday usually calls for a special observance.

WEDDINGS, BIRTHS, AND CHRISTENINGS

Because wedding gifts are usually displayed at the wedding reception, it is advisable to send the gift to the bride before the wedding. The usual household items are most appreciated; wedding gift registries are popular, especially in the cities. Money is not considered an appropriate wedding gift. The groom usually gives his bride a special bouquet on their wedding day.

Gifts are expected for births and christenings; however, there are no showers—birth or wedding.

FUNERALS

For a death, flowers are sent to the funeral home unless another gift such as a charitable donation is specified.

HOSPITALITY

Never go to visit a Dutch home without sending or bringing flowers. If you have the time, and especially if the affair is somewhat formal, it is preferable to send flowers ahead. There are no rules about numbers or colors of flowers, except for the standard associations of red roses for lovers and white lilies for funerals. You can also bring other small house gifts. If you are bringing a treat from your own country, don't give chocolates unless they are something special, such as filled with liqueur; and don't bring gin, as the Dutch have their own, called *jenever* (40 percent alcohol, drunk straight).

Business Gifts

For the most part, the business person will find no unusual customs or taboos associated with gift giving in the Netherlands. Typically gifts would be exchanged at the conclusion of a successful deal or long meeting. Business cards need not be translated. Appreciated gifts include illustrated books (possibly about your region of the world); high quality leather goods and desk items such as agendas; special gourmet food items, or fine French wine, Spanish sherry, or scotch. Good cigars are especially appreciated by cigar smokers, and brandy by brandy drinkers. If you are sending gifts to the Netherlands, be certain not to pack them in wood shavings, as they may have trouble getting through customs.

The Dutch enjoy giving their famous products to business associates around the world. If you are fortunate, you will receive in return a marvelous cheese, a beautifully illustrated book or calendar, or some of their exceptional liqueurs or chocolates. When traveling, Queen Beatrix gives her hosts gifts of Delft china, Dutch crystal with her royal crest, or her framed, signed portrait. And KLM, for example, sends clients and friends selected bulbs each Christmas.

There were many interesting gift exchanges during the 1986 Statue of Liberty celebrations in New York. Some of the most pleasing were the presentations from the captain of the Dutch naval ship *Abraham Crynssen*, which was participating in the parade of tall ships. Captain Kok gave the mayor of Port Jefferson, his ship's host, and the president of Operation Sail each a reproduction of a painting of the original ship (dating back 350 years) and an ashtray made from one of their grenades.

A Special Note

The legend of Saint Nicholas is based on historical fact. He lived in Asia Minor from 271 A.D. to 342 or 343. When his wealthy parents died in an epidemic, he distributed his fortune among the poor and entered the priesthood. Later, as the Bishop of Myra, the fame of his good deeds and saintly ways spread across the Mediterranean. After his death, an amazing series of legends and miracles appeared—stories about his becalming the sea for the sailors and his saving small children from the butcher's knife. Later, after Saint Nicholas became the patron saint of sailors, many harbor cities built Roman Catholic churches dedicated to him. He also became known as the traditional protector of children. As early as the fourteenth century, choir boys of the various churches were given some money on December 6. Their group leader, costumed as a bishop, would lead a procession of boys through the streets begging for "bishop money." Saint Nick's spirit also became entrenched in the convent schools. On his birthday the good pupils could anticipate a reward of gifts; the disobedient could expect the birch rod.

GIFT
GIVING CUSTOMS
IN SPAIN

Gift Giving Holidays

One of the most interesting Spanish customs takes place on January 6. On this occasion Roscón de Reyes, a round, sweet bread, is cut to reveal a prize. The recipient will experience good luck for the remainder of the year.

Spain has many national religious holidays, such as October 12, el Día de la Hispanidad, which commemorates the Virgin's appearance on top of a pillar; March 19, and August 25, Archangel Saint James' Day. On Cataluña—Saint George's Day—some couples exchange a rose for a book; he gives her the rose, she gives him the book. However, most of these holidays do not involve any special gift exchange.

At Epiphany, December 6, the children put their shoes out, hoping that the three Wise Men will bring small gifts rather than coal. Adult gifting centers around Christmas, with most families exchanging presents after their Christmas Eve dinner.

Valentine's Day (Día de los Enamorados), Mother's Day (the first Sunday in May), and Father's Day are celebrated with flowers, cards, or small gifts. Fathers are honored on Saint Joseph's Day—March 19—which is observed as a holy day. Birthdays are rather private celebrations; whereas saints' days are occasions for parties, presents, flowers, and telegrams. Easter eggs and chocolates are distributed to children and friends during Holy Week.

Special Occasion Gifts

WEDDINGS

Wedding gifts are usually sent to the house of the bride prior to the wedding. Any of the usual gifts of household goods are appropriate, except for linens—usually linens are already a part of the bride's trousseau.

HOSPITALITY

Guests to a casual gathering may bring a small "hostess" gift; however, it is preferable to send something such as flowers or a plant after the occasion. Chrysanthemums and dahlias are to be avoided, as they are used mainly for funerals; red roses represent passion, and in some areas, yellow roses stand for infidelity. The number thirteen is to be avoided. For a country weekend, bring a small gift for the house—crystal, leather goods, or elegant linens. The Spanish are quality and status conscious and appreciate fine gifts.

Business Gifts

Most business transactions are conducted over three-hour lunches. The exchange of business cards is popular, but business gifts are seldom exchanged before, during, or after a meeting or transaction. If you know your host well and/or will be working for some time with the same group, a small gift that is representative of your region of the world or a tasteful logo gift would be appreciated. Extravagant gestures may be regarded as bribes. At the Christmas season most businesses send Christmas cards; some exchange small gifts, often of liquor or wine.

GIFT GIVING GUIDELINES IN LATIN AMERICA

A very gift-oriented people, Latins enjoy both giving and receiving. Their emphasis on family life and lineage, their almost ceremonial courtesy, their desire to be "simpatico" and make you comfortable, and their cult of "machismo" are manifest in their gift giving customs. Friendship is highly valued. They appreciate gifts that recognize their individual qualities and interests, and they prize thoughtfulness above monetary value.

In many sections of Latin America people are influenced by gifts or money. This is an accepted practice that is not viewed as dishonest, but rather as part of their way of life. However, a business or friendship gift can be a legitimate communication that expresses your thanks, pleasure, or appreciation.

Remember, though:

- A business gift should not be presented until after all negotiations have been completed.

- A businesswoman should, in most instances, avoid giving a gift to a Latin man, as it is very likely to be misinterpreted.

- If you are visiting a family, American toys, small electrical appliances, and high-tech gadgets are special treats. Something from your region that the entire family can enjoy is a good choice.

- Logo gifts are considered "cheap" unless they are of excellent quality and have a subtle logo.

- Flowers are usually appropriate gifts; each country, however, has funeral flowers that would not be used for gifts.

- Except for specific thank-you gifts, do not give a gift to a Latin until you have developed a personal relationship.

- An imported product that is heavily taxed is especially appreciated (of course, you pay the tax).

- Maintain eye contact when giving or receiving a gift to show sincerity.

- Open a gift upon receipt and thank the giver as soon as possible.

- Do not expect thank-you notes—most thanking is verbal.

- Be certain that your gift is of the highest quality regardless of price; its quality reflects on the giver.

GIFT GIVING
CUSTOMS IN VENEZUELA

T he Venezuelans enjoy the art of gift giving. They give as a sign of affection, care, love, and gratitude.

Gift Giving Holidays

CHRISTMAS

For Venezuelans, as for the nationals of other Christian countries, Christmas means a mixture of religious commemoration and pagan entertainment. However, the lavish exchange of gifts, as practiced in the United States, is not customary in Venezuela.

The period from December 16 to 24 is called *Aguinaldos*, perhaps due to the fact that the year-end present or bonus given by businesses to their employees is called *Aguinaldo*. During this season young people enjoy playing at *"Aguinaldos,"* a game between a boy and a girl in which the loser is supposed to give a present to the winner. The winner is usually the girl because this provides the boy with a good excuse for giving her a present.

EPIPHANY

Children used to get their presents only on January 6, the Day of the Three Wise Men or Kings. At bedtime on the Eve of

Epiphany the children put their shoes on the window sill and placed wisps of straw inside them to feed the Magi's camels. When the children awoke the next morning, they discovered gifts in place of the straw. Now this charming custom is fading and presents for the children are usually given either in the name of the infant Jesus or from Saint Nicholas on Christmas Eve. Lucky children, in a blend of the old and the new, may receive both. Christmas gifts are placed around the crèche in most families. Adults exchange small gifts with one another.

SAINTS' DAYS

These are observed most often among the older and/or more rural peoples. Gifts are given to those who are named after the saint. For example, if your name is Catherine, you would receive gifts on Saint Catherine of Siena's Saint Day. Gifts are usually small tokens. Birthdays are celebrated by both friends and relatives in Venezuela with gifts and parties. Flowers are a customary gift. Children's birthday parties may be very elaborate; *penhadas'* contents are popular gifts for young guests (further described in the section on Brazil).

Special Occasion Gifts

HOSPITALITY

It is not necessary to take a hospitality gift to dinner. A gift of wine could even offend the hostess, who may think that her wine was not good enough for you. A better choice: send a small thank-you gift, such as fresh flowers. Flowers are usually presented wrapped. Red flowers mean passion; irises should be reserved for funerals.

WEDDINGS, BIRTHS, AND CHRISTENINGS

Wedding gifts are often given on the day of the wedding. The reception is usually held at the bride's home, where the couple display their gifts for the guests. The usual household presents are appropriate.

Gifts are given for both births and christenings.

FUNERALS

Flowers and cards are usually sent to the deceased's family for a death. Charity donations are not usually sent unless specifically requested.

THE ART AND ETIQUETTE OF GIFT GIVING

Venezuelans usually open their gifts immediately and thank the giver verbally and/or with kisses. If the giver cannot be thanked in person, he will receive a phone call. Generally, thank-you cards or notes are not necessary or expected, even for a wedding gift.

As seashells connote death, they are considered to bring bad luck. Gifts of shells or items with a shell motif, such as note paper, linens, or jewelry, should be avoided. Some of the older Venezuelans associate handkerchiefs with the shedding of tears.

Business Gifts

Gifts are not usually exchanged to start or conclude business in Venezuela. Entertainment is the predominant gift in the business world, perhaps with a restaurant celebration to mark a successful negotiation. There are no formal toasting customs. After all business is over, foreigners may present gifts from their homeland, office or desk items, or liquor such as good scotch or a fine wine. Logo gifts are acceptable but are considered "tacky" unless they are of excellent quality and the logo is very subtle. Business transactions can suffer if gifts are too personal (unless a personal relationship also exists). It is not appropriate to give wives and families gifts unless a personal relationship has already been established. Generally, American businesswomen should not give Venezuelan businessmen gifts—there is still the belief that American women are "free and easy." However, if they do, they must make quite sure that no connotations other than business can be attached to the gift.

Venezuelans enjoy many products made in the United States. Most things are available in Venezuela but are very expensive there. Good gifts include small appliances and high-tech items from either the United States or Japan, popular recordings, and American jeans. If you are going to visit a family with children, American toys are a top priority. When selecting gifts for Venezuelans, always consider the quality of the gift. Although thoughtfulness is placed above monetary value, a gift of poor quality reflects on the giver. Wrapped gifts will be opened by customs officials.

Historically, gifts have been exchanged as a gesture of friendship between Venezuela and the United States for many years. The United States gave a statue of George Washington that has stood in Caracas for over a hundred years; a statue of Henry Clay; a bust of Lincoln; and Martha Custis's son gave Venezuela a medallion that had on one side a lock of George Washington's hair and on the reverse his portrait. From Venezuela we have the modern sculpture that stands outside of the Smithsonian Institution's Air and Space Museum in Washington, D.C., and a bronze equestrian statue of "the Liberator," Simón Bolívar, who ended Spain's military power in South America.

GIFT GIVING
CUSTOMS IN BRAZIL

Brazilian society is still marked by pronounced regional and ethnic diversity, and this is apparent in their gift customs, which often change from region to region.

Two factors have been reflected in their customs: they are the single largest group of Catholics in the world; and their "cult of the family" stands out even among the family-oriented nations of Latin America. Family loyalty is the highest duty: one must assist one's kin in their needs. Many gifts are given as a spontaneous sharing of friendship and love.

Gift Giving Holidays and
Special Occasions

There is little commercial exploitation of Christmas. It remains primarily a holy, religious time, and gifts are given as a part of that religious tradition. Gifts, which are usually exchanged between relatives and friends on Christmas Day, are not as expensive or as lavish as those we exchange in the United States.

Easter is celebrated by gift giving, usually in the form of candy for both children and adults.

A gift in return for hospitality is neither necessary nor expected. Although a verbal thank-you is quite sufficient, a small token, especially sent as a thank-you, is a thoughtful gesture.

As an important family figure, the godparent is expected to give special presents to his child. There are no special restrictions on gifts for births, christenings, and weddings. Wedding gifts are often given on the same day as the wedding; they should be sent to the bride's house.

For funerals, cards, messages, and food go to the immediate family. Charity donations are usually appropriate.

Most gifts are wrapped at the store where they are purchased. Instead of a matching ribbon or bow, wrappers make interesting folded designs with the paper.

In order to show genuine appreciation for a gift, the recipient is expected to open the gift at once and thank the giver immediately. A verbal thanks in person or on the telephone is sufficient; thank-you notes are rare.

For special occasions, Brazilians enjoy *penhadas*, papier-mâché dolls stuffed with candies and small gifts. Blindfolded children gather around the *penhada*, which is hanging from the ceiling, and take turns trying to break it open with a stick. Once it breaks, they scramble around the floor to collect the fallen goodies. (This is more familiar to Americans as the Mexican piñata.)

Business Gifts

Business gifts should be given after negotiations have been completed. Logo gifts must be special and subtle. Liquors, chocolates, jams, and desk accessories are all appropriate.

Gifts from Europe are considered quality merchandise, especially leather goods or 18-karat gold. American high-tech products and small appliances are also appreciated. American toys are welcome as children's gifts. Wrapped gifts will be opened by customs officials.

Among the educated, there aren't any significant superstitions. Most taboos are associated with voodoo and black magic, which are still practiced in parts of the country. For this reason, homemade dolls may not be an appropriate gift.

GIFT GIVING
CUSTOMS IN CHILE

To Chileans a gift is a symbol of gratitude or appreciation; therefore, the value of the present is seldom as important as the feeling with which it is given. Quality, however, is important. Even with flowers, which are commonly sent to women for special occasions, the quantity is not nearly as significant as the presentation and quality.

Gift Giving Holidays and Special Occasions

Most gift giving centers around Christmas, birthdays, and weddings. In Chile, Christmas is not as commercialized as it is in the United States, and gifts are generally less extravagant. Small gifts are exchanged among family and friends.

Some people choose to celebrate their saint's day rather than their birthday. Whichever day the party celebrates, it is customary for guests to bring a gift.

Bridal gifts should be sent with a card of congratulations before the wedding. Although there now are wedding registries, this has not yet become a very popular custom, nor is it considered in the best of taste by some Chileans. It appears too contrived or commercial. The recipient(s) will acknowledge wedding presents with a thank-you note.

Small gifts are also exchanged at Easter time—primarily for children. As in Brazil, candies are given to the children.

Other gift giving occasions are baptisms, First Communions (Catholics), graduations, and important anniversaries. For a birth, visitors usually bring small gifts for the baby.

When visiting someone's home, especially for the first time, a token gift is appreciated. Flowers are best sent ahead by messenger so that the recipient receives them before you greet them. Red flowers, for some, are a symbol of love.

If you wish to send a gift for a funeral, flowers can be appropriate—also a "crown of charity," a donation to a good cause, preferably one selected or favored by the deceased's family.

Business Gifts

Business gifts are usually exchanged for public relations reasons and not expected to have any sentimental value. Frequent gift occasions include the initiation of major business negotiations, contract signing, and Christmas. On occasion, it is also customary to celebrate the successful conclusion of a business transaction with a dinner or banquet. Tasteful logo gifts are acceptable and recognized as a public relations gesture. Good-quality liquor is often exchanged. The selection of a business gift relates to the size and importance of the account and the title of the business person(s) involved. Bribes are not common.

In general, proper gifts are given or sent before or on the celebration date. It is the custom to open a gift in front of the person who gave it to you, when the gift is given in person. Except for formal occasions, such as weddings, thanks are usually given in person or by telephone rather than written. Gifts of clothing should not be exchanged between men and women who are not close family.

A gift of a handkerchief can be a symbol of displeasure or the cause of a break in a relationship. To prevent such "curses," the person who receives a gift of a handkerchief should give a small coin to the giver in return.

PART SIX

WHEN YOU CHOOSE ...

BOOKS AS
GIFTS

It could be a riddle. What gift is small in size, compact, not fragile, relatively inexpensive, and suitable for anyone on any occasion? The answer and the perfect gift is, of course, a book. A book can be an unlimited investment in the human mind and spirit. From comic books to historical novels, from rare antique volumes to large-print editions, from mass paperbacks to handmade small-press books, from a lush coffee-table photography book to a boxed set of children's nursery rhymes, the book's the thing.

There are books—and often particular bookstores—for everyone: books on design, stamps, telephones, travel, Egyptology, horticulture, college exams, anthropology, cooking, braille, aviation, business, flying saucers, spiritual inspiration, mysteries, the occult, yoga, sports, real estate, natural science, genealogy, foreign languages, child care, Americana, rare oriental antiquarian books ... the list is endless. As an example of a specialty bookstore: a Judaica bookstore—where all the books are on Jewish themes or by Jewish authors—carries hard-to-find first editions, volumes on the Holocaust, the Diaspora, guides to European cities pointing out the kosher restaurants, synagogues, and Jewish landmarks, favorite books translated into Hebrew, kosher cookbooks, records and tapes of Israeli folk songs, cantorial and klezmer music, and Jewish trivia books and board games.

Although books are no longer an inexpensive item, gift books generally give you real value for your money. When price is an issue—and even when it isn't—paperback books are an acceptable gift. The price difference may enable the giver to give two or three books by the same author or about the same subject. Put together several small books for the traveler or a bedridden friend. Paperbacks in boxed sets are attractive and popular gift items and range from a two-volume historical package by William Shirer to a deluxe gift box edition of Louis L'Amour's bestselling Sackett novels. More and more, book-gift givers are seeking that special biography or are giving two paperbacks and the new hardcover of a selected author because they want to share what they themselves love to read.

Many people enjoy buying books as gifts because they enjoy bookstore browsing. I often emerge with a gift or two for myself as well. Nowhere else can you find the wide variety and number of possible gift choices in such a small space: and bookstore personnel are usually helpful and knowledgeable, taking the time to make suggestions and to tell you about certain books. All of this helps to make your gift choice more individual. And if you still can't decide or feel that you don't know the person well enough to choose a book, a gift certificate for a book gives the recipient many choices as well as a reason to browse self-indulgently.

For those who do not have time for browsing and selection or are far from a bookstore, there are several book-locating services that are only as far away as your telephone. One, called Book Call, is a twenty-four-hour-a-day service. And, of course, the Book-of-the-Month Club has always sent gift books for its customers. The club's membership orders over forty-five hundred gift books each month—over eleven thousand in December 1985! Their membership director reports that the number of people taking advantage of this service increases each month; the only additional charge is $1 if you request gift wrapping. The club will also try to locate current books as an additional service to its members. In addition, most publishing companies distribute news bulletins or catalogs that describe their recent offerings.

For those with special interests, a book can be an exciting, imaginative—even unique—choice. A Texan would appreciate the two-volume illustrated edition of James Michener's *Texas* that was produced especially for Texas's Sesquicenntenial. For religious occasions a particular translation of the Bible, or, for Passover seder, Abrams's edition of *The Ashkenazi Haggadah* from the mid-fifteenth century, reproduced from the collections in the British Library of London, or perhaps *The Littlest Angel* for a child's Christmas. For food lovers, try regional cookbooks, for cat lovers, *The Indispensable Cat*. For speakers and have-to-writers, a book of quotations such as

Charisma or a speaker's treasury. For students, an abbreviated version of one of the desktop encyclopedias (usually in boxed sets of two). For the unwilling English student, one of Shakespeare's unabridged dramas in comic-book form (Workman, $7– $9)! For the fly fisherman, an antique angling book (Chatwell Booksellers, New York). For thoughtful executives *Individual Integrity* (Castlemarsh Publications). For serious gardeners, *The Vegetable Gardener's Book*, which includes pages to record in. And for the person who seems to have every book he desires, the *Bizarre Books* (St. Martin's Press)—an amazing compendium of titles and descriptions that range from "Manhole Covers in Los Angeles" and "The Romance of Leprosy" to "The Dentist in Art" and "Let's Make Some Undies"! (also "Teach Yourself Sex").

Finely produced, illustrated books—usually known as coffee-table books—cover a wide variety of subjects. There are elegant and beautiful science series, food books of all kinds (I once gave a magnificent book about caviar to a connoisseur of the same). The *Dining in France* book is a companion to the public television series; other choices are architecture, flower, decorating, and art books of all kinds. Harry N. Abrams and Stewart, Tabori, and Chang produce especially fine quality gift books.

There are appropriate books for every occasion—*Cole* after or before a musical evening of Cole Porter's songs; Anne Morrow Lindbergh's *Gift from the Sea* for a relaxing beach vacation or bon-voyage gift; a leatherbound appointment book for someone with a busy new job; *The Ultimate Householder's Book, Hints from Heloise,* or *Decorating on the Cheap* for a wedding shower. How about *The Kate Greenaway Baby Book,* filled with her famous Mother Goose illustrations for new parents?

The gift of a book becomes a useful tool for the recipient. For a young family, a set of animal encyclopedias; for the scholar and connoisseur, a leatherbound edition of the new *Encyclopedia Britannica,* a limited edition of one hundred at six thousand dollars. For the new homeowner, *The Complete Guide to Home Repair;* for the gardener a new *Farmer's Almanac.* Most travelers could use and enjoy an atlas. The best world atlases present convenient answers to geographical questions with carefully crafted graphics, complete indexes, and easy-to-follow coordinates for locating places. They are printed on heavy bond paper and beautifully bound in a cover suitable for display in office, den, or library. And there are many travel guides and other travel books for those who want to plan their itineraries.

Books are wonderful gifts to individualize by combining with practically anything. The new craze for caterers' cookbooks offers an almost automatic combination—*The Silver Palate Cookbook* plus a bottle of their balsamic vinegar or of one of their recipes you prepared. Or try a specialty cookbook with a related cooking tool or utensil, a *Born to Shop* book for London, France, or Italy, with a change purse or money converter; a book on indoor gardening with herb seeds and small pots or a grow light; a Dr. Seuss book or *Wind in the Willows,* or *Paddington Bear* with a stuffed animal; a coffee-table book such as *The Perfect Setting* with a table accessory. Look for a book designed to make someone's life easier or less hectic along with something for their new leisure—a hammock, tennis balls; a first aid handbook and kit for the new camper; a zoo book or book of elephants or giraffes with an invitation for a forthcoming trip to the local zoo. A book of *New Yorker* cartoons or drawings might accompany a subscription to the magazine for the nostalgic ex-New Yorker. A humorous sailing calendar-book combines with a seagoing mug or pair of sailing gloves for the boat owner.

Artists' books are an art form of which few people are aware. Many are traditional in form; some have wonderful hand-tooled leather bindings; others are more abstract, multidimensional multimedia pieces. Prices are not necessarily expensive: one of my favorites for an architect or new homeowner is an intriguing all-white "pop-up" book of various stairs and staircases designed by an architect from the Netherlands—twenty dollars. Others have cutouts or silkscreening. All are interesting ornaments as well as books.

For an uncommon gift, an autographed, first, or rare edition or a handcrafted book is an excellent choice. Or have someone's dog-eared antique volume repaired or favorite book rebound in leather. The commissioning of a handmade book for photos is a lovely idea for a wedding or anniversary gift.

It is also possible to commission a quality rendition of your own work—or someone else's—from a small press. There are several quality presses that will produce one hundred to five hundred copies for individuals or organizations who desire a lasting tribute to or for someone. Some binders will bind one to five copies of a special booklet.

Perhaps the most exciting gift for a bibliophile would be a membership in the Limited Editions Club (LEC, 551 Fifth Ave., New York, NY 10017)—an elite mail-order club. Their works are wonderfully illustrated, often by renowned artists, and made to last. Each year's two-thousand-dollar membership fee brings six richly handcrafted literary works—usually classics, both past and present. The valuable books, printed on special handmade Italian paper and on letterpress, hand sewn, and signed by author and artist, will increase in value. And for an extravagant gesture, a handmade reproduction (according to fifteenth-century methods) of The Gutenberg Bible. (Gutenberg probably printed 180 Bibles—30 on parchment and 150 on paper—and only twenty-four complete paper versions still exist.) The reproductions are available from Editions Les I nunables, 15 Place des Vosges, Paris 75004, for forty-five hundred dollars. Or, for the naturalist, the astonishing facsimile reproduction of Audubon's *Birds of America* with updated commentary by noted ornithologist/author Roger Tory Peterson (Abbeville Press).

Another thoughtful and useful gift is the blank book. This gift can be covered with classic leather, Italian marbleized papers, Japanese watercolors, flowered chintz, tailored linen, or humorous drawings. It can be presented for a specific purpose—for tour notes or diary on a special trip, to a new secretary for meetings' minutes, to fill with grandchildren's sayings, for birdwatching notes, or as a guest book for a party. Or leave it to the desires of the new owner—poetry, gambling systems, sketch book, needlework patterns, genealogies, memoirs, recipes, Christmas card lists, itineraries, decorating ideas, or memorable dates.

Children's Books

"Do you have *Chicken Soup with Rice?*"

I turned around to look at the speaker, certain that one of us was in the wrong place. We were both in a children's bookstore and apparently both in the right place. The speaker, however, knew exactly what she wanted, whereas I was feeling rather helpless surrounded by fascinating covers with other amazing titles.

It is never too soon to introduce children to books. There are even waterproof picture books for singing in baby's bath! Although you will usually find that publishers indicate the age level or grade level for which they think a book is most suitable, don't hesitate to choose a book that is suggested for an older child. The book can always be read to the child; and if it has an interesting story and good illustrations, the child will enjoy reading it later himself. Most classics have great universal appeal; however, often the giver is not familiar with the family's bookshelves and does not want to give a duplicate.

When selecting a child's book, take a few minutes to look at the books, and look for quality, whether paperback or hardback. If possible, select books that will appeal to the particular child's interests or needs. Most general bookstores offer a wide variety of children's books. Infants really enjoy books about babies—and there are several: for example, *The Baby's Book of Babies, What Do Babies Do?*, and *What Do Toddlers Do?* Well-known books such as those by Dr. Seuss or a *Sesame Street* book with a related audio cassette or *Where the Wild Things Are* by Maurice Sendak and a stuffed Wild Thing are always good choices for young children. And there are a myriad of books for special times—the birth of a new brother or sister, Purim, Christmas, a death in the family, adoption, a new pet . . . as well as posters for the child's room and seasonal gifts such as hatching books (small books inside plastic eggs) for Easter. One of my favorites to give is *The Gift* by John Prater—about a mysterious package that opens the world of a child's imagination.

The Children's Book Council makes some basic points to keep in mind about specific age groups when making your selections.

BABIES AND TODDLERS

• They are attracted by brightly colored pictures of simple objects.

• They are listeners, if a book with simple text and good rhythm is selected for them.

• They are visually and mentally stimulated by wordless books that encourage them to create their own stories.

• They are delighted with board books or cloth books (which have the virtue of being practically indestructible).

NURSERY SCHOOL AND KINDERGARTEN

• Mother Goose, nursery stories, and other books depicting familiar objects and experiences are enjoyable to children of this age.

• These children like listening to slightly more complex texts with good rhythm and effective word repetition.

• They are also coordinated enough to have constructive fun with pop-up and other toylike books.

EARLY SCHOOL YEARS (AGES FIVE TO EIGHT)

• There are children who begin to read as early as nursery school and others who may not be reading until the first grade or later.

• For reading to the latter type of child, select picture books with strong story lines and character development.

THE ART AND ETIQUETTE OF GIFT GIVING

- For the child who is reading independently, choose a book with a straightforward story employing words that will be familiar from everyday use. (Many publishers produce books termed "easy readers"; independent readers like them a lot.)

- Third-graders can usually handle stories of some complexity; the vocabulary should be relatively familiar while including some challenging words.

- A lot of informational books have been published for the early grades; these books encourage children to read about topics that interest them and to satisfy their curiosity about countless subjects.

OLDER CHILDREN (AGES NINE TO TWELVE AND OLDER)

- Consider *who* the child is—his or her personality traits and personal preferences.

- Make your selection with the child in mind; choose an informational book or a novel in an area of specific interest.

The Children's Book Council, a publisher's association that encourages the reading and enjoyment of children's books, sponsors National Children's Book Week and prepares a variety of material to help in the selection of children's books. *Children's Choices* is available free for a two-ounce stamped, self-addressed 6½-by-9-inch envelope from International Reading Association, 800 Barksdale Rd., PO Box 8139, Newark, DE 19714. *How to Choose Good Books for Kids*, by Kate McMullan, a clear and accessible guide, provides both criteria and book listings. *A Parent's Guide to Children's Reading*, by Nancy Larrick (Bantam paperback, 5th edition, 1982) contains an annotated list of "Books They Like." *The Kobrin Letter* (732 N. Greer Rd., Palo Alto, CA 94393), published eight times a year, reviews "children's books about real people, places and things."

Audio Books

Audio books, which are now sold in hotels, gift shops, and airport stores as well as bookstores, are rapidly becoming a solid gift category. Used both for entertainment and education, nonfiction, children's books, and bestseller fiction are most popular. People who drive a great deal or jog in the countryside or are bedridden are good candidates for audio books. Most audio books are abridged, with narrative bridges between excerpts. Some of them, such as *Iacocca*, include additional material—actual speeches and interviews—and others are dramatized in stereo sound. The aural drama is choreographed for the listener's enjoyment. Although unabridged versions are often available, they are considerably more expensive—forty dollars as contrasted with fifteen dollars. Many publishers including Random House, Crown, Warner Books, and Bantam Books produce these cassettes. Caedmon specializes in literary subjects including poetry. Unfortunately, the field has not yet developed enough to be reviewed in many publications. *The Village Voice* and *Publishers Weekly* (a trade publication) are exceptions.

Because promotions for audio books are usually organized around gift giving holidays, they should be easy to find in wide selection at those times—some oldtime radio tapes for Dad for Father's Day or meaningful poetry for someone for Valentine's Day are thoughtful, lasting gifts.

Books for the Visually Impaired

America's 11 million visually impaired people who are incapable of reading the print of the typical hardcover or paperback book are increasingly able to enjoy a wide selection of large-print books. Many elderly people who have never seen a large-print edition are truly delighted to discover the ease with which they can read again. G.K. Hall, a major publisher of large-print titles, prints these books on a special paper so that the books do not become too heavy or cumbersome; some are also produced in paperback versions. Large Print Books of Oxford (England) are also now available in the United States. Large-print titles range from dictionaries and classics to self-help and romances. Most bestsellers are usually out in large print within six months to a year after their first printing (depending on the restrictions of the original publisher). The Bible, *The Fathers' Book*, and cookbooks are especially popular large-print gift items. Many bookstores carry large-print books, and some have a special section and also will order these books for you—for example, most Waldenbooks stores carry a wide selection. Most large-print books come in a standard size print; however, there is an even larger size available in many books. A gift certificate to the Doubleday Large Print Home Library is also a thoughtful gift for those with eyesight problems. Recipients make their selections from the club's titles, which include both fiction and nonfiction. Each hardcover volume is unabridged and costs no more than a regular-print copy. The gift giver can give a year's membership beginning at fifty dollars; the recipient would receive the current introductory offer of books and premiums, then select books from the club magazine, which is sent fourteen times a year. For more information, contact the Doubleday Large Print Home Library, (800) 343-4300, extension 303.

For the blind, braille books are also available. Ask at your local bookstore, call an agency in your neighborhood such as Lighthouse for the Blind or the American Foundation for the Blind, or contact the American Printing House, 1839 Frankfort Ave., Louisville, KY 40206-0085, (502-895-2405) or the Library of Congress, divisions of National Library Services for the Blind and Physically Handicapped, Washington, D.C. 20542, for information and catalogs. Some newspapers and magazines also have braille editions; free braille calendars are available from the Lighthouse for the Blind.

Just as you can purchase flowers, fruit, and pasta "of the month" as gifts, you can subscribe to book series. The Franklin Library, for example, produces quality series in limited editions that contain illustrations by leading artists for its exclusive use. All bindings are stamped in traditional designs that make these books handsome additions to a home or office library. Some are leatherbound and ornamented with 22-karat gold; less expensive editions are bound in a good quality simulated leather. Series or collections vary from special first editions to great mystery classics to the world's great books. The Library also produces special single gift books such as *Gilbert and Sullivan Operas* and a leather-and-fabric-bound *Christmas Treasury and Personal Family Record*, personalized and gift wrapped—perfect for a new or young family's Christmas gift. For up-to-date information on their offerings, call Customer Service: 1-800-523-7622.

Don't forget that the perfect gift for anyone is *The Art and Etiquette of Gift Giving.* Combine it with a package of exciting wrapping paper, a single flower, or another book. . . .

MUSEUM
GIFTS

If you are seeking out the unusual, museum gift shops may well answer your needs. Whether the museum focuses on nature, history, anthropology, textiles, music, art, or architecture, its shop and/or gift catalog will be filled with pleasant surprises. The store extends the educational function of the total museum experience by presenting quality objects of excellent design. Reproductions, fine engravings, notecards, books, foods, sets of historical documents, photographs, ties, sculpture, calendars, audio tapes, wrapping papers, posters—all have been carefully chosen or adapted to reflect the museum's special range of interest.

Most cities have several museums—New York alone has over 150—most of which have some sort of shop area. Prices are usually fair, and many museums give member discounts.

Unlike most department and general gift stores, museum shops have the freedom of buying ten or twelve of something that you may never see again. They also produce and publish their own merchandise in limited quantities for each special exhibition. Often museums are given exclusive rights to reproduce certain works from an exhibition. Usually you will find the sales staff to be both knowledgeable and patient.

Many shops successfully establish the museum environment within, documenting the museum and/or part of its collection. The shops at museums like Mt. Vernon, the Textile Museum (Washington, D.C.), the Museum of Man (San Diego), the Albright-Knox

(Buffalo), and the National Building Museum seem to be extensions of the exhibits, reflecting the same quality as the institutions themselves. For example, the National Building Museum in Washington, D.C., offers a wide range of architectural books and materials along with items such as architectural jewelry, special pieces of artist's wrought iron, scarves designed by Frank Lloyd Wright, specially designed high-tech table accessories, designer desk appointment books, adaptable blueprints with scale units for interior design and landscaping (perfect gifts for new homeowners), cards and stationery with engravings of historic buildings, and a collection replicating the history of building nails.

Gifts I've found recently in New York museums include facsimile editions of manuscript scores by Mozart and Brahms (Pierpont Morgan Library); African beaded wedding necklace and Haitian popsicle-stick house (Studio Museum, in Harlem); antique carved wooden Asante stool, Native American pottery, and maps of rocks and minerals found in Central Park (American Museum of Natural History); cast iron mechanical bank of the Cheshire Cat (given with a special copy of *Alice in Wonderland*) and reprints of children's classics (Museum of the City of New York); hand-painted, hand-carved primitive crèche and reproduction mirrors (Cathedral Church of St. John the Divine); antique Russian lacquerware boxes and German matchbox fairy-tale puzzles (United Nations Headquarters); a contemporary espresso machine and a fascinating "executive" puzzle (Museum of Modern Art).

For whom are museum gifts most appropriate? Of course, for those with a particular interest in the museum subject. However, museums also offer unique children's toys and games, interesting puzzles and stationery for older people, uncommon coffee-table books, or lovely scarves and limited editions of unusual jewelry for the fashion-conscious collector.

You may select a museum gift for its design and beauty, function, information, and/or educational value. Collections of various objects such as minerals, insects, or textiles are valuable not only for their own sake but enhance the principle of orderly observation; scale models of buildings or bridges or boats can be exciting as well as contribute to one's knowledge of architecture, construction, and historic evolution; a brilliant Chinese kite can illustrate aerodynamics; an art poster can also give information.

Although American museums, schools, and other cultural institutions have been creating special gifts and mementos for many years, many museums in other parts of the world have only recently begun to fashion gifts that represented the institution or its collection. One reason for this is that most American museums were started and are supported by individuals, whereas most European museums are state museums. Those who operate them do not have the same reason, interest, or passion to do the extraordinary as do the volunteers. Fortunately, however, there are some wonderful exceptions—many of them in Paris. The Calcography Department of the Louvre has produced a collection of engravings printed on thick handmade vellum with the Louvre's imprint embossed. Selling for moderate prices (beginning at about five dollars for a small architectural print!), approximately two hundred of these are available from the collection of sixteen thousand at any given time. The shop provides an inexpensive source of original works of art spanning more than three hundred years of French engraving. The main shop of the Musée du Louvre has one of the largest collections of reproductions from top museums all over the world, and the jewelry counters are a delight: for your friends who aspire to the "Best Dressed List," sterling silver cuff links reading in hieroglyphics "he who dresses the gods." While you're canvassing Paris museums, don't miss the boutique in the Musée des Arts Décoratifs, which features contemporary French crafts as well as antique reproductions and unique children's gifts. In the annex of the Bibliothèque Nationale one can purchase an assortment of French literary memorabilia. An interesting assortment of French designers' gifts—playing cards, scarves, stationery, and shawls—can be found at the Musée d'Art Moderne. The newest Paris museum shop, at the long-awaited Musée des Arts de la Mode, specializes in reproductions of French fashion and jewelry treasures—from Elsa Schiaparelli's perfumed earrings to Louis Vuitton sewing kits. In addition to marvelous replications of Bauhaus lamps and famous Egyptian murals on papyrus, the Museum Boutique at the Montreal Museum of Fine Arts offers contemporary jewelry and the stone sculptures of the Inuit Eskimo tribe.

Suggestions for museum gift shopping:

- Next time you need a gift, instead of heading to the shopping mall, treat yourself to a museum trip. Discover a local folk, native arts and crafts, or nature museum, or explore the gifts offered by your community symphony or state university, if appropriate.

- Search out those gifts that are unique to museums. Many museums offer products that are available in department stores; avoid those that are mediocre and kitschy.

- After gift wrapping, deliver the gift in the museum bag; this adds authenticity and cachet.

FLOWERS
AND PLANTS AS
GIFTS

Flowers have been part of history and legend in every age and every country: the hyacinth and narcissus were half-divine, half-human creatures who, according to ancient mythology, were transformed into flowers when they died; in ancient Persia, the tulip became the symbol of love when tulip flowers sprang up where drops of blood had fallen from a tragic lover's suicide; an old Flemish custom has it that on her wedding day a bride was expected to hide a pink somewhere on her person, and her bridegroom was expected to find it; the peony has long symbolized wealth and honor to the Japanese; the red rose was created when Venus pricked her finger on one of its thorns, staining it forever; as a knight and his lady were strolling along a river, he was picking small blue blossoms that grew in the swampy areas, then he slipped into the river and, as the current carried him to his death, he tossed the bouquet to his love, shouting "forget-me-not." Today flowers still perform a symbolic function—we celebrate spring and rebirth with white lilies, use rosemary for remembrance, sometimes still give lilies-of-the-valley at a christening, mischievously use mistletoe at Christmastime, and believe (especially if we're Spanish and not Texans) that the yellow rose connotes jealousy.

A universal expression of appreciation, a symbol of beauty and luxury, a manifestation of love, an instantaneous transformation, flowers add something lovely and festive to the recipient's life.

WHEN YOU CHOOSE ...

Interest in flowers has not been as great since the Victorian era; each year more people are becoming more knowledgeable about flowers and more demanding of their gardens and their florists. Perhaps, some have speculated, this is an expected reaction to our technological age. Or maybe it simply accompanies our new emphasis on interior design and renewed interest in glamor.

TRENDS

There are trends in flowers. Most of them follow current fashions in home decorating from the high-tech stark look to the soft rustic French country arrangement. In our changing and mobile society we have an increasing need to surround ourselves with more traditional things—objects that look as if they've always been there, thus accounting for the recent interest in English gardens, botanical flower prints, and the massed floral arrangements of the English country house.

A number of blooms that until the last few years have been considered rare have increased in availability. The "exotic" flower has become trendy in both the United States and Europe—the more unusual or foreign, the better. Tropical varieties that seem ubiquitous in Miami and Los Angeles are exciting accessories for an office or home in Paris, Chicago or Boston. There is a fascination with flowers which have come all the way from India, the Caribbean, Hawaii, or Africa. New York's popular Palladium changes its arrangements of exotic blooms twice a week.

The most popular of exotics include the anthurium, freesia (fragrant), bird-of-paradise, ginger (smells wonderful), protea, rubrum lily, cymbidium, oncidium, or dendrobium orchids, euphorbia, ixia, gerbera daisy, eryngium, agapanthus, amaryllis, and nerine. These flowers—with their asymmetric, irregular shapes—in themselves make a dramatic, distinctive arrangement, often a single stalk makes the desired statement.

Although rare, exotic, out-of-season flowers and plants are considered elegant and worldly symbols, those that are truly fragile and short-lived are even more chic. Blossoms that are open for only a day, stems that lose their rigidity in a short time—these convey a message of value and extravagance as well as ephemeral loveliness. Bunny Mellon calls her favorite ten bunches of violets in a clear glass soufflé dish her "fleeting beauty."

Small and miniature flowers carry the feeling of preciousness. Thus, *fleurs minceurs*—masses of lilies of the valley, miniature daffodils, or crocuses—are very popular.

Another trend is the call for "garden flowers"—larkspur, corn-flowers, peonies, and poppies. Easy, casual pluckings straight from the garden make the loveliest of gifts. Also popular are potted perennials—for patios, decks, terraces, or indoor pleasure. I enjoy living with entire flats of tulips, and recently received the gift of a potted blooming double hollyhock for my New York apartment.

There is a new attitude toward arrangements too. Today's most exquisite floral designs are fresh and natural, a long way from wired, woven, tied, and unnatural configurations and formal, self-conscious containers. Single blossoms, mosses, wild grasses, or squash blossoms combine with found objects to create a down-to-earth environment in small urban apartments. Ralph Lauren's "welcome to the family" gift for the openings of his new franchised shops is blooming amaryllis with roots and bulbs exposed in a clear glass bowl.

In addition, lavish, Victorian arrangements with a sense of the past are popular in certain environments; and the centuries-old orien-tal discipline of ikebana is flourishing. Ikebana, Japanese flower arranging, re-creates nature on a reduced scale through the arrange-ment of all types of plant materials gathered from their original settings. These arrangements are designed to preserve the distinctive beauty and characteristics of each plant and flower, their containers are well suited to their "essence," and many of them are seasonal in theme.

Of course, there are regional trends and traditions as well. Many of the designs of noted Houston florist Leonard Tharp tend to be Texas-colossal in size—he once felled an Oregon cherry orchard, transplanting it to an oil heiress's birthday party in a hotel ballroom.

Conversely, for the concerned, sophisticated gift giver, as well as those who give flowers to impress others, some flowers have become unchic. Referred to by florists as the "bucket trade," old standbys such as carnations, daisies, gladiolia, and chrysanthemums are over-used and thus "out." Flowers that are easily grown and obtained seem to have lost their cachet in favor of those which—if not exotic—are at least out of season, such as lily-of-the-valley and tulips for the Christmas holidays.

As Americans become more European in their attitude toward flowers as the perfect gift, they continue to adopt and adapt Euro-pean chic—such as the sophistication and elegance of all-white or all-yellow bouquets and the additional pleasure afforded by fragrant blossoms such as jasmine. And fragrance itself is becoming more important with a revival of some old-fashioned roses such as peach Kyries and lavender Sterling Silvers. Henry Moulie of Moulie Savart in Paris, purveyor to Karl Lagerfeld and Yves Saint Laurent and the accredited florist to Élysée Palace, calls the white orchid the fashion flower of the moment, but personally favors the white anemone and has many requests for his famous miniature white tulips.

Flowers—Gifts for All Occasions

I really cannot think of an occasion when you could not give a gift of flowers—and neither could Emerson. Flowers make appropriate business gifts, remember-me gifts, compromise gifts, congratulation gifts, I'm-sorry gifts, thank-you gifts, and even, as FTD advocates, "Pick-Me-Up Bouquets." Unfortunately, however, the flower gift is often a last-minute choice, the result of having forgotten a special occasion and the convenience of finding a bouquet at the grocery store or train station. If this is the position you sometimes find yourself in, here are some guidelines. First and most important, look for quality. Select the freshest, most colorful, largest blooms; second, remember that the number of flowers is not nearly as important as your choice of flower; third, if you are giving a small number (under ten), an uneven number is more graceful; finally, one perfect single bloom can be simple, magical, and just as flattering to the recipient.

According to my New York designer, Pat Braun of Salou, when people don't know the recipient well, they sometimes spend too much for flowers. He suggests some classic presents that are suitable for almost any occasion: long-stemmed roses, massed sweetheart roses, stems of freesia, ten tulips, one perfect orchid, peony, or lily—and for that special occasion, champagne with Champagne roses.

You also give the gift of flowers when you grace your home or office with them. Tasteful flowers help guests, clients, or business acquaintances to feel welcome, comfortable, and special. One bank in the Midwest has an extravagant display of changing orchids, mosses, and hanging baskets all year long; a real estate firm in the Southwest keeps a collection of blooming cacti for its clients' pleasure; Charles Masson of New York's famous restaurant La Grenouille creates unique bouquets each day in eight rare Baccarat-crystal vases for his patrons.

FLOWERS AS HOSTESS GIFTS

For your special host or hostess, an interesting topiary, miniature pineapple, bonsai or specimen tree, or orchid plant can be a wonderful gesture of appreciation. However, do not give plants that require considerable attention to those who travel a great deal or who do not live all year at that location unless you are certain that they will arrange to have them cared for. I recently brought a new apartment dweller a basket containing several varieties of bromeliad. She travels a great deal and lives part of the time near her business in Connecticut. These bromeliads require only an occasional misting and look even more interesting as the outer leaves dry. You might also consider giving a novel dried arrangement of wildflowers, thistles and weeds, or exotic leaves for low-maintenance locations.

If you wish to send flowers for a formal dinner party, it is thoughtful to ask the hostess if you can send the centerpiece or another decorative arrangement. If she is not using a particular florist, you might ask her colors or decorating scheme for the event so that your gift enhances rather than clashes with her plans.

Working with a Florist

When purchasing a special gift of flowers, choose your florist carefully. Again, the quality of the flowers is most important—and so is the florist's willingness to work with you in selection and/or design. Tell him your budget, the occasion, and as much as possible about the recipient. For example, a truly practical person may be offended by something expensive that will by nature endure for only the evening but be delighted with a pot of growing herbs or a shade tree for the patio. A good florist will make several suggestions and will be open to your ideas as well.

If you are sending flowers to a city where you don't know a florist, you have several choices: ask your florist if he or she has a reference; call FTD or Teleflora, but be very specific about your choice of flowers and arrangements and ascertain that what you want is available; call a Texas firm 800-FLOWERS, Inc., a twenty-four-hour flowers-or-plants-by-phone service that allows you to order from one of six thousand florists in the United States and many overseas by credit card. U.S. florists in this program promise to deliver within forty-eight hours; however, delivery can be made the same day if the order is received before 11:00 A.M. List your first and second choices, and if neither is available, you are consulted, with guaranteed replacement of flowers if they're not satisfactory. When sending flowers, often it's more prudent to be a day late in order to get what you want than to send something less desirable.

Flowers for Men

Braun has some special hints for the growing number of women who give fresh flowers to men. Keep it simple rather than frilly; give one type of flower rather than a mixed bouquet; and, unless you know that he has containers and he (or you) enjoys arranging them, send them in a container. Some popular choices for men are French tulips, snapdragons (I wonder why), and flowering branches such as quince.

Signature Flowers

Some people have delightful flower trademarks—Woody Allen likes to send white roses; Diana Vreeland always gives red flowers; Mary Wells Lawrence has made tulips her year-round signature. You can do the same. From my small rooftop garden or greenhouse, I select whatever is available: fresh herbs or tomatoes for my cooking friends, Peace roses (in June, July, and August) for those who appreciate the fragrance and fragility of these flowers, camellias in late winter, or orchids for special occasions. When nothing appropriate is blooming, I call my florist.

Silk Flowers

An arrangement of silk flowers can be an exquisite gift. Artist Diane Love—for years the designer of beautiful flowers and wonderful potpourri at her Madison Avenue shop by the same name—cautions to be certain that they are of silk, not polyester, and to check the assemblage for quality and flexibility—every petal and leaf should be carefully wired. Silk flowers can be an especially appropriate gift for a hospital patient when oxygen is at a premium; for an older person who cannot care for plants; as a lasting memento for a mother at her baby's birth; for a busy office area with lots of traffic; or for unusual keepsake bridesmaids' bouquets. They can be arranged into a nosegay to place on a pillow or as a bouquet for a favorite bowl.

Extraordinary silk arrangements that re-create old-master paintings are the creations of the owners of Decoration Day in Larchmont, New York. Just send them a picture of the painting and they'll reproduce it. It's an unusual gift for someone who treasures a special flower painting.

Specially selected silk flowers are an easily packable choice for traveling gifts and a welcome hostess gift. The King of Morocco for years sent silk flower arrangements to his hostess the day after a function.

Potpourri

All of my blossoms that are not given away as fresh flowers are used for potpourri—one of my favorite gifts. Many people enjoy making their own. Diane Love had a wonderful signature scent that she used in candles and sachets as well. Calvin Klein once sent elegant bowls filled with her potpourri to his personal friends for Christmas. My potpourri is made of my herbs—mainly lavender— rose petals, and orchids. I enjoy drying them in baskets and selecting the container for each recipient—crystal bowls, antique inkwells, original North Carolina pottery, mustard jars, Navaho baskets, brass or wooden boxes, old cheese crocks, oriental bulb containers, incense burners. Everyone seems to like gifts of fragrance from flowers.

If you still are not persuaded to give flowers, call Unforgettable in Los Angeles to order long-stemmed chocolate chip cookies. They'll please the stomach but not fill the soul.

GIFTS FROM
CATALOGS

Catalog shoppers have discovered how to perpetuate Christmas 365 days a year, enjoying the thrill of selection without leaving their home or office. Instant gratification is the mail order industry's most recent goal. Not only will catalogers deliver wherever, whenever—they will now accomplish this overnight if you desire.

Observers of our sociological scene refer to the four C's— computers, convenience, credit cards, and crime—as manifestations of modern lifestyle trends. Clearly, the rapid-fire growth of the mail order industry correlates with the first three of these. And when shopping by mail, you no longer have to remember "don't leave home without it"; the catalog credo is "don't leave home." Since Benjamin Franklin's book catalogs, "shopping by mail" has become an over $45 billion business each year. It is estimated that by 1990 one of every four sales will be a direct sale.

Last year nearly 7 billion catalogs—perhaps 6,500 different ones—went to consumers last year. There must be at least one catalog for every interest and every lifestyle: catalogs specialize in music boxes, Corvette supplies, rare books, products with pigs on them, photographic equipment, bath accessories, left-handed products, and popcorn; and the gourmet cook can select from an abundance of catalogs from Williams-Sonoma to Whole Earth Access. And there are the continuity programs that are sold only by mail or phone order—for example, a year's membership to receive fresh/

gourmet coffee beans from General Foods' Gevalia Caffe is a wonderful gift for the coffee lover or a year's gift of Hawaiian orchids—a different one each month. Catalogs are an entire gift world. Sears Roebuck might have instituted the purchase of goods through the mail, but Neiman-Marcus' famous Christmas catalog spawned the upscale gift catalogs that fill modern mailboxes.

Jo-Von Tucker, reknowned international catalog consultant and producer, estimates that about 60 percent of purchases made from non-department-store catalogs are for gifts; catalog mogul Roger Horchow (originator of several catalogs including The Horchow Collection) states that at least one-third of the products he sells are for gifts—at Christmas at least two-thirds—and this out of an annual volume of $90 million. You will find that many of today's catalogs are geared to the gift market, with suitable gifts for Mother's Day, Valentine's Day, and so on in the catalogs preceding these holidays.

Why do so many people prefer to find gifts in this manner? For many people—especially working women—shopping is no longer a social activity. Current figures indicate that the majority of upscale catalog customers are women. Tucker states that 85 percent are women and that 65 percent of them work outside the home. Another catalog market is the elderly; more than 26 million Americans are over the age of sixty-five. In addition, the often obligatory nature of gift shopping puts one under pressure and/or encourages one to wait until the last moment to choose the gift. Thus, these shoppers want the quickest, easiest, and most convenient way to select and send presents. Other reasons for the popularity of catalog gifts: accessibility to merchandise that is not usually available where the consumer does most of his or her shopping; avoiding the hassles of store shopping, such as parking, crowded stores, finding out immediately whether the product you want is in stock and available in the size or model you want, and rude clerks at the holiday season; fashions displayed on models rather than on hangers; and the knowledge that the catalog you are using is both reputable and quality-conscious.

Many shoppers feel that the clear display of individual items with sufficient information about the product, possibly followed by further information from knowledgeable telephone salespeople is reason enough to purchase gifts in this manner. Bettie Bearden Pardee, founder and former president of Papillon catalogs, observes, "The copy alongside the products in our catalogs can tell you more about them than a salesclerk, if you are lucky enough to run into a salesclerk, much less one who knows anything about the product."

If you are not familiar with the catalog or its reputation, how do you know that it is reputable? Tucker says that a good catalog makes a promise, then lives up to its promise in every respect. She lists several clues to its credibility: the look and feel of the catalog (is the catalog itself a quality production?); the type of guarantee—it should offer an unconditional guarantee as well as an easy way for you or the recipient to return the gift; you should be able to call an 800 number to have it picked up and your refund should include your postage and handling; the fidelity of reproduction (if the skin tone appears yellow, what might the color of the fabric be?); accuracy of copy (have you ever seen a product described as blue, but appearing to be very purple?); the simplicity of the order form and/or ease of ordering; and their acceptance of major credit cards. Today's better catalogs, such as Hammacher Schlemmer's, possess and communicate a certain personality—an underlying philosophy; they are often clearly identifiable without their cover page. Horchow tells his buyers not to select anything for the catalogs unless they know someone to whom they would personally give that item as a gift. At the same time, beware—a good catalog can also use subliminal techniques, evoking emotions that may lead you to buy five gifts instead of two—three of them for yourself.

Catalog gift shoppers can look forward to several interesting trends: increased global catalog marketing, giving us more international options; the megalog—a combination magazine and catalog, containing editorials and articles of informational and topical interest; more upscale catalogs for the consumer with discretionary income; videologs—video cassettes of the available products. Tucker points out that some of the best catalogs inform, entertain, and enhance your lifestyle; they're no longer throwaway pieces—some even offer leather binders for shelving them in organized fashion.

Tips for Shopping by Mail from the Direct Marketing Association and the Federal Trade Commission

Before ordering, be sure you understand the company's return policy. When placing an order, fill out the form with care.

Keep a record of your order, including the company's name, address, and phone number; identifying information about the item you purchased; your canceled check or copy of your money order; the date you mailed the order.

If you order by telephone and use a credit card, keep the same detailed information.

Never send cash through the mail. Send a check or money order. Many companies also accept credit card charges, but then special credit rules apply.

If merchandise arrives damaged, contact the mail order company immediately. If you're asked to return the product, get a receipt from the shipper.

If you return merchandise to a company for any reason, it's always a good idea to get a return receipt from the shipper.

If you don't receive your order because your package is lost in transit, the mail order company will probably take responsibility for tracing it.

If your prepaid order doesn't arrive when promised, you may cancel the order and get a full refund. If the company didn't give you a delivery date in its solicitation, the company must ship your order within thirty days of receiving it.

If you cancel a mail order purchase charged on your credit card, the seller must credit your account within one billing cycle following receipt of your cancellation request.

Some additional hints. If you order by phone, fill in the order blank to keep for your own records; check to see that your catalog is a current one; ascertain that handling/shipping charges are not more than you would save on the "bargain" price of the item; send unresolved mail order complaints to Mail Order Action Line, Direct Marketing Association, 6 East 43rd Street, New York, NY 10017 (a no-charge consumer service program established by the DMA in 1971); if you have trouble with a company that has no phone number listed and only a post office box number for address, write to the postmaster of the city in which the box is located—include a copy of the ad or the appropriate catalog page citing the P.O. box—the postmaster will then send you the name and street address of the company; in instances of mail order fraud or misrepresentation, contact the local postmaster or write to the Chief Postal Inspector, U.S. Postal Service, Washington, D.C. 20260-2161.

Another important point is checking to find out what action the company takes in relation to late-arriving gifts. A reputable concern should first consult the giver to advise of the lateness, giving him or her the opportunity to cancel; then, with the giver's permission, the company should offer to send to the recipient a notification of lateness that includes the name of the sender. Otherwise, poor Uncle George is left wondering why his niece, after twenty-five years, stopped sending those thoughtful birthday presents.

PHILANTHROPIC GIVING

People give gifts to charities and institutions for a wide variety of reasons: most people care—they have a desire to give something back to society; some people enjoy the program involvement—the actual helping or doing; many people like to be needed; sometimes peer pressure is a factor; some people enjoy the prestige and/or publicity they receive; certain tax advantages help people to give more than they otherwise might have; or the importance or position of the person who makes the request may influence one to contribute. Whatever your reasons, give wisely.

Your gift can be in the form of a donation, bequest, gift in kind, grant, or time. As a volunteer you will be one of almost 90 million dedicated Americans who work—for no pay—to help others. The time and effort spent performing volunteer service is a rewarding gift for both recipient and giver.

For the person "who has everything," a donation made to the church, hospital, museum, health organization, or library he supports is a wonderful, caring present. To give a donation, send your check to the organization, with the information that the gift is to be made in the recipient's name. Be certain to include his or her address as well as yours. The organization will then write to the recipient to inform him of the gift (but not the amount) and to the donor(s) to acknowledge the gift.

Most philanthropic organizations—charitable, religious, or

educational—have a high degree of responsibility because of their public trusteeship. The over $70 billion that Americans give annually to about 300,000 agencies, organizations, and institutions can improve the lives of millions. However, competition for your philanthropic dollar has increased substantially over the last few years—particularly as a result of the government's slashing of moneys for domestic programs, including some designed to help charitable organizations and those they sevice.

It is most important to all of us that our charitable dollars be properly managed and used to achieve the organization's stated purpose. One of our country's greatest strengths and most precious legacies is our willingness to help others. The informed giver will help to accomplish his cause and, at the same time, strengthen the practice of private philanthropy.

How can one make an informed decision about a philanthropic gift? Even a genuinely honest charity can be managed so poorly that it spends most of its funds on administration and fund-raising.

Wise giving is the result of understanding between the donor and the donee. As a potential donor you should be certain that you know the organization's purpose, what it does, and for whom. How effective do you think its programs are? Is the organization registered properly with the state in which it's soliciting? The organization should have available an annual report that includes an audited financial report showing how much was spent on each of the organization's main activities, plus management and fund-raising activities, and a list of board members or trustees, preferably with some identifying information about each.

If you are unfamiliar with a charity—even though the name sounds similar to that of a well-known organization—ask for information in writing. Avoid contributing to street solicitors, radio or TV appeals, and—especially—telephone calls asking for help for causes that you have not heard of before. Do not give to any organization about which you cannot find sufficient information. And when you give, make your gift by check or money order so that you'll have a record for tax purposes.

For the concerned giver, there are watchdog groups that supply evaluations based on information that each agency sends in. For example, the National Charities Information Bureau, Inc., provides information to the public about four hundred organizations that solicit funds nationally from the general public and evaluates national agencies on their compliance with set standards in the areas of board or governing body, purpose, program, expenses, promotion, fund-raising, accountability, and budget. The bureau's objective is to maintain and enhance the American tradition of private initiatives for the public good by setting standards for the integrity and credibility of individual charities. Copies of their "Standards in Philanthropy" may be used to evaluate your local charities as well. The Council of Better Business Bureaus reports on ten thousand charities throughout the country; and various religious organizations belong to local or national umbrella organizations such as the Evangelical Council for Financial Accountability, whose code of ethics includes financial disclosure.

In the regulatory area, the National Association of Attorneys General is developing a model state law for regulating charitable solicitations. To date, almost forty states have their own statutes, and these vary tremendously from state to state. Although these laws do require secular charities to make their annual reports available to the public, charities affiliated with religious groups do not have to register or file financial accounts—in line with separation of church and state.

Patterns of growth in philanthropic giving in the United States have been fairly consistent over the last few years: for example, contributions from individuals continue to grow, comprising over 80 percent of all giving; giving from both foundations and business corporations has risen substantially; and religious organizations, which traditionally receive the largest single share of all charitable giving, have gained even more, accounting for almost one-half of all philanthropy in the United States. Americans have more than doubled the amount contributed as recently as seven years ago. Contributions to nationally/internationally televised concerts aimed at relieving economic strife among Americans and Africans have helped substantially to boost donations in the last few years. How durable this method will be remains to be seen.

As potential givers, we should be pleased with philanthropic trends—professionalism in fund-raising and in fund-raising management has improved greatly over the last few years; governing boards have become more active and responsible; there has been a large growth in the number of capable professional women in the field of fund-raising; there is an increasingly closer working relationship between government and private funding as well as between donor and donee.

Although Americans are known for their charitable efforts, international philanthrophy is beginning to gather momentum. Even Asian countries, such as Japan, are becoming aware of the needs of other groups, contributing to higher education in the United States and other countries. According to Jack Schwartz, president of the American Association of Fund-Raising Counsel, Inc., many other countries have yet to learn the value of dialogue or partnership between donor and donee; but many of the lessons learned here are portable, and we are already helping other nations. Several non-American groups have organized to foster international philanthropy—for example, Interfil and the Institute of Charity Fund-Raising Managers, both based in London.

This new interest is in part a result of the welfare system's inability to provide the same level of funding for charitable and educational institutions. In countries such as England, where one is allowed to contribute one hundred pounds per year through payroll deductions, and France, where one must receive permission from the government to give a gift over five thousand francs and still must leave his heirs 75 percent of his estate, philanthrophic giving is severely limited. Schwartz points out that their recognition of a need for growth in philanthropy is leading them to explore tax advantages for donors.

Agencies That Provide Information About Charities

NATIONAL CHARITIES INFORMATION BUREAU, 19 Union Square West, New York, NY 10003

PHILANTHROPIC ADVISORY SERVICE OF THE COUNCIL OF BETTER BUSINESS BUREAUS, 1515 Wilson Bl., Arlington, VA 22209

EVANGELICAL COUNCIL FOR FINANCIAL ACCOUNTABILITY, P.O. Box 17511, Washington, D.C. 20041

INTERACTION, 200 Park Avenue South, New York, NY 10003

GIFTS OF
MONEY

Some consider a money gift vulgar and a "last resort" for those who lack time and imagination. Although this can certainly be true, a gift of money can also be a thoughtful and gracious gesture.

Presentation is particularly important with money gifts. Occasion, timing, and discretion all play a part. Money should not be flaunted, nor should it be presented or received so that the amount is revealed to others.

There are recipients for whom money is the most appropriate gift: for children going on a holiday; young people saving for something special; a newly married couple who live far away; a college student; a young relative you haven't seen in a long time and whose tastes and lifestyle you are not familiar with; an elderly person of limited means.

Money may be given in the form of cash, check, money order, or traveler's check. If you mail the gift, indicate on the card or in a note that a check is enclosed; don't send cash in the mail.

When several people contribute as part of a joint money gift, a clearly written or typed list of donors should be provided so that the recipient can thank each one.

Another form of money—the gift certificate—can be a marvelous choice, especially if it is for a store of special interest to the recipient. Some examples: a music or record shop, a travel-book store, a sporting goods chain, a photographic supply warehouse.

People who are disabled, homebound, or live far from urban centers would appreciate a gift catalog with a certificate enclosed.

Savings bonds, stocks, and bonds are traditional money gifts for births, graduations, and weddings. A life insurance policy purchased when a baby is born or when a child is young becomes a very significant gift when he is older—a perfect choice for grandparents or godparents.

LIQUORS, WINE, AND BAR ACCESSORIES AS GIFTS

M any givers regularly send wine or liquor because it is an easy gift to give. However, the successful gift of wine or liquor requires some thought. Sending a selection of name brand liquors may help someone with his or her entertaining but shows little consideration for his or her preferences. A case of vodka is a good idea for someone you know drinks it, but only if you know the recipient's favorite brand.

Although it is helpful to know something about the recipient's preferences to give a bottle or two of wine, it is enough to know that he or she appreciates good wines. Those who drink only white wines enjoy sharing their reds with their friends.

Aperitifs and afterdinner drinks such as cognac, sherries, and liqueurs are good gifts for those who entertain at home. Quality is important; it is probably best to stick to familiar liqueurs for gifts, as some of the more innovative are not especially good-tasting.

Gifts of wine or liquor need not be dull. Each Christmas season, packagers work hard to create beautiful bottles and seasonal packagings that transform the drinks into attractive gifts. A little imagination, however, will do a lot more. For example: The recipient—a high-powered executive; a world traveler; a scotch drinker; a woman. The occasion: return from Japan after winning a large contract. The gift: a mellow single-malt scotch, Glenmorangie, heretofore available only in Europe—tucked into the most elegant basket of bath accessories amid aromatic oils, fluffy bath powder puffs, and bubble bath. You might add a short crystal glass, bath pillow, bath tray, and a light paperback book. For another occasion, tuck the bottle into a Tartan blanket and send with a cord of wood, or add a robot to serve it.

Guidelines

- Do not send alcohol to someone who doesn't drink.

- Do not give a gift of alcohol to someone who is not of legal drinking age.

- Champagne is a traditional gift for celebrating, but don't give it unless it is of good quality; give a nice bottle of wine instead.

- When you bring wine to your host or hostess, indicate that it is to be used at a later time (unless you were asked to bring the wine for dinner). Hosts who have carefully selected their wine may feel obliged to use yours. You can always send it as a thank-you the day after the event.

- Send gifts of alcohol to one's home, not his or her office, even if it is a business gift.

- One or two bottles of wine, a bottle of liquor, a bottle of liqueur, sherry, or aperitif is a sufficient gift for a meal, unexpected event, or gesture of friendship.

- A bottle of well-chosen rare wine (for connoisseurs only), or a case of good champagne, wine, or liquor is a good selection for significant occasions.

Bar gifts can be small or large, for office or home. If you know that someone can never find ice tongs or that his corkscrew doesn't seem to work properly, it's an easy choice. If you are buying something as important as a wine rack, be certain it is needed, will fit, and matches the decor. If you buy bar glasses, get at least six (matching, of course).

Some bar accessories can mark special events—a silver or crystal jigger with date, initials, or college logo; paper cocktail napkins with name and occasion imprinted; ice bucket or wine cooler with date engraved.

Other ideas: wine or liquor bottle lables; ice crusher; bar towels; lime squeezer; martini pitcher and stirrer; coasters; fabric cocktail napkins; brandy snifters or champagne flutes (you could send only a

pair of these for a newly married couple); cutting board with bar
knife; cocktail strainer; decanter; crystal drink stirrers; milkshake
mixer; blender; small bar pitcher; serving tray; bottle and can
opener.

PETS AS
GIFTS

Pets are not appropriate gifts unless you are certain that the potential recipient as well as those he or she lives with want this type of pet and are able to care for it responsibly.

A few general guidelines:

- Find a pet that suits the needs, personality, and lifestyle of the recipient(s). Does the potential owner work during the day or travel a lot? Will the pet be alone much of the time? Will there be someone to groom the pet regularly? (Some pets require more grooming than others.) Are there other family pets? Are there young children? Is there adequate space for the pet's needs? Is noise level a consideration? Has the recipient always wanted a pet cobra, monkey, parrot, or nonbarking basenji? When selecting a breed of puppy or dog, decide whether the recipient's need is for security, companionship and playfulness, or stylishness.

- Always deal with a recommended pet shop or well-respected breeder. If you buy from a breeder, you will probably pay much less (one-third to one-half) than the price charged at most pet stores. Prices, however, vary greatly depending on location, reputation, and pedigree.

- If you receive a pet from your local ASPCA or other agency, the pet should be in good health, usually having had its shots and with some type of guarantee.

WHEN YOU CHOOSE . . .

- Insist on a written "seventy-two-hour health guarantee"—especially for purebreds. This will enable you to take the pet for a physical examination.

- If you purchase a purebred pet, be certain to get a registration form filled out by the breeder, and give it to the recipient when you present the pet.

- When selecting a puppy or a kitten, decide whether you want a purebred or a mixed breed. Both can be affectionate pets; however, if you want to know what to expect, the purebred offers greater predictability. The most popular dog breeds registered with the American Kennel Club are as follows:

> Cocker spaniel
> Poodle
> Labrador retriever
> German shepherd
> Golden retriever
> Doberman pinscher
> Beagle
> Chow Chow
> Miniature schnauzer
> Shetland sheepdog

Each breed has its advantages and disadvantages. The official publication of the AKC, *The Complete Dog Book*, is a valuable reference for purchasers of purebred dogs. Currently fashionable breeds are the Akita and Shar-pei as well as the aloof Lhasa apso and Afghan hound.

GIFTS
YOU SHOULD NEVER
GIVE

At a party, a gift considerably more expensive than anyone else's

A pet, unless parents agree or adults request

Anything vulgar or in bad taste

Liquor to someone who may not drink

Something oversize or fragile to someone who will have to travel home by train or plane (offer to send it)

Personal gifts to people you do not know well

A substantial gift to a business person with whom you are negotiating a deal

A gift with obvious sexual overtones

Perfume or cologne unless you know the recipient's choice or preference

Citrus fruit to people in Florida or California

Fine chocolate to someone on a diet

A very expensive gift to an employee

Anything of inferior quality

An item that conflicts with that person's image of him- or herself

Anything illegal, immoral, or unethical

Perfumed stationery to anybody

PART SEVEN

SPECIAL INTERESTS AND SPECIAL RECIPIENTS

Perhaps the easiest person to find a gift for is an enthusiast. Those with a passion for skiing or needlework enjoy gifts that reflect that interest—but may require something new, different, or imaginative. The most difficult to select for are those whose interests we may not know, group gifts (such as families), and those with special problems. Gifts for each category range from inexpensive to costly and from utilitarian to fantasy. Most can be found in department stores and shops throughout the United States as well as in catalogs.

This section was originally intended to be only an example of the wide range of gifts available in a given interest category. Once begun, it continued to grow almost uncontrollably until I read the title of one of William Safire's columns in *The New York Times Magazine*, "Gifts for Glossolaliacs." At this point I realized that there is really no end to a "Gifts for . . ." section.

GIFTS
FOR FAMILIES

Giving one gift to an entire family is not only simpler for the giver but can be more exciting for the family to receive than several small presents—some of which may not be well suited to family members one sees infrequently.

These suggestions are for families with children; additional gift suggestions for couples can be found throughout the book.

The two gift categories most often used for family gifts are the magazine subscription and food. Magazines can range from *National Geographic* to *TV Guide*. *Family Travel Times* is filled with tips on family travel programs, information on hotels, and what families can do together in various cities ($24 for twelve issues). *Children's Video Report* helps parents choose quality cassettes for youngsters ($35 for six issues). Food possibilities are almost endless. If a family used to live in another section of the country, a package of familiar regional foods is always welcome. Presents of smoked fowl, fish, or meat, a box of steaks, a country ham, special sausages, or bacon are hearty choices.

More food suggestions: sweets such as a collection of jams and jellies, ice cream sauces, fudge, a gingerbread house, a holiday cake such as fruit cake or panettone, a box of candy, your own Christmas cookies or coffee cake; other gift foods—attactive large cans of popcorn, assortments of cheeses and crackers, salad dressings or vinegars, freshly baked bread or croissants, mustard, homemade spaghetti sauce and/or pasta, frozen quiche or hors d'oeuvres, nut assortments, paté, a box of fruit or fruit-of-the-month, or a homemade casserole in an attractive dish.

Other Great Family Gifts

Barbecue grill or utensils
Ice cream maker
Patio furniture or umbrella
Bulbs, tree, or bush for yard
Pool or water floats, games, or toys
Exercise equipment
Family outdoor game such as badminton, croquet, or horseshoes
Jigsaw puzzle
Games such as Trivial Pursuit, Monopoly, Chinese Checkers
Tickets to special entertainment or sports event
Bookends
Ice-cream scoop and sugar cones
Coasters or glasses
Large beach towels
Ice bucket
Place mats with matching napkins
Something for a boat (see Sports section, p. 280)
TV trays or tables
Ping-Pong table
Membership in a dinner club
Records, discs, or tapes
Bubble gum machine
Popcorn popper with popcorn
Family book such as atlas, encyclopedias, travel guide, book of
    wildflowers, trees, birds, astronomy, sea, or wildlife
Cellular telephone or telephone amplifier
Photo album
Family tree or genealogy
Picnic basket or equipment
Beach umbrella
Bulletin board
Membership in local museum, educational TV station, symphony, or YMCA
Bird house, feeder, or bath—perhaps with a bag of bird seed
Holiday tree ornament, door decoration, or wreath
Wind chimes
Pet door

Water purifier
Smoke detector
Microwave oven
Fireplace equipment, logs, or cord of wood
Matching T-shirts—maybe with name of family boat
Calendar
Music box
Place card or napkin holders
Large tray
Candles and candle holders
Door mat
Flowering plant
Rolling cart
Playground equipment
Tree house
Playhouse or sandbox
Picture frame with a composite of their family photos
Video or computer game
Clock
"Good-for" card for a special outing
Rocking chair
Barometer/thermometer
Fan
Lawn mower
Garden hose
Door knocker
Fire starter
Bookshelves or storage units
Pet
Lamp
Wall hanging
Gift certificate for family portrait
Camera
Telescope
Binoculars

GIFTS
FOR TEENS AND
GRADUATIONS

I made this a separate category because so many people seem puzzled when it comes to appropriate gifts for young people. Although it is true that many teenagers follow the fads and/or traditions of their peers in their dress and musical choices, they do have their individual interests and pleasures as well. If you know a young person's hobby, pastime, or sport, consult the appropriate "Special Interest" section.

Young people who are graduating from either high school or college will probably need practical items for dorm rooms or apartments. The graduate who is embarking on a career also needs presents that help to support his or her work efforts.

General Suggestions

Record crates
Posters (if you know recipient's interests)
Walkman cassette player with good earphones—some have radio
    built in
Books or calendars in area of interest
Sunglasses—especially Ray-Ban or Vuarnet
Popular inexpensive watches—may wear two or three at a time
    (Swatch is good)
Subscriptions—*Rolling Stone, Dance, Omni, Circus*
Jewelry

Stereo or compact disc equipment
Concert tickets
Clothing—Ralph Lauren, Esprit, Guess, Laura Ashley
Perfume or cologne, if you know the recipient's preference
Party or dance for special occasion such as birthday
Bicycle
Back pack
Camera or other photographic equipment
Gold Saint Christopher's medal
Folding umbrella
Wallets, clutches, and key cases
Monogrammed silver pocket mirror
Monogrammed robe
Natural bristle makeup brushes in case
Trip with historical interest—Washington, D.C.; Williamsburg; the Alamo
Trip with sporting interest—fishing, white water rafting/canoeing, skiing, mountain climbing, back packing
Popcorn popper with popcorn
Thermos for cold weather sports events—perhaps with stadium blanket
Musical instrument and lessons
Private telephone line
Typewriter or home computer
Season tickets
Photo album
Picture frames
Evening bag in gold, silver or black
Dressing-table set
Portfolio
Quality stationery with monogrammed die included
Good pen
Pocket calculator
Portable radio or radio/alarm clock
Shares of stock
Telephone answering machine
Binoculars or opera glasses
Small TV set
Stuffed animals
Gift certificate for records or cassettes
Electric rollers or small hair dryer

Although most of the items above are appropriate for graduation gifts, some gifts seem especially suited for the graduate who will
soon be making major life changes.

Instead of giving cold cash to a new graduate, consider a gift
that might turn him or her into an investor: think about an investment gift. Stuart Varney, financial anchor for Cable News Network,
suggests a zero coupon bond. You can buy one now for a couple of
hundred dollars that will pay back one thousand dollars in seven to
ten years—just about the time your favorite graduate will need some
extra cash for a home or family. In addition to helping financially,
you will help the student understand something about money and
investing. Many parents open an individual retirement account for
their children just leaving college. The advantages: the graduate has
a ready-made investment account as a start for managing money; the
cash can't be touched until age fifty-nine and a half, so it will grow
significantly over the years; and it's a gift of money that cannot be
spent and/or squandered because it's locked into the account. Another
useful gift, according to Varney, is shares in a family of mutual funds.
You can buy into a mutual fund that invests in, say, stocks. If it's part
of a group or family of funds, the recipient can switch that cash into a
bond fund or a money market fund anytime he likes. Another
popular gift is a savings bond. It's low-priced, safe, and pays high
interest if held five years. Then there are dividend reinvestment
plans: with some stocks, dividend payments are automatically rein-
vested in extra shares—a useful way to accumulate stock long-term.
If the graduate is interested in literature or art, many books and
works of art will increase in value while your graduate enjoys them.

One of the most treasured graduation presents I received was a
beautiful sterling serving spoon with my school and graduation date
engraved in the bowl. Each time I use it I am reminded of my Aunt
Laura's thoughtfulness. For those graduates going off to school or
moving into a new apartment the gift possibilities are almost endless:

Organizers such as barrels, plastic space savers, foot lockers that
can double as seats or coffee tables

Reference books such as a thesaurus, atlas, dictionary, encyclopedias, law, or medical texts

Luggage and luggage tags with name and address

Linens for dorm room or apartment

Stationery printed with name and new address

Small refrigerator

Canvas director's chair

Electric blanket or sheet

Flannel sheets
Handsome corkscrew or other bar accessories
Beanbag chairs or attractive floor pillows
Set of coffee mugs, wineglasses, or beer mugs (with name of school if appropriate)
Kitchen utensils and accessories
Small appliances such as food processor or battery-operated vacuum
Basics for dormitory or apartment cooking such as mixing bowls and frying pan
Watering can and plant
Airtight container for storing food in one's room
Waste-paper basket
Subscription to hometown newspaper
Framed prints
Lighted mirror
Frame for diploma
Class ring
Laundry bag
Address book
Autograph book
Bookends
Iron or travel iron
Sewing kit
Beach towel
Ice chest
Pajamas, nightshirt, or nightgown
Scrapbook
Homemade food
Heating element for coffee, tea, soup
Portable bookcase
Pencil sharpener and pencil holder
Personalized labels
Telephone credit card
Mop and broom
Coin bank filled with quarters
Desk lamp
Gift certificate for two or more to special restaurant in new town

The graduate in his first job might appreciate any of the following: desk accessories; picture frames; portfolio or briefcase; desk agenda; thermal water pitcher and glass for desk; subscription to professional journal or *The Wall Street Journal* or *Advertising Age;*

small leather notebook and agenda for briefcase or handbag; personalized, leatherbound atlas, thesaurus, or other appropriate reference book; gift certificate to dental, medical, architectural, or other job-related supply house; membership in professional or alumni association. The "ultimate" gift for the graduate: a job offer!

ENTERTAINING IDEAS FOR HOSTS/ HOSTESSES AND GOURMET COOKS

T hese are suggestions for those who enjoy entertaining and/or cooking as well as gifts for the host or hostess who is entertaining you.

House Gifts

It is always considerate for a guest to bring a "house" or "bread-and-butter" gift. Gift selection should be based on (1) the extent of hospitality and duration of your visit (for tea or a planned weekend?); (2) how well you know the recipient; and (3) what you know about the recipient. Although flowers and gifts of food and wine are usually appropriate for a meal invitation, even these can be offensive if not chosen with care. Flowers brought to a formal dinner can create confusion while the hostess or others search for a suitable container, then attempt to integrate the flowers into the design and color scheme that has already been chosen. If you know the hostess well, tell her that you would like to provide a special floral arrangement for the occasion and ask if she has a color scheme, florist, and such. Sending flowers or a plant with a note the following day (having seen the decor) is also a thoughtful gesture. The same is true of wine brought to a dinner party. It is best to hand it to the recipient with the admonition that it is for him to enjoy at a later time, lest he be concerned that he is to use your gift of white wine with the beef course. Also be aware of others' religious beliefs and taboos—some people do not condone the drinking of any alcoholic beverages; others eat and drink only kosher foods.

The houseguest may wish to bring some small token, then wait until after the visit to select a suitable thank-you gift. For those who entertain outdoors a great deal, try citronella-scented candle torches; for outdoor play and a large lawn, a croquet set; for game-players, the latest rage; for the elegant host, a classic smoking jacket; for anyone, a carefully chosen book.

Gift Ideas for Those
Who Entertain

Most people enjoy entertaining others—in their homes, at restaurants and clubs, or at special events. Entertaining can be exceedingly simple or extraordinarily complicated. To produce an elaborate dinner party, the host or hostess may be responsible for menu selection, shopping, cleaning, flower arranging, shining of silver and crystal, seating charts, and general organization. Each of these functions offers an opportunity for the knowledgeable gift giver.

FOR COOKING

Any cook appreciates utensils that make food preparation easier or more attractive. Gourmet cooks, however, may have definite preferences, such as a certain line of copper cookware, wooden spoons, or particular knives.

The general cook appreciates new cookbooks. Knowing that the recipient has recently installed a microwave oven or food processor makes your selection easy. A cookbook holder with a book of quick meals, German recipes, or entertaining suggestions makes a welcome presentation.

Other General Suggestions

    Covered mixing bowls
    Freezer-to-oven cookware
    Potted herb garden
    Food scale
    Pizza pan, paddle, and brick
    Vegetable steamer (perhaps bamboo)

Collection of small, useful utensils such as pineapple corer, melon baller, garlic press, grapefruit knife

Wheeled chopping block

Cake or pie carrier

Coffee grinder and beans

Fondue pot

Omelet pan

Sausage maker kit

Pressure cooker

Poultry shears

Electric knife or knife sharpener

Sprout kit

Wine rack

Corkscrew set

Hanging space-saving toaster

Meat slicer

Electric griddle

Oyster and clam openers

Waffle iron

Spice rack

Electric wok

Microwave popcorn popper

Ice cream maker

Egg poacher

Microwave bacon rack

Professional knives

Butter warmer

Electric drink mixer

Grater/slicer

Vegetable washer

Cotton or linen kitchen towels

Over-the-sink cutting board

Juicer

Knife block

Sandwich maker

Bagel slicer

For the More Serious Cook

Gourmet cooking class, wine-label album, or book about fine wines

Asparagus, artichoke, or fish steamer

Special dishes for soufflé, au gratin, quiche, or paté en croûte

Bread pans (clay or black steel)
Canape maker
Steak hammer
Cheese or wine tasting course
Pasta maker
The Cooks' Catalog—a comparison of over four thousand kitchen
    items, utensils, appliances, and machines (Harper & Row)
Nonstick copper rolling pin
Food processor or an accessory for one
Deep fryer
Food scale (you can buy a talking one with memory)
Belgian waffle iron
Large pepper mill
Electric crisper
Espresso machine or pot
Tabletop barbecue/rotisserie
Videos of great chefs' cooking techniques
Rolling cart with cutting-board top
Cappuccino maker
Marble mortar and pestle
Copper cookware
Electric crepe maker
Pastas
Pasta of the month
Specialized cookbooks such as *Feast of the Olive, Asian Pasta,
    Martha Stewart's Hors d'oeuvres*
Pressure cooker
Electric mincer
Extra-virgin olive oil
Confectioner's dipping-tool set
Truffle scoop
Stock pot
Oil can
Sun-dried tomatoes
Basting brush
Nacho skillet or tortilla warmer
Taco fryer and rack set
Garlic paste
Special vinegars
Herbs
Soda siphon
Kitchen fire extinguisher

Zester/lemon stripper
Ejector fork
Cherry stoner
Poultry shears
Dumpling maker
Paella dish with saffron
Shitake mushrooms.

The real culinary sophisticate of—for instance—various oriental cooking would require more exotic equipment and ingredients: a Malaysian *Kulai;* a Burmese *Dare-oh;* an Indonesian *Wajan;* the Korean *Kalbi* (lava stones perfect for grilling at the table); or a Thai *Tom Yum* set or Japanese *Otoshi-Buta.* The key, of course, is to discover the cook's latest exotic interest.

Those who pride themselves on baking with a professional flair might appreciate parchment paper; colonial dough bowl; cast iron muffin or cornbread pans; pastry scraper; French tart/quiche pan; baker's icing and cooling rack; black steel popover pan or croissant set; ceramic pie weights; vanilla and almond extracts; antique cookie or chocolate molds; mini-loaf rack; charlotte mold; bundt pan; rolling cookie cutter; jelly-roll pan; classic European cookie molds; checkerboard cake-pan set; icing and decorating set; French madeleine mold; gugelhupf pan; professional chef's cap; liqueurs; professional chocolate in ten-pound blocks.

Outdoor entertaining offers its own set of possibilities: wicker paper-plate holders; steak serving plates and knives; grill cleaning brush or attachments; terry cloth napkins; outdoor cookbooks; basting and barbeque sauces; insulated or unbreakable glasses; fire starter or electric charcoal lighter; sturdy shish kabob skewers; corn set (brush for desilking and corn-on-the-cob butterer, corn cob holders); wooden salad bowl(s); terry towels; rechargeable portable electric can opener; shears; hickory chips; mesquite wood; ice cream maker; Texas barbeque sauce; party-size storage cans; trays; picnic basket.

FOR ENTERTAINING

Presentation and decoration are an integral part of entertaining. Crackers can be beautifully served in rustic grapevine baskets or on ornate antique silver trays; place mats can be of cork or lace; dishes of shells or crystal. Those who enjoy entertaining also enjoy creating new settings, decors, and ambiences for their guests.

THE ART AND ETIQUETTE OF GIFT GIVING

Silver storage bags
Quilted protectors for china
Drip catchers for candle holders
Drink glass froster
Japanese hot towel basket
Apron
Special or scented candles
Serving pieces, such as a tray for deviled eggs or a deep dish pie
    baker and server
Decanter, ice bucket, or wine cooler
Gelato dessert dishes
Chili pot
Sangria pitcher
Place mats and napkins
Mugs or soup bowls
Selected pottery pieces
Place card holders
Fondue bourguignonne set
Antique fish servers
Berry or fruit dish or set
Coffee-table book
Casserole dishes
Heated trays
Unusual baskets
Dust buster
Air purifier
Tissue valet
Telephone-book stand or cover
Tasteful bathroom accessories
Potpourri and scented candles, soaps, or sachets
Floating puzzles
Canape trays.

Food is almost always an appropriate gift: beautifully packaged cookies, biscuits, wafers, or candies; selected cheeses; preserves, jellies, or marmalades; choice hams; smoked salmon; herbs; vegetables or fruits from your garden; special dressings or sauces; a selection of ice cream toppings; imported mustards; gourmet popcorn; pesto sauce; caviar; truffles; double hickory-smoked bacon; special breads;

sausages; patés; teas or coffees; plum pudding; nuts; vintage maple syrup; box of frozen steaks; chocolate wine bottle filled with candies; wine or liqueur; reception sticks (for stirring coffee); fruits; or something you made.

GIFTS
FOR THE ELDERLY
OR DISABLED

While there are many very active and healthy elderly people as well as young persons with disabilities, some gift items are common to both age groups. These suggestions focus on gifts that will help to make life easier and more comfortable, rather than those that relate to the particular interests of an individual. (See other Special Interests sections.)

Persons who are in full-care facilities seem to be especially difficult to select gifts for. Usually, however, their needs are simpler than you think, and they enjoy your visits, calls, and letters more than anything else. Be sure to consider any dietary restrictions that the recipient may have as well as nursing home or hospital restrictions concerning homemade or "outside" food. And, if you are looking for gift ideas for someone in a nursing home, remember that some local fire regulations do not allow plastic items.

For Improved Comfort

> Bed wedges for head or leg elevation
> Tension or cervical pillows
> Special car or chair seats
> Massage pillows
> Heating pad or blanket
> Electric or flannel sheets

Afghan
Foam-covered curlers
Shower/bath bench
Down comforter
Small electric heater or fan
Lap robe or shawl
Washable bedroom slippers
Electric foot massage
Specially designed curved and/or cushioned pen that takes the
    pressure off the wrist and fingers
Car seat posture cushions
Bench backrest
Book holder attachment for exercise bike
Sound sleep machine
Electric mattress pad
Steering-wheel cover that keeps wheel cool when auto has been
    parked in the sun
Sun deflectors for car
Walking shoes
Heat massager
New mattress
Hospital bed
Neck pillow and cover

For Convenience

Dressing-aid stick
Stocking pull-on
Zipper puller
Folding cane
Pill splitter
Button aid
Lightweight scissors
Door grip
Swivel car cushion
Travel chair
Automatic card shuffler
Folding bed board
Cutting board with suction tips
Under-shelf jar opener
Bath bench
One-hand can opener
Remote switch for TV or lamp

Arm for holding telephone receiver
Fully stocked lap desk
Telescoping magnet
Folding shopping cart or shopping bag on wheels
Elastic shoelaces
Harness for one-handed fishing
Foot mop
Pan-handle holder
Telephone amplifier
Small, convenient appliances
Folding TV or bedside table
Lighted magnifying glass
Blood pressure monitor
Wash-and-rinse shampoo tray
Universal cuff—eating and writing utensils slip into these for
    easy use
Ramps
A couple of hours of visiting time relieving someone who must
    be constantly with a patient
Handicapped clothing (easy to get into and some of it is very
    attractive)
Electric wheelchair
Electronic, digital thermometer
Electric snow shovel
Handicapped silverware (in a wooden handle so it doesn't turn)
Clamp-on umbrellas for wheelchairs
Fancy canes
Three-wheel carts (especially good for going outdoors)
Medicine dispenser
Electric time-projecting clock (look up at ceiling)
Magnifiers to clip on to sunglasses
Vertical hand mixer with natural grip
Silver-storage bags (to keep silver tarnish-free)
Hand mirror
Lighted magnifier
Visor
Organizer for car
Basket with legs
Roll-out underbed storage
Overbed table
Pure-water pitcher (special filter in the cap)
Long appliance cords with tension reels

Money belt
Fold-up dish rack
Digital scale
Comfortable "extra" chair
Desktop organizers or file cabinet
Small thermal tote
Lightweight ironing board

In addition, there is a variety of tools made for reaching places that are usually difficult to get to—long-reach pruners, magnetic window washers, light-bulb changers with different length extensions, magnetic pickups, claw pickups, long-handled bath brushes, shoe and sock aids, folding reachers, and telescoping mirrors.

For Safety

Tub bar or rail
Nonskid bath or shower mat
Two-step stool
Power failure security light
Smoke alarm
Railing for outside steps
Safety arm rest for toilet
Portable raised toilet seat
Flashlight
Grab bars for halls, stairs, or entrance areas
Remote controls for phone (can blow into the phone to answer
    and hang up—check with your local phone company)
Alarm light (flashlight with alarm)
Night light
Portable fire-escape ladder

• For the hearing impaired, gift suggestions include a course in lip reading; personal television amplifier; clock with flashing lights or vibrator; wake-up device or clock; telecommunication machine (tele-typewriter that transmits to similar machines via telephone); sub-scription to *Deaf American* magazine; a Dog for the Deaf, trained to respond to phones, smoke, or fire alarm, oven buzzers, alarm clocks, a baby crying, and so on. (Dogs for the Deaf, a nonprofit tax exempt organization, is located in Jacksonville, Florida.)

If you have difficulty locating some of these items in your area, there are a number of catalogs that specialize in products for the disabled or ill or simply sell products that make life easier and more comfortable for all of us—Sears' *Home Health Care* as well as *Comfortably Yours* and *FashionAble*, to name a few. The National Association of the Deaf and the American Foundation for the Blind are both excellent sources of information as well as some products.

GIFTS FOR
ILL PERSONS

T he best gifts for people who are ill and recuperating for any period of time are your visits, your letters, your time to run errands, take care of children, answer telephone and mail, and your thoughtfulness.

When you ask a sick person what he needs, be as specific as possible and make suggestions about food choices, clothing requirements, and cosmetic or toiletry articles. Be certain that the patient will be permitted to receive the gift you select, and choose gifts that are appropriate to the patient's condition.

Although flowers are the most popular gift for the ill, they are not always the best choice. A room filled with plants and flowers can be confusing and claustrophobic—even depressing to patients when the blooms droop and die. Most hospital and nursing-home rooms are already small and crowded; busy nurses sometimes do not have time to tend to all the greenery; and patients who wish to keep the arrangements may not want to make several trips to the family car carrying flower arrangements. Fruit can be an equally annoying gift. It is a temptation to patients who should not be eating it and probably too much effort and mess for those who should. Fruit baskets are especially good for visitors. If you know the patient's *favorite* flower or fruit, by all means bring or send it. Favorite foods—which the patient is permitted to eat—are special treats unless he is taking advantage of his convalescence to lose weight.

On occasion I have put together "get-well" kits for hospitalized and recuperating friends. The selections vary with the individual but have included the following:

Satin or linen pillow cases to put over the regulation hospital ones
Small bell
Shawl
Eye shade and ear plugs
Slate and writing utensil (after a throat operation)
Gift certificate or offer to help with a shampoo and blow-dry
Neck pillow
Lap desk with stationery, post cards, and stamps
Bed rest
Basket to hold cards and notes
Bed caddy to hang at bedside
Puzzles and crossword puzzle books
Flower in a crystal or silver vase
Audio books
Automatic TV changer
Bed tray with cheerful china
Pencil and notepad
Bag with dry shampoo, hand and body lotion, lip pomade (a must for everyone), baby powder, cologne, and toothbrush
Homemade cookies or muffins
Decorations for the IV pole
Potpourri
Scented candle
Champagne
Harmonica or musical sweet potato
Current magazines
Executive puzzles
Dresser set
Small boxes of china, silver, or brass
Note saying that a floral arrangement will be delivered where and when the patient wants it
Collection of paperback books (hardback books can be heavy for a bedridden patient)
Ice cream
Luxurious soap
Teddy bear
Playing cards
Bed sheets

Washable slippers
Bulletin board
Kaleidoscope
Long switch or braid of false hair
Hospital gown in a pretty and soft printed material
Chocolates
Newspaper articles of interest
Slide projector and slides to show

A lengthy convalescence deserves extra attention from friends. As an illness drags on, flowers, fruit, and friends all seem to die away. However, there are many ways to show that you still care: a marvelous catered dinner; a special meal once a week; planned weekly visits; a telephone answering service for a certain period or an answering machine; regular grocery shopping; videos or video club membership; subscription to guide for educational channel or special music station; a car and driver for two hours per week; gift certificate or credit at book or music store; a portable party, complete with food, drink, hats, and balloons, given by individuals or a group of friends. Bringing a slide projector and slides or a video of a vacation or the grandchildren is an especially lovely gift for both the ill and elderly, as are newspaper clippings and magazines about items of particular interest.

Sick children require many diversions. Many enjoy an autograph pillow or book or guest book for their visitors to sign; quiet games and puzzles that they can do by themselves are helpful to busy parents. Boxes or bags of art supplies such as crayons, construction paper, glue, tape, scissors, activity book, colored pens and pencils, coloring books, ruler, paper dolls, and origami paper and book can help to fill hours pleasantly. Hand puppets can be used for both play and teaching. Small toys such as miniature cars can be played with in bed. There are dolls available that help explain to the child what is happening to him. With parents' permission, a small pet such as a bird or a hamster in the child's room at home can really change attitude and outlook. A book accompanied with a promise to read it aloud will bring rave reviews. For additional ideas, see "Gifts for Children," p. 313.

GIFTS FOR
THE TRAVELER

People who travel a great deal are both a challenge and a pleasure to shop for. No matter how worldly he or she may be, that perfect paperback, essential mineral-water spray, private newsletter, or new high-tech pocket gadget will be welcome.

Most travelers enjoy reading about places they will visit as well as places they have been. The more sophisticated appreciate subscriptions to special newsletters that keep them up-to-date. For example, *Connections* is for the traveling businesswoman; each month describes a major U.S. city and reports on a subject of particular interest to the woman traveler; *Passport*, a newsletter intended to be more current than standard guidebooks, covers a wide range of topics and places worldwide; *The Hideaway Report* is for the leisure traveler who is looking for unspoiled, peaceful places to visit in the United States and the Caribbean; several newsletters focus on restaurants or particular areas—*The Restaurant Reporter* keeps its readers current about Manhattan restaurants sixteen times a year.

Various books and guides can be wonderful presents. In addition to the many current guidebooks for almost each part of the globe, there are specific books for various interests—*Born to Shop* guides (Bantam) for major European cities; *Who Lived Where in Europe* (Facts on File) for those who want to look up the addresses of over three hundred famous persons who lived in Europe; *Tracking Treasure: Romance and Fortune Beneath the Sea and How to Find It*

(Acropolis) for treasure seekers and beachcombers; *Rado Guide to Metropolitan Fitness Centers* gives information about facilities and services for working out in major U.S. cities and lists fitness centers that accept short-term members; *French Farm and Village Holiday Guide* for those wanting to rent a rustic farmhouse for a week; *The Women's Travel Guide: 25 American Cities* (G.K. Hall), commonsense advice and suggestions for dressing and dining alone. Some world travelers and armchair travelers with a particular interest in certain regions or countries collect travel books. There are beautiful modern photographic renditions as well as interesting antique tomes of most places. There is even an unusual publishing concern in London— Eland Books—which specializes in reprinting travel books of distinction. More general gifts—the *Inworld Guide*—a definitive soft-bound leather reference that may be monogrammed, or Abrams's *The Travel Book*, a lovely vacation journal for the traveler's prose, illustrated with miniature paintings by artist Carol Inouye. Subscriptions to travel magazines such as *European Travel and Life* or *Travel and Leisure*, are options that will last throughout the year.

I enjoy putting together kits, bags, or boxes for my traveling friends. Many additions can be both inexpensive and thoughtful:

Ear plugs and eye mask
Miniature mineral water Evian face spray, lip moisturizer, pill box, cotton terry slippers in matching pouch, 9-by-12-inch or 10-by-14-inch manila envelopes for organizing, storing, or sending home printed materials
Pressure-sensitized labels that can be preaddressed for quick post-card mailings
Packets of facial tissue and lemon-scented damp towels
Small neck pillow
Traveling dental kit
Small terry-cloth towels
Tape measure with inches marked on one side and centimeters on the other

The pampered pilgrim will also enjoy the following sybaritic additions:

French cachou licorice
Elegant writing paper and Mont Blanc pen, perhaps with leather lap desk
Perfume purse spray
Favorite scented soaps

THE ART AND ETIQUETTE OF GIFT GIVING

Small antique frame for special photo
Makeup travel case with lighted mirror
Silver canister with travel toothbrush
Leather shaving kit
Staffordshire enamel sewing kit
Luxurious pillow case
Vintage silver flask
Hon folding bike to take in car, boat, or plane—twenty-eight
    pounds, folds to nine-by-eighteen-by-twenty-eight inches in
    thirty seconds

The array of small, compact products available for the modern
traveler is vast:

Converters for portable or electronic equipment
Worldwide adapter plug kits
AC/DC adapter/charger
Dual voltage immersion heater
Travel irons and hand steamers
Pocket curler wand or curling iron that operates with lighter fluid
Two-face extension mirror that folds flat
Remote control personal stereo the size of a cigarette pack (Aiwa)
Food Informer, which lists over 650 foods and drinks and their
    nutritional content
Wizard of Wine II calculator with a data base of 549 vintages—it
    lists vintage years of 27 types of red and white wine, even
    rates each year's harvest from poor to excellent, and you
    can give the recipient an updated microchip each year
Pocket translator that doubles as a four-function calculator for
    instant currency conversions comes in French/English,
    English/ French, German/English, and English/German edi-
    tions, with a built-in memory bank for storing additional
    words or phrases
Currency converter
Security accessories such as portable door or dresser locks
Kit of magnetic safety signs for the stranded motorist
Wallets that clip over belts or loop around one's neck
Money belts
Portable smoke detectors
Snap-on extra handle
Traveler's medical kit
Laundry kit with adjustable clothesline, clothespins, detergent,
    and waterproof laundry bag

Reusable film pouch to protect film against X-ray damage
Lap-top portable computers
All-in-one desk kits with all the essentials from tape to clips
Voice-activated travel alarm

A gift of luggage must be selected with the recipient's specific needs and tastes in mind. There are bags that expand in ingenious ways for filling with collected gifts and souvenirs; tote bags that are compartmentalized for holding toiletries; weekenders of every description and in every price range. There are many good-looking lightweight bags in almost every color from pale lavender to silver; and for those who are looking for the best way to go, a black crocodile traveling makeup and jewelry case lined with bordeaux calf leather by Gucci, a grained calf writing case or expandable jewelry case from Asprey, an ostrich train case with jewelry and cosmetic compartments by Mark Cross, Vuitton signature cases, and hanging bags all contribute to tasteful travel.

They call themselves "travelers," are traveling more for the cultural experience than for the sights, and are insulted to be referred to as "tourists." These—mostly—young people, who travel via almost any type of transportation and often stay in Youth Hostels, have special needs that include a day pack for shorter trips, small map of world or country, Walkman, travel books (before and during), complete sewing repair kit, and lightweight camera and film. Other very welcome contributions—especially if they have been traveling for a while—include jeans; a collection of shampoo, body lotion, insect repellent, sunscreen, and lotion; zip-lock plastic bags; pens, air mail cards, and stationery; water bottle, rain poncho, wool sweater, cotton pants, shorts (but not for women in many warm cultures), long-sleeved shirts, skirt, T-shirts, and money belt; small, compact notebook for recording experiences; address book, locks/chain; bed sheet—can purchase or make by sewing a full-size sheet into a sleeping bag—sometimes required by Youth Hostels; new, comfortable tennis shoes.

The thoughtful giver can arrange for special gifts or treatment for someone almost anywhere in the world. Gifts of fruit and cheese, flowers, or champagne are classic and usually appropriate; however, there are many other options that can put a traveler at ease or make him or her feel especially honored. So they're going to Paris for their honeymoon or anniversary—use Paris en Cuisine, a service that will reserve good tables at legendary restaurants or suggest excellent lesser-known cafés; or wire chef Guy Vendome at The Ritz to prepare an elegant food hamper suited to their mode of travel and their tastes—it can be arranged with china, cloth napkins, and a Hermès leather thermos containing an herbal tea to help one fall asleep—perfect for the return trip or a train to their next destination.

Many stores and catalogs are devoted primarily to travel accessories; prices for identical items can vary substantially, so, if you know what you are looking for, comparison shopping is a good idea.

GIFTS FOR
THE OFFICE

For the Desk Dweller

 Paperweight
 Personal directories or yellow pages
 Desk organizers
 Kits—such as a collection of small-size makeup, skin freshener,
   hand lotion, or sewing and repair supplies, or sample-size
   mustards, honeys, hot sauces, and so on
 Magazine subscription
 Desk nameplate
 Holders for tape
 File folders
 Pencils
 Clips
 Telephone shoulder rest
 New desk chair or pad
 Dictionary, thesaurus, or resource book, such as *The Art and*
   Etiquette of Gift Giving
 Vase and weekly flower
 Rotary file or index
 Stapler
 Pencil sharpener
 Small calculator
 Picture frames or holders

Place setting including place mat for desk meals
Thermal carafe
Basket of interesting instant teas, coffees, and boullions
Clock for desk or wall
Set of underlining or marking pens
Gift certificate
Drawer organizers
Bookends
Decorator waste paper basket filled with favorite munching
    foods or homemade cookies
Desk gym

For the Executive

Career fortune cookies (decorated Chinese take-out container
    with choice of lawyer, stockbroker, or physician fortunes)
Personalized wine or champagne
Executive puzzles
Leather agenda or appointment book
Photo album
Appropriate office coffee-table book
Magnifying glass
Certificate for color or wardrobe analysis
Membership to health club near office
Massage
Personal trainer
Chocolate business or logo card
Antique letter opener
Basket with sports equipment (tennis or golf)
Luggage
Personalized leather atlas
Candy jar with promise to keep filled
Bookends
Bar tools/accessories
Umbrella
Popular book on management or investing
Box of steaks or salmon
Tickets to event
Travel kit
Frame an award or picture
Commissioned portrait

GIFTS FOR
THOSE WITH SPORTS
INTERESTS

Most people today are involved in some way with sports or fitness—even if only as armchair fans. From the competitive sailor to the person who bicycles alone on country lanes, there is an appropriate gift. However, if the giver is unfamiliar with the sport, selecting the gift can be confusing and intimidating. This chapter is intended to give this giver some guidance.

General Tips

• Do not purchase serious sports equipment for the serious sportsperson, such as a gun for a hunter or clubs for a golfer, unless you are certain that the selection is perfect in every respect—size, brand, type, color, and so on.

• Tickets to games, exhibitions, sports shows, tournaments, or races are an excellent present for sports fans. They become more special when accompanied by a picnic basket, shooting stick, thermos, or special note—or when tucked into a new wallet.

• Books and subscriptions to sports periodicals are especially good choices for those who enjoy dreaming about their favorite sport during the off season.

• Many sports buffs take pleasure in various reminders of their favorite sport—figures in porcelain, metal sculptures, needlepoint, chocolate golf and tennis balls, even assortments of fortune cookies containing specific fortunes for various sports enthusiasts.

• Gift certificates to the appropriate sporting goods store or catalog can solve the problem if you are unsure about equipment or know little about the sport.

• Memberships in racket, shooting, golf, tennis, or health clubs and/or lessons are a personal and thoughtful gift. Has she always wanted to learn karate? Does he need to find a health club near his office or a lunchtime exercise class?

• The sports fan, in addition to enjoying all of the above, could probably use a small ice chest, stadium blanket or cushion, binoculars, a TV remote control, or (for an enthusiastic supporter) anything with his favorite team's logo on it—mug, bumper sticker, poster, clock, or license plate frame.

• There is a variety of new training equipment that can be used by the serious athlete. For example, Sports Scan is a device that volleyball, tennis, racquetball, and softball players can use to help them improve athletic responses and performance by increasing their visual perception of the ball.

Snow Skier

Is this person an avid skier or a novice?

Small gifts for either level of accomplishment could include a ski-wax kit; a ski lock; lip emollient and face cream; ski gloves, waterproof gloves, or glove liners; goggles; sunglasses with wind visor; a belt or fanny pouch; wine bota; or a book of ski-lift tickets. Turtlenecks are used in layering, and long underwear—especially thermal silk—is very light and warm. Caps, masks, scarves, and heavy socks often need replacing. More serious gifts might be a car rack for skis, a parka, a warm-up suit, after-ski boots, or a trip to a ski lodge.

Scuba Diver

The giver must first ascertain whether the diver has his own equipment or rents it wherever he travels.

Basic equipment ranges from small items such as safety whistles, divers' knives, and weights to wet suits and cylinders. Gloves, depth or pressure gauges, hose protector, regulator, masks, fins, snorkels, and diving vests are all necessary equipment for the serious diver.

Underwater lights and repetitive dive charts would be special additions.

If the diver owns all of his own gear, he may still need accessories such as a diving watch, an international "Divers Below" flag for the boat, or a snorkel lock. You might fill a catch bag or duffel with de-fog solution, rubber-marking paint, rubber preservative, and other small practical items.

Jogger/Runner

For runners, there are many small, useful gift choices. Many new books on running—philosophy, technique, aerobics—are small and will fit into a purse or briefcase. The *Jim Fixx Running Calendar* is always a good choice. Other ideas to help jog your memory: sweatbands; visors; pedometers; reflective clothing; athletic socks; jogging shorts or suit; monogrammed neck towel; or key holder to attach to shoe lace. The really earnest runner might appreciate leg weights, earphones, massage oil and liniment, or a massage from a masseuse or masseur or from you!

Hunter

You need certain information before selecting most gifts for a hunter: What does he hunt? Where does he hunt? What time of year does he hunt? What does he hunt with?

Some gifts are general enough for most hunters, such as a weather radio, a hunting knife, an ice chest, a first aid kit, or a thermos.

Clothing, of course, varies with climate, season, and type of hunting, and can range from camouflage suits and thermal underwear to shooting gloves and rainsuits. For traditionalists, the ultimate foul-weather gear is the British-made Barbour jacket. Made of waterproof 100-percent cotton, these jackets have protected wearers including Theodore Roosevelt and members of the British royal family since 1890. Although these jackets acquire a worn, seasoned look and gain status with age, owners can retreat the jacket with thornproof dressing.

Archers might welcome a target, a bow and arrow rack, gloves, an arrow straightener, fletching tools, broadheads, small game points, or a kit for making arrows.

For the bird hunter, decoys, bird bag, calls, duck blind, and items for bird dogs, such as dog grooming aids or training kits, are practical items. Bird hunters might also like to collect porcelain birds or bird dogs, old hunting prints, or antique decoys. In addition to enjoying his hunting dogs, industrialist Peter Grace collects figures and prints of retrievers, especially those that remind him of his light-colored favorite.

There are many possibilities for gun equipment; however, most accessories relate to a particular type and size of gun. Gun cleaning supplies, gun case or sling, scope, racks, and safes are suitable gifts.

If you know where the hunter is planning to hunt, you may be able to obtain a detailed map or aerial photo of the area from the local highway department or agriculture office.

For the serious hunter, the itinerary for a trip to hunt grouse, pheasant, moose, and so on can be presented with a hunting license for that area or country.

Fishing Fan

What kind of fishing does he enjoy—surf fishing, fly fishing, spin fishing, deep sea fishing?

There are lots of opportunities for innovative collections of things for the fishing fan: a box of assorted hooks and weights; an assortment of knives—filet, scaling, pocket, floating; or a tackle box with fishing pliers, hook hone, folding scissors, hook remover, and stringer. Other ideas for this sportsman include rain gear; a stream thermometer; a floating flashlight or keycase; chest waders or hip boots; fisherman's vest; a pocket camera to record the one that didn't get away; live bait tank or bait bucket; or a fishing guide for a day or weekend. And for the successful fisherman, a fish cookbook, fish-mounting kit, or smoker.

When not fishing, the avid fisherman enjoys reading about his favorite sport. Most bookstores stock a variety of titles ranging from the tying of trout flies to the art of tarpon fishing.

More substantial gifts for major occasions might include a guided fishing trip—to announce the gift, a box of specially selected flies and/or lures for the area. And there is always a week at either the Orvis or the Joan and Lee Wulff Fishing Schools for the serious fly fisherman to brush up his skills. A gift certificate from a well-known taxidermist such as J.T. Reese of Florida would also be welcome.

As a gag gift, you can always include a gift certificate to a fish market.

Cyclists

Whether racing or touring through city or country, the cyclist finds certain gifts always suitable. Special gloves, repair tools, pants clips, or a water bottle that clips to the bike are safe choices.

The racer, who wants to carry as little weight as possible, could use a helmet or cycling cap, cycling shorts with a chamois seat, or toeclips and straps. The motocross enthusiast may want number plates or grips for handlebars. The touring cyclist can use many practical items for the traveler, such as guidebooks, small transistor radio, compass, rain poncho, or Swiss army knife. The casual biker, who often uses his vehicle for carrying packages, books, or other people, might need a basket or carrier rack, a child seat, a padded seat, a lock and cable, or a horn or bell. A tire pump, personalized license tag, reflectorized clothing, or bicycle rack for the car could be equally welcome.

Bowler

Often bowlers are already members of teams and have most of their sports clothing and equipment. Personal bowling balls are drilled individually to fit fingers. Gloves, wrist supports, towels, bowling ball buffers, or passes to a bowling alley are all options. Some avid bowlers enjoy various items with a bowling motif—posters, mugs, key chains, and so on.

Rugged Outdoorsperson

Is the recipient a camper and/or backpacker or just someone who enjoys hiking occasionally?

For anyone who spends much time out doors: **clothing**, such as beachwear, humorous or monogrammed beach towel, beach bag; wool shirts and jackets; appropriate gloves; warm or electric socks; sunglasses, hats, or visors; rainsuits; down vests or jackets; **eating gear**, such as folding drinking cups; waterproof matches; outfitted picnic basket; thermos or ice chest; portable grill; solar tea jug; drying rack for fruit, vegetables, and flowers; **practical items**, such as beach, sun, or rain umbrella; hammock; campstool; flashlight or lantern; all-weather blanket; binoculars; range finder or compass; waterproof camera bag.

Kits or collections are fun to put together: a survival kit might include a candle, a compass, dehydrated food, a signal mirror, paper cups, a whistle, first aid supplies, and extra socks for wet feet.

Membership in the Sierra Club, various field guides, and topographic quadrangle maps from U.S. geological surveys are interesting alternatives to subscriptions and books.

Campers specifically might require various types of portable heaters or fans, portable toilets, baby-carrying devices, roof racks for automobiles, or fire extinguishers. Basic gear can include folding chairs and table or canvas water bucket. The choice of cooking gear is almost endless, with continued improvements in nesting cookware, collapsible ovens, and camper toasters. Small gifts are easy for campers—long-oven mitts; tablecloth clamps; insect repellant and sting stopper; reflective blanket; dried food; unbreakable dishes; whistles; durable plastic bottles; inflatable pillow; elastic clothesline; laundry bag; fly swatter. Special updated park and campground guides are an excellent gift suggestion for traveling campers.

The very nature of backpacking makes the backpacker selective in his choice of gear and supplies. Special lightweight versions of regular outdoor gear are a good solution. Remember that certain gear is seasonal. Special insoles for shoes, identification bracelets or necklaces (possibly with medical alert information), water purifier, plastic tube for carrying maps and papers, GI can opener, aerial flare, and walkie-talkie are other good ideas.

Golfer

All golfers receive golf balls, golf ball monogrammers, golf shirts, tees, golf club covers (fuzzy, crocheted, knitted, needlepointed or monogrammed), personalized golf towels, and golf umbrellas in excess. So what's left? An electric putting cup, a golf practice net, a golf swing analyzer, a carrying case for golf bag (for travel), a golf club care kit, a golf lesson from a famous pro, a gift certificate for custom-made golf shoes, or a week of golf school. For the special golfer, take videos or movies of his or her swing for analysis, or—the ultimate—arrange for him to have a special fitter come to his office to fit him for a putter or set of Pedersen quality hand-crafted custom clubs (include a special trip to their factory in Connecticut to view the entire process) in a Gucci golf bag. Then add the ultimate golf cart, complete with phone, TV, refrigerator, and bar.

There are also charming golf prints, such as those by Leroy Neiman, and scenes of famous Scottish golf courses, Irish crystal decanter and glasses with etched golfers, a wrist computer for computing your (and your opponents' scores), designer scarves like Hermès printed with golf designs, and golf games—Trivia Golf or Ultimate Golf. Sterling ball markers, tees, and divots, or a crystal club with the recipient's name might enliven the golfer's desk; Hoya's miniature crystal golf clubs or an elegant trout; Tiffany's sells handsome sterling key chains and pins in a golf club motif. Interesting small items (under twenty-five dollars) include golf motif leather coasters; custom-etched glasses and barware; bag tags; golf bag mugs; belt buckles; money clips; paper weights; jewelry boxes; leather shoe valets; and golf pro kits containing divot repair tool, ball markers, and cleat fastener.

Tennis Player

An invitation to a tennis ranch or camp would be the perfect gift for the serious player. Other, less-expensive possibilities include a tennis racket press; a practice rebound net; a tennis bag; a hanger for racket and balls; tennis glove; assorted tennis clothing; leather sneakers; sweatbands; an ice chest; a canteen; kits for stringing or regripping a racket or a gift certificate for this repair; a tennis ball belt; or a tennis trainer (a base with attached ball on string). Videos or movies of player's technique for his or her study or tennis technique books would usually be appreciated. Many tennis players enjoying using anything with a tennis motif, from key rings to stationery to sweat shirts to calendars.

Health and Fitness Devotee

There are all kinds—some for fun; some for figure; some for health. How serious is your recipient?

The varieties of attractive exercise clothing for both men and women offer lots of potential—lxurious monogrammed terry robes and towels, warm-up suits, leotard-and-tights combinations, or shorts. Small-scale equipment for home or compact items for travel enable the health-conscious to exercise wherever he is: jump ropes and travel gyms fold into briefcases; there are compact rebound joggers and small doorway gym bars and punching bags. Exercise mats, gymnastics balls, barballs, ankle weights, digital watches, inclined exercise boards, or exercise tapes or videos to follow are sensible choices for these devotees.

Fitness buffs often are concerned with all aspects of their health—what they eat and drink, their weight, and so on. Many gifts enhance this holistic approach to living: faucet water filters; blood pressure monitors; dust masks; air purifiers; humidifiers; bathroom scales; shower or heat massage; biofeedback tapes; diet and nutrition books and charts. Vegetarians and those who eat only organically grown foods will be pleased with a yogurt maker, a Crock Pot, a bamboo vegetable steamer, an herb garden, a sprout kit and seeds, a pottery soup tureen, bread-making utensils, a mixture of dried fruit and nuts, a food processor, a wok and Chinese recipe book, or special cookbooks for vegetables or breads.

Boaters

Be advised that power boaters and sailors differ greatly in their outlooks, interests, and needs. It is also important to learn whether your boater races his boat or cruises for pleasure. Often a gift that would be greatly appreciated by one would be of little value to the other.

For those who cruise on either a sailboat or a power boat, there are many convenience items available—antiskid, unbreakable place settings or mugs marked with nautical terms or the name of the boat; floatable cushions; a buoyant jacket; special towels; colorful streamers or flags; place mats; a set of charts for their local area; or a set of compact liquid-tight plastic containers.

Boaters who race competitively are careful not to load their vessels with unnecessary gear because extra weight will slow the boat. Thus, racers are more interested in items that will help them be more competitive. For example, a good pair of racing gloves, a countdown timer/stopwatch, warm watch cap, spotlights and flashlights, and freeze-dried meals are good ideas.

In addition, sailors can use wind and wind speed indicators, winch covers, sail ties, foul-weather gear, a dodger, sun hats, and safety harness—even a gift certificate for a new spinnaker. Special courses such as navigation or chartered cruises are a more extravagant gift selection. A detailed handmade model of the recipient's yacht can be commissioned if you have the plans available—price: four thousand to five thousand dollars, with two to six months' order time.

There are some gifts that any boater would receive with pleasure—boat shoes, binoculars, depth indicator, speed indicator, navigational instruments or tools, or safety devices such as flares or man-overboard modules. How about stationery imprinted with house flag and club burgee, or a box of Godiva chocolates packaged and trimmed with your choice of ship's wheel or anchor? The real aficionado may enjoy antiquarian nautical books, the creation of a house flag, or The Sailor's Game (by Sparkman and Stephens).

Horseback Rider

Before making most gift selections, the giver should know what kind of riding the recipient does, how serious he is (in competition?), and whether he has his own horse. Belts, buckles, tie pins, and some items of clothing are common to most riders; however, the interests of the polo player and the hunter as well as their dress and equipment differ greatly. Appropriate books and video tape lessons, riding lessons, knee guards, a horse trailer, a groom brush, a comb and sweat blade, riding boots, a bridle, a crop, or a saddle are fine gifts if tailored to the recipient's requirements. And for the horse—a supply of carrots, apples, sugar cubes, or hay—or Hermès handsome leather sugar cube carrier.

GIFTS
FOR GARDENERS

The world of the gardener is delightfully diverse—from herbs and vegetables to cacti and miniature fruit trees, from ornamental grass seeds and orchid flasks to dahlia bulbs and lily-of-the-valley pips, from orchards and farms to window boxes and greenhouses. There are few of us who would choose to live without growing plants around us, and an amazing number of people who do grow special types.

For the General Gardener/Putterer

    Sprayer
    Harvest basket
    Bedding plants
    Collection of gourmet lettuce seed packets in a small basket or cloth
        bag
    Gardening tools (pruning shears, gardening fork, trowel, clip-
        pers, dibble, weed remover) and bucket or holder
    Soil test kit
    Cordless grass or hedge trimmer
    Wheelbarrow
    Sun hat and garden gloves
    Subscription to gardening magazines or a collection of catalogs
    Gardening charts
    Timely *Farmer's Almanac*

Compost bin
Knee pads and rubber boots
Hose or hose hanger with nozzles
Special rake
Leaf eater
Rain gauge
Gift certificate to favorite nursery or catalog
Weed puller
Desk accessories, address books, and so on, decorated with designs of peonies, spirited birds, butterflies
Small garden ornamentation such as sculptures, bronze cranes, sundials, bird baths
Tree or shrub
Collection of spring bulbs
Garden lamp
The Garden Game, in which players must plant four gardens with compatible plants—has seed packet cards, weather report cards, act of God cards, and compost cards

For the Food Producer

Cold frame
Tomato stakes
Frames and bedding plants
Bean poles and seeds
Onion sets
Tub of sprouting seeds and sprouter
Book on canning or freezing
Canning jars, labels, lids
Pressure cooker
Garden tower
Strawberry jar already planted
Plastic markers for plant and garden identification
Fruit tree
Herb garden
Farmer's Almanac
Vegetable cookbook
Kit for drying fruits and vegetables
Herbal soaps
Solar-powered ventilated pith helmet
Vegetable seeder (hand or tractor mounted)
Seedling flats
Automatic cold-frame opener

Seed catalogs for miniature vegetables and European vegetable seeds

Unusual hydroponic forcing kit such as Belgian endive

For the Flower Gardener

Bulbs or bedding plants

Bulbs or seed packets in the appropriate pot or vase, or tulip or hyacinth bulb kits

Flower cutters or clippers

Class in or books about flower arranging, such as ikebana

Botanical flower prints

Flower-arranging materials

Planter

Collection of flowering meadow seeds

Botanical note cards or stationery

Flower-drying equipment and instructions

Unusual vase

Start collection of botanical flower plates

Flower calendar or plan book

Potpourri jar, oils, and instructions

Flower-shaped cookie cutters

Chocolate flower pots filled with silk or real flowers

Flower garden planner

Bird house, bird bath, or bird feeder

Garden ornaments (garden sculpture is becoming increasingly popular—antique pieces with good graphics and sculptural forms are highly prized)

For the Indoor Gardener

Grow light (small telescoping lights mount on the edge of the pot)

Humidifier

Herb kit

Cachepot

Collection of pots

Garden shears

Potting soil, bulbs, and gravel

Moisture reader

Small greenhouse

Small gardening shears and trowel

Attractive watering can

Plant hanger and bracket

Plant

Window box

Baskets

Membership in indoor gardeners' club in the area or in plant
society, such as the Orchid Society

Rolling plant stand

Books on indoor plants and gardening

Small sprayer

Tickets to garden or plant show

Bonsai plant

Miniature fruit tree

• For the specialist, consider giving something relating to his or her
gardening interest, such as bonsai materials; orchid pots; pebbles for
bulb forcing; a particular rose bush, perhaps a very old English or a
new variety; or historic plants—flowers or fruit—that are being restored, cultivated, and preserved at the Historic Plant Center at
Monticello, in Charlottesville, Virginia.

GIFTS
FOR THE CLERGY

If you know your minister, priest, or rabbi well enough to give him or her a gift, you probably also know his/her special interests. Gift certificates from a shop that caters to that interest or to a book or music store are always received with pleasure. Food—homemade or favorite imported delicacies—is a popular gift; however, not necessarily a practical one if he regularly receives a great deal of perishable food for certain holidays or occasions.

Engraved or printed personal stationery and writing implements, subscriptions to magazines or newspapers, membership in a museum book club or hobby-related organization, a special dinner invitation, or tickets to a sporting or cultural event are thoughtful presents.

As clergy usually cannot afford some luxuries, group gifts are often the most successful—some examples: a car; membership to a local golf club; a TV set, VCR, or stereo; sporting equipment or fishing gear; a boat; luggage; a vacation trip; an elegant briefcase.

Nuns who do not wear a habit would perhaps enjoy a gift certificate to a local clothing store or good mail-order catalog. In addition to enjoying the same gifts as the clergy—see above—they might appreciate a blooming plant, gifts of china or crystal if they live in an apartment, or a basket of scented soaps, lotions, and potpourri.

If you are concerned about a gift for the Holy Father, you might wish to emblazon it with the papal crest (the Holy See mission to the United Nations can give you a copy of the tiara and the keys of Saint Peter); and remember that Pope John Paul II likes to ski, kayak, and read, and is especially fond of hats and the foods and drinks of his native Poland.

Don't be disappointed, however, if your gift is not accepted by the Holy Father for his own use. Perishables go directly to the apostolic pantry; most of the other gifts go to a clearinghouse where plans are made for dispersal of the presents to parishes.

Francis Cardinal Spellman often gave Pope Pius XII modern gifts that he enjoyed using—an electric typewriter and a microscreen shaver.

Prince Charles and Princess Diana presented Pope John Paul II with the book *Bede's Ecclesiastical History of the English People*, which was written by the English historian and theologian called the Venerable Bede in 731—eight centuries before King Henry VIII broke with Rome and established the Church of England. The Pope accepted it, saying that he was familiar with the work and that Bede was "a great person of the common and universal church."

GIFTS
FOR THOSE INTERESTED
IN THE ARTS

People who enjoy music, art, theater, or dance can be easily satisfied in the gift department. The giver must know some specifics, however, in order to give effectively. Does he or she paint, play, or dance for pleasure? What type of music? What instrument? Favorite dancers? What medium—oils, pen and ink, watercolor? How serious and/or advanced is the recipient about studying the art?

The possibilities in this gift category are so diverse that these general suggestions are meant only to stimulate your imagination.

For Appreciators of Art and Artists

Magazine subscriptions
Tickets to exhibitions, the exhibition catalog, and perhaps your
    company and a gallery lunch as well
Utilitarian or decorative easel
Gift certificate to favorite art-supply house or picture-framing shop
Studio smock or apron
Mat cutter
Collection of frames and stretcher strips
Portfolio
Course, lessons, or seminar
Artists' books or books on design or technique
Quality brushes

Bristol board or paper
Brush holder
Calligraphy set
Art bin or box for supplies
Adjustable wooden mannequin
Canvas
Tracing paper
Posters of exhibitions
Jewelry or amusing items with artist motif
Frame an invitation to his or her exhibition

For Appreciators of Music and Musicians

Music stand (maybe antique for propping a painting or book)
Unusual foreign or antique instrument (a balalaika from Russia)
Offer to do invitations and program for recital
Magazine subscriptions
Tickets to concerts
Concert in park with picnic
Record or tape holder
Tape of his or her music
Jewelry, mugs, or figures with musical symbols
Old sheet music—possibly autographed
Photographs or sketches of favorite musicians
Frame musician's program
Staff paper
Headphone that plugs into instrument
Record, disc, or tape in field of interest
Copies of famous paintings with musical instruments (i.e., Picasso's *The Blue Guitar*)
Swimming pool in shape of musical instrument (I once had a neighbor whose pool was in the shape of a cello!)
Scrapbook for programs/recitals
Music dictionary
Lessons or classes
Blank cassette tapes
Gift certificate to music store or music catalog
Metronome
Antique hymnal for your church organist
Piano tuning
Laminate or frame music that is special to the recipient
Case for carrying music
Membership in musicians' union

Case for transporting or carrying instrument

Complete collection of a group of works by one artist or composer

Caricature or silhouette of musician

Recording or sheet music related to the occasion and/or the recipient—Christmas music, "Tea for Two" if you're coming for tea, a recording of a symphony Wagner wrote on the birth of a baby for your grandson's birth

For Appreciators of Theater and the Movies

Wall masks or bookends (of comedy and tragedy)

Costumes

Signed programs (perhaps from an important opening night)

Framed autographs of actors and actresses

Leatherbound editions of plays

A pair of tickets presented with an accompaniment (an umbrella with tickets for *Singing in the Rain*)

Subscriptions to repertory companies

Membership in a theater guild that offers admission to rehearsals or cast parties

Recordings of great plays by well-known actors

For the theater scholar, unique reference books (a Shakespeare *Concordance*, for example)

For the aspiring actor, an adult education or college class in acting, speech, or movement

For the musical comedy buff, a pair of tap shoes and lessons

When money is no object: a London theater tour

Tickets to the Tony Awards, where recipient can mingle with Broadway's best

Posters of favorite shows (try the Triton Gallery, 323 West 45th St., New York, New York, 10036)

Scripts of plays or screenplays

A course in how to write a screenplay at a local college or film school

A scrapbook of movie stills featuring a favorite actor or actress

A video camera and tapes for raising home movies to a higher art

Invite the recipient and his/her friends to a film retrospective for which you provide videotapes and popcorn

Memorabilia belonging to a legendary star (watch for auctions and bid for yourself and others as high as you dare; you may come home with a pair of Ruth Gordon's shoes or Joan Crawford's false eyelashes!)

A bit part in a movie or television series, offered as a bonus at celebrity benefits for worthy causes—rare, but a special treat for the right fan!

For Appreciators of Dance and Dancers

Subscription to *Dance Magazine*

Books about the history of dance—ballet, modern, ethnic

Old photographs of great dancers

Autographed programs

Posters of dancers or of great ballet companies

Autographed toe shoes (The New York City Ballet Guild sells used toe shoes signed by the dancers as a fundraising method)

Jewelry or sculpture of dancing feet or famous dancers

Videotaped performances of great ballets or dance films (*The Red Shoes, A Chorus Line, The Turning Point, Sleeping Beauty*)

Subscription tickets to a new dance company

For a beloved child, tickets to *The Nutcracker* at Christmastime, and an invitation to a grown-up tea or dinner

Classes or seminars on the dance given by active or retired dancers and choreographers (check with local theaters and museums)

For the experienced dancer, a chance to attend a master class given by a well-known dancer or choreographer

Dance clothing—spectacular leotards and tights, unitards, jazz shoes, a chiffon dance skirt (even leg warmers you knitted yourself!)

Biographies of great dancers, often heavily illustrated with photographs

Cassettes of well-loved dance music, or compact discs

A backstage tour of the performance venue of a favorite company (this may include visits to costume shops, rehearsal studios, and a moment onstage)

Membership in a volunteer organization or dance guild that offers attendance at rehearsals as a benefit

GIFTS
FOR SOMEONE AWAY
FROM HOME

Boarding school and college students, service personnel, workers with jobs overseas, members of the foreign service, continual travelers, and expatriates form a special category with unique needs.

If you are regularly sending packages abroad, be certain you understand customs limitations and regulations.

Particularly for the Student

    Mail from home
    Iron/ironing board
    Bed and bath linens
    Bookcase or shelving
    Insulated ice chest
    Desk or bed/book reading lamp
    Restaurant dinner
    Stationery with school address
    Memorabilia relating to school
    Class ring
    Popcorn popper
    Coin bank (filled?) for laundry, drink machines, telephone
    Prints or wall posters
    Gift certificate from school bookstore
    Plant

Christmas tree
Passes to local driving range, movie, fast food restaurant, ice
    cream parlor
Food
Typewriter or personal computer
Car insurance
Loud alarm clock or clock radio
Car accessories or gift certificate for car wash
Personalized labels

For Others Living Away from Home

Mail from home
Nonperishable food package
Camera, film, protective bags for film
Clothes-drying rack or line
Photo album
Addressed, stamped postcards
Heating element for liquids
Sewing kit
Telephone credit card or coupons for long distance calls
Tickets home
Travel alarm clock
Cassette tape recorder-player and regular cassettes from family
    or friends
Subscription to hometown paper
Magazine subscription
Luggage
(See Gifts for the Traveler, p. 273, for further suggestions)

GIFTS FOR
PETS AND THEIR OWNERS

Both pets and their owners enjoy pet gifts. Owners whose pets are their friends like to delight them with special tokens. And owners appreciate gifts given to their pets—one of the current gift trends for dogs and their owners is the mother-doggy/ father-doggy look meant to match the owner's lifestyle—gray flannel collar and lead for the business person's dog, crystal and onyx collar to match milady's diamonds, camouflage rainwear and overalls for the outdoors-type owner, or bomber jackets and mink wraps to match the owners'. Pet outfits of mohair, suede, marabou, and sequins are no longer unusual among pampered pets.

Beauty and grooming aids are fine gifts. There are shampoos for different colors of fur, shampoos that disentangle and loosen matted coats, shampoos with color intensifiers (a little more apricot?), and shampoos with special fragrances and conditioners. Also available are flavorful toothpastes and breath fresheners, deodorants, perfumes, colognes, and makeup for covering poodle and Persian tearstains.

Many pet gifts help make life more comfortable for both owner and pet: a portable pet taxi for traveling to hotels or vets; a pet door so pet can come and go without its owner's being on call; special nontangling leashes; sturdy indoor gates; raised bowls for pregnant or back-problem owners; automatic or self-feeding sets for when owner is away; training manuals, such as *How to Be Your Dog's Best Friend* (Little, Brown) or a training class; a certificate for pet sitting or dog walking; customized leashes or collars; handmade sweaters, boots, and rainwear; a gift certificate for a grooming appointment; bird feeders that hold up to seventeen pounds of seed—great for bad weather; Cat Can Trainer; some sessions with a pet therapist; an all-in-one pet-feeding tray that can't tip or move; a kitty cabana—a collapsible metal frame that comes with a choice of tentlike covers—camouflage, plaid, ticking . . . appropriate for putting over litter boxes or food dishes, especially in apartments where the bathrooms seldom afford room for litter boxes.

Especially for an animal companion: favorite food, pet candies, catnip, or chew-sticks; a sleeping bag for cold weather; a new bed, cage, or basket; pet toys; a scratching post, pyramid, or house window perch for the curious; custom-made cat furniture; balls, or a Pet Cruise (American Cruise Lines), price $1,095.00 for pooch, parakeet, or puss. Masters and Mistresses sail free. Travelers board ship in New Orleans and navigate the Mississippi for 7 days. The ship accommodates 65 pets and 125 people.

For proud owners: sweat shirt or tote bag with appliqué of recipient's breed of dog or cat in a choice of colors (Pets on Sweats, New York); sculptures, figurines, pictures, or other decorative items depicting cats, dogs, birds, monkeys, and so on; jewelry relating to recipient's love of horses, cats . . . could be stirrup tie clip or bracelet, a charm, a pocket pet (pin of animal's head to appear above pocket), or a miniature portrait of pet done in ivory for a locket; a framed and/or enlarged photograph of a favorite pet; a pet portrait in oils, charcoal, or pencil; a special family portrait including pets.

GIFTS FOR NEEDLEWORKERS

Needlework is rapidly becoming a popular pastime for those who want to see and feel the results of their own efforts and ingenuity. The stressed working woman and man of today especially enjoy this patience-building form of relaxation.

The great variety of needle crafts include sewing; weaving; free-hand embroidery; needlepoint; petit point; knitting; blackwork; counted cross-stitch; pattern darning; pulled work; canvas embroidery; patchwork; quilting; smocking; cutwork; drawn thread work; needle lace; tatting; crocheting; metal threads; bead work; and on and on. These often remarkable forms of needlework have been handed down from generation to generation in all countries of the world, and each has its own traditions and stitches to admire. The museums and churches of the world display beautiful examples of rugs, vestments, tapestries, and clothing that seem impossible to duplicate. Perhaps they had more leisure time in those days, but today many people are rediscovering the joy and satisfaction of creative needlework.

Today's needleworker has the advantage of using the ancient techniques and traditional designs of these masterpieces as well as discovering a far greater choice of materials, threads, patterns, and—sometimes—machines found in needlework shops worldwide. Many shops now also teach their customers particular skills and offer help with problems.

A handmade gift from a needleworker is a gift of love. For this reason, those of us who haven't the skills and do not take the time to create gifts for others feel especially inadequate when we want to reciprocate.

There is no need, however, to search far for a gift that a needle hobbyist will use and cherish. According to the kind of needlework the person enjoys, there is a wide selection of appreciated items:

Scissors—large, small embroidery, folding, or pinking shears

Thimbles—all sizes and kinds

Needles—sets of all sizes and types for the knitter, embroiderer, or crochet enthusiast

Pattern books from around the world, as well as kits containing all the necessary material, needles, and thread, along with a design and instructions

Lamps—for good lighting and magnifying for extrafine work

Bags—of all descriptions; some are specially designed to hold needlework, others can simply be beautiful, ample containers

Comfortable chair, pillow, or back rest—often a necessity for those who spend many hours doing fine work—particularly appreciated by the elderly or handicapped

Subscription to a needlework magazine

Sampler-of-the-month program—the recipient receives materials and instructions each month for making a different item depending on the program you select, for example, beginner's needlepoint, pastiche, silken sampler, German blackwork, and so on. (This could also be the perfect gift for someone who is recently confined because of illness or accident and who is a willing novice.)

A sewing machine—a wonderful gift for some brides, also for people who enjoy or want to do their own monogramming and certain embroidery stitches

Unusual scissors and thimbles usually appeal to the needleworker. It is easy to assemble an international collection of these items; but unless they are only for display, they should be well made and functional as well as decorative.

Gifts for needleworkers are easily orderd by mail. One of the best sources for a variety of types is *The World of Stitches*, 82 South St., Milford, NH 13155.

GIFTS
FOR ROCK, MINERAL, AND
GEM ENTHUSIASTS

Have you ever picked up a pebble or a small stone—just because it was bright or colorful or an unusual shape? Stones, both precious and semiprecious, delight people every day, providing a rewarding hobby, avocation, or interest for many throughout the world. Some people polish the stones, others facet them, and still others enjoy fashioning settings for them. Many people just collect them; and almost everyone enjoys receiving them.

Aside from their mineral worth, stones are valued for their beauty, color, transparency, luster, refractive index, durability, and rarity. The Mohs' scale of hardness is a very useful tool in judging stones. Only the harder minerals (7–10) retain their beautiful appearance when used in jewelry or other items.

Mohs' Scale of Hardness

1. Talc	Talc can be scratched by any other mineral.
2. Gypsum	
3. Calcite	
4. Fluorite	
5. Apatite	
6. Feldspar	
7. Quartz	Diamond will scratch any known mineral.
8. Topaz	Diamond is many times harder than corun-
9. Corundum	dum; nevertheless, if tapped at strategic
10. Diamond	points of its atomic structure, it will shatter!

Diamonds, rubies, sapphires, and emeralds, are usually considered the precious gems, and they maintain a steady demand although their per-karat price fluctuates. Various nationalities and religious groups place special value on certain stones. For example, rubies would probably cost more in India, where red is regarded with reverance. In Russia, alexandrite is especially popular because of its discovery there on the day the future Czar Alexander reached his majority; its twin colors, red and green, are the military colors of the Imperial Guard. Jade is the gem of China, where it is prized more highly than in the Western world; and our American Indians have enhanced the value of turquoise by their passion for it and their artistic use of it.

There are a few other gems, such as pearls and coral, the products of animal organisms, and amber and jet, which are evolved from tree sap and vegetation. Ivory and bone are also used in design.

Birthstones are a most welcome and appropriate birthday gift for anyone, including an infant. (See "Birthday Gifts," p. 59, for complete listing.) Specific gems and minerals are suggested for particular anniversaries. (See "Anniversary Gifts," p. 71, for complete listing.) There are countless other gifts for those who enjoy rocks and gemstones—handsome stone bookends; items of marble; clocks set into interesting rocks; various desk accessories and display pieces, such as a beautiful slice of a geode; small and large boxes carved of stone; sculpted figures; and stone vases.

When selecting a gift for a rock collector, be certain that you know what type of collection he or she is working on. Some collectors want minerals and gems from all fifty states or from every country, worldwide; others specialize in collecting certain types of jade or geodes such as Florida's agatized coral. For the lover of nature, rocks that contain the fossil remains of plants and animals can be fascinating to own—even more fun to hunt for (on a birthday excursion).

If your recipient is recently retired or is a workaholic who needs an enjoyable hobby, tumbling stones, faceting gems, and making jewelry are interesting choices. The machinery and tools for these activities are readily available. This will also help to solve your future gift giving problems.

A beautiful crystal is an elegant gift for anyone—for almost any occasion. Have you ever peeked into a basalt amygdaloid from the Syhadree Mountains near Bombay, India? You would glimpse a view of pearly white, soft fibrous crystals—a miniature world of snowflakes and snowballs lining the cavities. A breathtaking experience, and a temptation to possess. These rare, flexible crystals are called okenite.

A favorite—and very special—gift of mine is a gold tree (cast of a fire ant nest) on a base of deep blue fluorite. It is blooming with a colorful collection of beautiful gems which my father hand-faceted for me.

People enjoy owning and giving God's gifts of beauty. Rocks, minerals, and gems provide an endless source of gifts. If you desire to learn more about rocks and gems as well as their gift possibilities, *The Lapidary Journal*, published monthly in San Diego, California, is a prime source. For your gift-hunting pleasure, it lists all the mineral and gem shows held worldwide by the month and gives the place, date, and hours, as well as the sponsoring organization. At these shows you will find jewelry and other gifts from all over the world for display and for sale—also specimens of rocks and crystals that are collectible in various sizes from the perfect miniature crystals sold in small magnifying boxes for apartment dwellers to huge museum-quality specimens to entice those with huge rooms to fill and strong backs to carry them.

GIFTS
FOR TEACHERS

Although many schools, both public and private, have rules concerning gifts for teachers, there are some teachers who deserve a special thank-you. From the kindergarten teacher who stayed late with your child when your car broke down to your long-suffering dissertation director, the successful gift is more likely to be thoughtful than expensive.

The best gift for a teacher is a sincere note of appreciation—I still treasure mine from parents of seventh-graders to university juniors. Homemade fudge, cookies, bread, or preserves are always appreciated.

If the gift marks spring break or summer vacation and the teacher is planning to travel, find out where he or she is going, then supply paperback travel guides, language tapes, traveling accessories, or a tote bag.

Teachers who have worked at the school for a long time might appreciate a special book's being given to the school library in his or her name or a special teaching aid for the department or room.

Other suggestions: gift certificates to a book or music store; tickets to lectures or events; subscriptions to magazines of interest; picture frame for desk; flowers or plant; bookends or bookplates; potpourri; crystal or pottery vase; magnetized notepad; drawer or desk organizers; filled candy dish or bowl; basket of gourmet foods.

GIFTS FOR CHOCOHOLICS

For lovers and addicts of that incredible edible there is a variety of sauces and fudges to keep their ice cream properly flavored, tins of powdered rich Dutch and French cocoas to change their drinks to the right color, and chocolate newsletters and catalogs to keep them dreaming between the bites and swallows.

Chocolates come in shapes and sizes for almost every interest: dominoes, initials, teddy bears, puzzles, automobiles, animals, flower pots, dessert cups, business cards and personalized messages, Christmas tree ornaments, bottles, and portraits. How about a chocolate pizza or a can of chocolate tennis balls? Chocolates cover cherries, flowers, citrus peel, nuts, cookies, creams, mints, caramel and nougat, pineapple slices, marshmallows, bananas, molasses, apricots, orange slices, peanut butter, coffee, liqueurs, truffles, strawberries, marzipan, rum, and ants.

Chocolate lovers would enjoy a chocolate-colored baker's apron with their favorite word in twelve languages; a chocolate cookbook; a copper double-boiler with bars of bittersweet German cooking chocolate; a chocolate fondue set; chocolate-flavored coffee beans; chocolate, chocolate chip, or super-fudge-chunk ice cream; a confectioner's dipping-tool set; a chocolate mousse or truffle cake; a hot cocoa set; an ice cream maker; parfait dishes and spoons; an old poster advertising chocolate; four different types of fudge; a "the best things in life are chocolate" mug; a basket filled with different white chocolates; a piñata filled with chocolates; or a variety of chocolate bars.

For major occasions, even more spectacular chocolate gifts are available. Give someone a portrait in chocolate—his, yours, or one of each grandchild (see page 46 for source); present a handmade oak lap-desk filled with luxurious chocolates; pass Go and collect three thousand calories with a 174-piece thirty-pound chocolate Monopoly replica—edible from the Boardwalk, bills, and deeds, to the hotels, houses, and dice or send a personalized chocolate greeting card.

GIFTS
FOR DEBUTANTES

Local traditions prescribe who give gifts to debutantes. Usually they are given by family members, godparents, old family friends, and, sometimes, the deb's close friends. Gifts from the family are often family heirlooms such as a piece of jewelry or an antique dresser set. Godparents often give an engraved or monogrammed memento. Although gifts can be given at any time during the festive period, significant gifts are presented prior to her ball, sometimes at a special family dinner.

Escorts are not expected to give the deb a gift, but they may send bouquets of fresh flowers to her and her mother. An escort who is also a close friend or a regular date may wish to give a gift; if so, it should be a token and not too personal.

Some givers select gifts that she can use throughout her busy social season—an evening bag; leather gloves; a traveling makeup kit; a silver belt buckle; a fur muff or hat; a cashmere scarf, shawl, gloves, or sweater; an evening jacket; an elegant robe or dressing gown; a silk blouse; a classic leather handbag; or an evening scarf. Good jewelry is a popular present for debs; this is an occasion for classic pieces rather than costume—a ring; a gold charm; a string of pearls; bangle bracelets of gold or silver; silver or gold barrettes or combs; a diamond or heart pendant; or a gold neck chain. Other possibilities—a trip; a set or a piece of luggage; new sports equipment; monogrammed stationery; a pair of season tickets to theater, ballet, symphony, or opera; sterling compact or other purse accessories; sterling frame for her debutante photograph; or something that she needs for her apartment, dorm room, or car.

GIFTS
FOR CHILDREN

Selecting children's gifts can be both fun and frustrating. Fun because most children's toy, clothing, and book stores are a delight; and frustrating because we don't know the child's sizes or reading level, nor do we know how to choose the appropriate toy for his or her age. (See "Books as Gifts," p. 211, for information on how to choose children's books.)

Children's clothing ranges from the most functional overalls and T-shirts to silk and velvet coats and European flannel blazers from top designers. A gift of clothing—especially for very young children—can often be considered more of a gift for their parents. Grandparents, godparents, and proud aunts and uncles seem always to know the child's correct sizes. However, if you are uncertain, buy too large rather than too small—especially if the gift is not returnable.

Classic toys such as the Teddy bear, the first baby doll, fire engines, and ABC blocks will always be popular. However, electronic toys present a whole new world for the gift giver. Talking toys, whether Mother Goose or Mickey Mouse, and learning/teaching machines for everything from the alphabet to music are an entirely different category. In addition, the uninitiated toy shopper will discover that an amazing number of products are related to children's TV shows and personalities. I believe that unless the child or parent suggests a gift related to TV, you would be better advised to select something else, as the child may already have the trendy item or may not enjoy that particular show.

A child's room should be his own special place. If the child's room is new or needs to grow with the child, a beanbag chair, height chart for wall, lamp, blackboard or bulletin board, decorative or personalized waste paper basket, personalized light-plate switch, book-ends, nightlight, pencil sharpener, or desk could be a thoughtful treat. Other room ideas—shelves; a colorful quilt or blanket; posters; a jewelry box; pictures; a case to display dolls or models; a toy box; a small table and chairs; amusing pillows; a rocking chair; printed sheets; a radio or clock. Or for his or her yard, a jungle gym, swing, basketball hoop, or sandbox.

Almost all toys are gifts, and choosing one can be especially baffling. Should I buy a toy that teaches new skills? Is this toy too simple for a five-year-old? Will the child think this toy is fun? Fortunately for the consumer, some of the guesswork is eliminated by the *age label* on the toy package. Its purpose is to help the giver select an appropriate toy matched to the average abilities and interests of a child within a particular age group. Their guidelines consist of four main criteria:

• The physical ability of a child to manipulate and play with the features of a toy.

• The mental ability of a child to understand how to use a toy

• The play needs and interests applicable to various levels of child development

• The safety aspects of the toy itself

Of course, no two children are exactly alike in development, skills, or interests—so, if possible, consulting the parent is a good idea. The Toy Manufacturers of America suggest other factors to consider in toy selection: its safety, its warranty or guarantee policy, and the child's or family's lifestyle or space limitations.

The best playthings should enhance the three main areas of development, according to the TMA—thinking/cognitive skills, muscle/ motor skills, and social/creative skills—as well as develop mastery in play activity. They should also provide some degree of realism, be functional, and provide a variety of play experiences.

There are entire books that describe suitable toys for children of various ages. However, knowing the individual child's interests, needs, abilities, and limitations is the best way to select his or her gift. When possible, involve the child in the selection of the toy.

THE ART AND ETIQUETTE OF GIFT GIVING

The following suggestions are offered merely as a guide to help you select within age groups.

Under Eighteen Months

TMA's selection guide suggests choosing playthings that are:

Too large to swallow
Lightweight for handling and grasping
Without sharp points or edges
Brightly colored
Nontoxic for exploring mouths

Babies enjoy brightly colored, lightweight toys of various textures as well as sound or music makers and moving objects that enable them to "play" with their eyes.

Suggestions: soft dolls or stuffed animals; crib mobile; strings of big beads; floating tub toys; squeaky rubber toy; rattle; crib exerciser; blocks with rattles or pictures in them; simple picture books; nesting or stacking toys; push-pull toys; musical boxes; large, soft ball; simple train set; toy telephone; hammering toys; well-made, sturdy model cars and trucks; rocking horse or riding toy. Gifts other than toys: water-baby swimming class, child's portrait, step stool, or toy chest (if it has an attached vertical lid, be certain it has a spring-loaded lid support that will prevent the lid from closing shut on its own).

Wonderful and extravagant! A special rocking chair from Off Our Rocker—since children are not just miniature adults, they don't make miniature adult rockers. These are beautiful, imaginative, hand-painted, limited edition, signed chairs—choose your own colors, then personalize it with the child's name, if you like. The purchase price includes a fifty-dollar tax deductible contribution made in the buyer's name to a selected charity that promotes either research for the cure of childhood illnesses or the preservation of the environment, worldwide.

Toddlers—Eighteen Months to
Three Years

The two-year-old usually enjoys unwrapping packages more than he enjoys their contents; and he needs toys that encourage physical activity—a small indoor gym, a low tricycle, a wagon, a wading pool, a stick horse, inflatable toys, a swing set or slide, or a riding toy. He or she can also master take-apart toys, large bead stringing, and simple puzzles and games, and enjoys imitating adults with dolls, animals, play utensils and furniture, and dress-up clothing. They enjoy putting their toys into colorful tote bags, talking on their toy telephones, and playing their close-and-play record players. Other gifts for toddlers: their own junior silverware, dishes, or cup; light-switch extender; decorated and/or musical toothbrush; bath toys and bubble bath; special child's bath towel; jewelry—almost anything "just like Daddy's or Mommy's."

For special fun, try Bedtime Buddies' charming dog or dragon quilt; the pillow is the head, it has hand-puppet paws.

Preschool—Three to Six Years

Many children of this age group spend a great deal of time in the land of make-believe. Carefully selected old clothing, complete with hats and junk jewelry or ready-made cowboy, Indian, or fairy costumes; puppets; play money, food, store, or house; small-scale household or carpentry items such as brooms, hammers, tool set, tea set; miniature villages, circuses, farms, cities, doll furniture, space stations; trucks, planes, boats, and cars—all help children to imitate grown-up roles and create imaginary situations.

For less active moments, appropriate toys include construction sets; records with read-along books; coloring books; art supplies or paint sets; sewing cards; craft sticks; activity books; magnetic board with letters and numbers; space toys; Nerf® toys; Slinky®; ant farm; gerbil or bird (with parent's permission); toy clock; magnifying glass; Silly Putty®; flashlight.

Other gifts for the preschooler: slumber bag; tooth-fairy pillow; own personalized Christmas tree ornament; bank; items for starting school (lunchbox, notebook, pencil box); personalized beach towel; teaching doll with buttons, snaps, or zippers. They also would enjoy a special outing to the zoo, amusement park, children's movie, fast food restaurant, or fire station, as well as lessons in swimming, art, and tumbling.

Trends for tykes: KPVs, or kid-powered vehicles, are aerobic-conditioning and workout vehicles for kids. The Tuff Trike tricycle, Road Rower rower-race car, and Workout Wagon wagon-rower are intended for children age three and over. Also recommended are amusing cotton animal T-shirts that teach the alphabet (the A has alligators) and come with a matching coloring book—called Learning

Shirts, by Judith Weiniger. For the more traditional tot, try the Montgomery Express, a nine-car railroad set of Vermont hardwood: it reaches a length of seven and a half feet when its all-wood pieces are all linked together, a personalized brass plate is available, and surely it will become a family heirloom—from Montgomery Schoolhouse Toys.

Six to Nine Years

This age enjoys experimenting with various work worlds—dolls of firemen, fashion models, doctors, and so on are appealing gifts. They enjoy social games and sports such as kite flying; marbles; Frisbee; jacks; jump rope; pogo stick; stilts; sports equipment (football, helmet, pads; small-size basketball, backboard, hoop; baseball, bat, glove, outfit); yo-yo; bicycle and related equipment such as basket, horn, reflectors, carrier rack; roller or ice skates and socks; beach and water toys; checkers; safe darts; tether ball; bingo; dominoes; ring toss; croquet; scooter; sled; skis; junior set of golf clubs; baton and twirling lessons; tennis racket and balls.

They are interested in doing and making things—printing sets, snap-together models, more advanced construction sets, child's cookbook, apron and own omelet pan, magic set, science kits, crystal radio, microscope, art supplies, child's sewing machine, and Boy Scout craft kits are all good choices.

Children of this age group are developing their own interests. Any of the following would be appropriate: pocket calculator; walkie-talkie; inexpensive camera; scrapbook or diary; stickers; model racing car set; items with Girl Scout or Boy Scout emblems; stuffed animals; special trip to a zoo, museum, park, ball game, circus, movie, or a ride on a train, plane, boat, or balloon; addition to a doll or model collection; tools; lessons in dance, swimming, gymnastics, musical instrument, art, karate, or magic; a book of passes to a skating rink, fast food restaurant, swimming pool, or ice cream parlor; addition to bank or savings account.

They are now old enough to appreciate a watch or good simple jewelry, a fancy comb and brush set, decorative items for their rooms, video or computer game programs, collector dolls or models, record or cassette player, a globe, or a pet (ask parents first). And of course they are interested in the latest fads.

The giver is at a great advantage if he or she knows the specific skills and inclinations of the child. Model kits, hobbies, crafts, science sets, and jigsaw puzzles are popular with the older child. Various board, card, and electronic games help develop social skills, and dramatic plays—with puppets, marionettes, costumes, and props—sometimes become complete productions. Magazine subscriptions relating to the child's interest can be an excellent choice—and they do not necessarily have to be children's magazines. (A subscription to *Popular Mechanics* for a nine-year-old mechanically inclined grandson was a wonderful success and gave him and his interest instant adult status.) Tuition for a class or lessons, Little League outfit or equipment, a leotard, shoes, or costume for dance or gymnastics, a public library card, a visit to a museum—all are related to the child's special needs or interests.

Other appropriate gifts: wall posters; fun T-shirts or sweat shirts; personalized jewelry; wallet or key ring; locked box for treasures; sleeping bag; sunglasses; model train set; clock-radio; records or tapes.

A special treat—an Earth-in-Space globe from the Museum Shop at the American Museum of Natural History, New York. Or send him or her to cooking camp near Bordeaux, France; extra benefits—he or she will return to prepare you an authentic four-course French meal and, hopefully, have learned to speak the language.

Two free pamphlets—*The ABC's of Toys and Play* and *Learning About Labels*—will give you more comprehensive consumer information about toys, toy selection, and safety tips. To order, send a postcard with name, address, and zip code to Toy Booklets, P.O. Box 866, Madison Square Station, New York, NY 10159.

All children love extra money. For a birthday, or a holiday, cash or a check is an entirely suitable gift. And if you don't see the child often and you know little about his or her interests and lifestyle, money would be a wise choice.

Almost all ages would cherish a special birthday gift of a clown, magician, Walt Disney character, balloon person, or rented video for his or her birthday party.

TMA's Toy-Buying Tips for Adults

There are over 150,000 toy industry products on the market. They range in price from under one dollar and many cost less than fifteen dollars! According to the U.S. Department of Labor, toy industry retail prices have never kept up with inflation and are lower than prices for other consumer goods. *Many* items such as craft kits, construction sets, puzzles, and board, card, and video games can be enjoyed by the whole family and are inexpensive alternatives to the high cost of family entertainment outings. The following are tips from TMA, the industry trade association:

- Before buying toys, check packages for recommended age *guidelines* and special instructions, keeping in mind the age, level of development, and interests of the person for whom the toy is intended. Look for the words *nontoxic; flame retardant; flame resistant; washable; hygienic*; and, on electrical items, *U.L. Approved* (for Underwriters Laboratories). *Discard all wrappings immediately.*

- When in doubt, check with parents or older siblings about such things as possible duplication of toys, the child's preferences, and the *total* play environment, i.e., younger siblings, space limitations, and so on.

- Consider the cost of power sources and accessories to the recipient's family.

- Buy from a reputable store and make sure the manufacturer's name and address is on the box, in case you have any questions. Ask a salesperson if there is a demonstration model of an unfamiliar product.

- Comparison shop from your home by reviewing local print and broadcast advertisements. Check for *special promotions* and *rebates* offered by manufacturers and retailers. Many stores will lower prices on popular toys, selling these items as *"loss leaders"* to attract customers. When shopping *throughout the year*, check toy departments for unadvertised specials and *stockpile* these products as you would for other consumer products! Store them and use for *year-round gift-giving* for "children of all ages," such as graduations, Valentine's Day, Easter, Mother's and Father's Days, anniversaries, and so on. Also, many people give inexpensive toy industry products such as stickers, clay, balls, pens and pencils, and so on, as nonedible, tamper-proof Halloween treats.

- S-t-r-e-t-c-h your dollars by purchasing "classics," i.e., products that have been available for several years and are usually less expensive than newer items.

- Consider multipurpose playthings such as shape sorters that are also water toys; construction sets that build push-pull toys; or ride-ons that also serve as storage units.

GIFTS
FOR LEFT-HANDED
PEOPLE

When all other gift suggestions fail, find out if your recipient is a lefty. After years of having to adjust to a right-handed world, they appreciate not having to cut with an upside-down scissors, peel vegetables backward, or break watch springs by mistakenly winding them the wrong way. When teaching in China, I purchased a small wind-up alarm clock that I discovered wound in the opposite direction from Western clocks. I never did remember to turn it the right way and was relieved to return to its Western counterparts; one of my left-handed friends, however, was overjoyed to receive it.

Left-handed shops and catalogs as well as some department and specialty stores carry an assortment of items with openings or handles reversed or altered for the use of lefties. Some examples: numerous kitchen tools including a serrated knife, vegetable peeler, can opener, and ice cream scoop; playing cards with numbers in all four corners; a watch that winds on the left; a camera with controls on opposite side; sports equipment such as catcher's mitt, archery bows, and golf clubs; notebooks bound on the right; cups and mugs with handles on the right; special musical instruments; kitchen and pinking shears; carpentry tools; and manuals for teaching lefties various skills.

For a more humorous token, give lefty bumper stickers, calendars, posters, stationery, T-shirts, or badges.

FOR
CHILDREN
ONLY

F inding the right gift for the right person is difficult and confusing—even knowing where to go is not easy. In fact, it's so hard that I've written this entire book to help adults with their gift problems.

The best gifts are often the treasures that you find, the presents you make, and the special things you do for someone else. My favorite gifts from children—my own and others'—are things that could not be purchased in any store in the world. I remember especially a prehistoric-appearing elephant that my son sculpted from clay when he was about four or five years old, and a lovely small garnet (dark reddish pebble) that he carefully pried out of a rock in the mountains. My son is twenty-two and I still have them both. The nicest Mother's Day I can remember began with a lovely breakfast in bed, prepared, served, and cleaned up by my children when they were quite small. My daughter's photographic designs from her first photography classes last year hang in my den; and I couldn't forget the gift of nieces who helped me with some of the filing and research for this book.

When we love people a lot, we want to give them the whole world—anything they want. Unfortunately, this is not possible. It is possible to give someone you love a small piece of the earth— flowers, a pretty stone, seashells, dried grasses, colored leaves, even a ladybug from the garden. Remember, however, that your mother may have to adjust to—maybe even refuse—some things that you think are wonderful. For example, my cats, Rangoon and Tigger, bring me their nicest gifts—lizards, snakes, and chameleons, and once a very frightened tiny bunny—and place them in the middle of my bed. I'm not always grateful for these gifts.

Of course, you know that you can make things. You've done lots of that in school. You can paint and draw, and you design interesting gifts sometimes for Mother's Day and Father's Day. So we won't talk about that. I'll just leave making gifts to your own imagination.

In my family we often give "good for" cards—meaning this is good for one car wash, a closet cleaning, five planned and cooked meals, doing the dishes or clearing the table for a certain period of time, weeding the garden, chopping wood, taking out the garbage, walking someone's dog, visiting a sick or elderly person each week, keeping our room clean, or any of a number of other things that this person might especially appreciate.

But sometimes we do need to buy gifts.

Be sure that your parents are clear about how much money you have to spend for a gift or gifts. If you are given one amount for several presents, you may wish to ask someone to help you decide how much to spend for each person on your list.

The first thing is to think about the person for whom you're buying the gift. For example, does he or she like to read? have any hobbies? play any sports? enjoy watching television? work in the garden? cook a lot? have a desk in an office? like to entertain and have company over? enjoy funny jokes? play games? belong to a special club or organization? love certain foods?

As parents and other adults are usually the most difficult people to buy for, let's start with them. If you want to spend more time with the adult, buy a gift that you can enjoy together—a model plane, car, or boat kit that you can work on; gift certificates for ice cream cones or hamburgers; a game, puzzle, or magic trick; a book you would both enjoy; tickets to a school or sports event; or a kite.

Now that you've thought about the person, let me give some ideas about gifts to get you started thinking:

If he or she likes to read, magazines or magazine subscriptions of interest are wonderful gifts. Almost every magazine has a tear-out section for ordering a subscription. There are paperback books on every subject. Ask the salesperson or your school librarian for suggestions. Bookmarks, bookends (you can make these yourself), highlighter pens, or a tiny light that clips onto a book might also be good ideas.

THE ART AND ETIQUETTE OF GIFT GIVING

If he or she has hobbies, even the most exotic hobby requires certain important small items. For sewers: small scissors, pretty pin cushions, fancy thimbles. For handypersons: a pocket tool kit, tape measure, carpenter's pencils, tapes, multihead screwdriver.

If he or she plays sports, the list is endless. For the golfer: tees, golf gloves, golf hat, a ball and tee pouch that attaches to a belt, a score-card holder, or a book of golf cartoons or jokes. For the tennis player: sweat band, wrist band, tennis hat, tin of good balls, book about tennis or favorite tennis stars, tickets to tennis match, sweat socks, or an invitation to play a game with you.

If he or she enjoys staying at home watching television, let's make the recipient comfortable. How about warm slippers, a TV tray, a large mug or special glass for his or her favorite beverage, a supply of munchies, a neck pillow, a large ashtray, a decorative candle, a box of candy, a footstool, or a subscription to *TV Guide*?

If he or she enjoys working in the garden, make it easier for him or her. Give garden gloves, a nice basket for picking vegetables or flowers, garden scissors, a knee pad for weeding, packets of seeds (especially nice to give at Christmas when it's cold), row markers, bedding plants, fertilizer for indoor plants, pots or small vases, a garden catalog, weeder, garden tools, or a sprinkling can. Other suggestions: tomato stakes with a tomato plant; small tree, plant, or bush for a new yard; some bulbs for outside or for forcing inside; one amaryllis bulb; a small cactus plant.

If he or she enjoys cooking, there are lots of fun things to buy: a garlic press; a pineapple corer; a cherry pitter; a lemon-wedge squeezer; a meat or candy thermometer; peelers; a good paring or bread knife; a soufflé dish; a baster; a pastry brush; cookie cutters (choose some you like); a butter curler; a hamburger press; a bagel slicer; corn holders; an apron; a chef's hat; a cookbook; a calendar with beautiful place settings or food displays; a magnetized pad to keep the shopping list on refrigerator; decorative magnets; or spices and herbs.

If he or she has an office desk, the nicest gift is your picture, maybe in a frame. Other suggestions: a pencil holder; a paper weight; a small vase; a mug or glass; a small box for holding paper clips, rubber bands, and so on; drawer organizers; a thermos bottle or pitcher; an infuser to heat water; a collection of instant soups, teas, or coffees; a nice pen or mechanical pencil; a photo rotary file; a paperback thesaurus or dictionary; a small, easy-to-care-for plant; flowers or special cookies to take to the office the morning of his or her birthday.

If he or she enjoys entertaining company, there are many small touches that add to the pleasure: candles; napkins (paper or cloth, cocktail size or larger); a vase or candy dish; salt and pepper shakers or a pepper grinder or salt mill; a nice tray; a container of fancy toothpicks; cheese markers; a cheese board and/or cheese knife; a serving basket; fruit knives; special coffee or tea; swizzle sticks; ice tongs; a butter dish; WELCOME or other type of door mat; candle holders; a mustard jar; or vinegar and oil bottles.

If he or she enjoys jokes or likes to play games: magic tricks; difficult puzzles; crossword puzzle book; jigsaw puzzle; jokes, such as imitation ants or fake sandwiches; family board games like Scrabble, Monopoly, Yahtzee, Trivial Pursuit; or a book of jokes or tricks.

If he or she belongs to a special club or organization that is important to him or her, you may be able to purchase certain items with the organization's emblem or logo on them, such as ties, hats, belt buckles, mugs, pins, tie tacs, picture frames, change purses, scarves, and so forth. You could also find books about the subject or organization.

If he or she loves certain foods (and who doesn't?), give a special treat. When my daughter was little she would use part of her allowance to buy me a supply of my favorite junk-candy—of course, then she could join me in eating it! So, consider whether this person would like a special jar of mustard; a can of popcorn; lots of corn chips and dip; a DoveBar (my favorite); an ice cream cone or a favorite ice cream; fudge; a juicy steak; a can of peanuts; a bag of pistachio nuts; a jar of pecans; chocolate chip cookies; fresh fruit like strawberries or raspberries; diet foods; health food bread or muffins; or something he or she enjoys but doesn't eat because no one else in the family will eat it—like anchovies or smoked oysters.

Think along the same lines when looking for gifts for your friends. Often you already know what they would like because you want one too. Don't forget that you can give your friends tickets to sports events or concerts, magazine subscriptions, museum memberships, gift certificates or tickets for amusement parks, hamburgers, bookstores or music stores, and "good-for" cards.

Parents are usually pretty much help when it comes to presents for your brothers and sisters. Try to give them something that they will enjoy rather than something you would like to have, unless it's something that you can help a younger brother or sister with.

You can find the gifts listed here and many others at your local grocery store, hardware store, drugstore, five-and-ten-cents store, or bookstore. For Mother's Day, a trip to the bakery might produce a large chocolate chip cookie that you could talk the baker into putting a frosting "M" on.

Finding, making, and buying gifts can be fun; but the most enjoyment comes from giving someone something that he or she really likes. It makes you feel good.

Because I'm a parent I can't resist telling you always to thank people for gifts that they give you—either in person, on the telephone, or in a note or letter. Even if the gift is not your favorite or even if you dislike it, remember that the person who gave it was trying to select something that you would like. As you will discover, gift givers are not always successful.

To Parents

Dr. Spock tells us that by the time children are around the age of three, their feelings of enjoyment and affection toward other children have developed sufficiently for them to want to share.

Children who live in a thoughtful, caring environment will be able to give and receive with grace. If the job of the child is to learn to live happily in today's society, he should also learn something about consumerism in a positive way. There are a number of stores, schools, communities, and other organizations throughout the country that help children shop at holiday time. The experience is made as pleasant as possible, and some programs emphasize the good feelings one receives from the act of giving. One such program, called Santa's Secret Shop, offers teacher workshops and lesson plans along with good-quality, useful merchandise that ranges in price from fifteen cents to fifteen dollars.

PART EIGHT

PRESENTATION

Do you want your gift to say something before it's opened? Do you want your gift to appear to be something it's not? Do you want the packaging and giving of your gift to enhance the gift itself, or to display the gift in all its splendor?

Presentation is a gift's first message, and thus the giver's as well. Our feelings are reflected in the way we wrap and bestow our gift. Its presentation sets the tone, conveys how the giver views the recipient, reflects the giver's taste and mood, and makes promises about the contents.

There is an increasing regard for quality products that are distinctive and well made. People seem to be more concerned about what they're wrapping with. It's the growing realization that the packaging of a gift says something about you. And there are many ways to say it!

SIGNATURE
WRAPPING

Many givers have made their gifts recognizable through "signature" wrapping. Official gifts from the White House and the State Department are formally and elegantly wrapped in white or gold foil paper embossed with the Great Seal. One friend wraps all her gifts in shiny white-on-white patterned paper and ties them with white and silver ribbon. If the recipient is a woman, she often adds a small cluster of silk violets; if a man, acorns or leaves sprayed with silver. A more frivolous and flexible giver may use a polka-dot paper with a striped ribbon; a combination like this permits almost unlimited color combinations as well as a variety of sizes of dots and stripes. Newspaper works well for some people's more casual gift giving situations: one acquaintance enjoys selecting the appropriate section for each recipient—sports pages, comics, gardening, and so forth. Many givers simply have their names or initials printed on ribbon, which they use on any type of wrapping. Gift wrapping can be another way of making a statement, visually expressing your own taste, preferences, and sense of color and design. At the same time, once you have determined your mode of wrap, you will have avoided some future decision making and will always be prepared because you will be able to buy your supplies in quantity.

TRADITIONAL
JAPANESE PACKAGING

For me, the most aesthetically perfect packaging is seen in the vanishing art of traditional Japanese packaging—one form of Japan's cultural heritage. The use of natural materials, the obvious relationship between use and shape as well as between hand and material, the refined artistic sensibilities, the wisdom of their utilitarian wrappings, the ability to create beauty from the simplest natural elements—all became manifestations of the Japanese package as a work of art. Wrapping eggs in rice straw, dried fish in rope, oak leaves around rice cakes, and magnolia leaves around bean curd enhance the freshness and natural textures of these gifts; and the patience and skill applied to the wrapping of a simple object in a square of cloth demonstrate consideration for others. Remnants of the art can still be found in Japan—particularly in Kyōto, where confectionary comes packaged in sections of bamboo or packed in baskets of woven bamboo strips or wrapped and tied in imitation of the packs carried by oldtime travelers in Japan. Examples of this packaging can be enjoyed in Hideyuki Oka's entrancing book *How to Wrap Five More Eggs* (Weatherhill, New York and Tokyo, 1982).

We are no longer able to take the time and care to perform wrapping and packaging as a ritual. However, there are times when you want your gift to appear festive, artistic, elegant, or suited especially to the occasion. Whatever your choice, the gift should always look inviting.

STORE WRAPS

Many stores have their own elegant trademark wrapping that automatically bespeaks the treasured contents. Bergdorf Goodman in New York uses silver boxes with its name in unobtrusive purple letters in the middle of the cover. Last Christmas one of BG's employees added silk velvet purple ribbons to the silver gift boxes that he gave to his friends. Gucci's classic tan box with red and green stripes on each side as well as their beautiful shopping bags automatically convey a certain sense of quality. The gold of Godiva, the robin's egg blue of Tiffany's, the sienna and brown of Hermès, and the perfect Cartier box and ribbon are recognized by recipients worldwide.

Many travelers and urban people who take buses or taxis carry their gifts from one locale to another in "status" shopping bags. Despite the fact that these people will tell you that they just "love the design," in these situations rarely is a bag just a bag. Foreign bags and museum bags are just as important as those from recognized stores.

I must admit that—totally lacking the skill, coordination, and patience required to measure and cut wrapping paper, fold neat corners, and tie bows—I have stood in department store lines waiting for dexterous high school students to wrap my packages. And many stores these days have lovely wraps that they change to reflect a new theme or image or to create a certain fashion statement. The wrappings of local department stores and boutiques convey messages about their contents, quality, and—often—price to people in each city. Neiman-Marcus was the first department store to offer the giver a choice of creative gift wraps.

Susan Crane, one of the most innovative custom design houses for store papers, produces distinctive quality papers that range from parchment to four- or five-color lithographs from original artwork. Neiman-Marcus's unusual signature wraps based on various cities, such as the skyline of San Francisco, and Bloomingdale's Statue of Liberty paper, are good examples. Many specialty stores have developed unique designs: one of my dinner guests last night brought a package so lovely I was reluctant to open it—a small shiny white paper bag trimmed with pink and white bows and streamers and a pink, white, and green seal. It was from Manuel Canovas of Paris.

CONTAINERS AS PACKAGING

Sooner or later, however, each of us is confronted with an unwrapped gift that needs appropriate covering and presentation. One of my solutions has been to search out containers so delightful, beautiful, clever, or utilitarian that no other wrapping is needed. Baskets are the most versatile containers. They can be found in almost any shape or size you require in oriental stores, houseware departments, and mail-order catalogs, and many are inexpensive. They can be quickly stained or sprayed with colored or metallic paints, as can wood-slotted mushroom or berry boxes. Baskets can also be lined with colorful tissue paper, calico, or any number of other materials.

Many plant containers can become the perfect packaging for other objects; for example, attractive cachepots, Mexican, Indian, and Italian pottery, various glazed and unglazed hand-thrown pots, and traditional Japanese-style receptacles.

Certain presents can be appropriately placed in laundry bags or tied in a silk or cotton scarf. At houseware and five-and-dime stores you can purchase handsome, inexpensive glass bowls, teapots, bottles, and other vessels. Or use a costly crystal decanter, champagne glass, martini pitcher, or caviar holder. These see-throughs, including clear and colorful plastic containers, can be handsomely stuffed with tissue. Small gifts can be cached in one of your collection of boxes—china, tin, glass, fabric-covered, ceramic, brass, or wood. Tool boxes, buckets, and watering cans can be used to hold their related implements.

It is often difficult to hide the identity of a plant gift; so you enhance it by placing it in an interesting and appropriate container. Shells, glass bowls, grape vine baskets, decorative straw, fiber, metal waste baskets, or bird cages of bamboo or reed (wonderful for ferns and trailing plants)—all can be used to enrich your plant's appearance. The proper pot—one that matches your plant in scale, shape, color, and design—will double its attractions. If your container has no drainage, place the plant in a pot which does have drainage before placing it into the decorative container. If possible, remove the shiny paper from a commercial plant before giving as a gift. These wrappings often detract from the beauty of the plant. Repotting in a ceramic pot and adding a saucer is always an improvement.

BASIC
AND CREATIVE
GIFT WRAPPING

Appealing wrappings can be very simple or exceedingly lavish. Most gifts can be fitted into two basic shapes—the cube and the cylinder or sphere. These may range from the smallest (matchbox, golf ball) to the most gigantic (boxcar, hot air balloon). One can learn to measure, fold, and tape to cover these shapes. The crispest rectangles are achieved by carefully folding and mitering the corners and by using double-stick tape. Cylinders can be wrapped like the snappers used for children's party favors, sleekly around the container with accordion folded ends (use only lightweight papers, such as tissue or crepe for this), or rolled like a croissant with the paper cut diagonally.

If you are adept with wrapping paper, layers of colored or white tissue paper always look crisp and inviting—both inside and outside the package. You can stamp, stencil, and marbleize your own papers. Children often enjoy making their own wrappings with a potato or block print.

There are several excellent books that offer suggestions, hints, and step-by-step descriptions for wrapping techniques and ways to enhance packages. Following the instructions, the enterprising wrapper can design and decorate packages to resemble sneakers, mailboxes, bookworms, ice cream sodas, bees, turtles, diapers, hobo packs, buses, clowns, aprons, or planets. One can learn how to use old vitamin jars, cardboard tubes, milk cartons, and flower pots for the

THE ART AND ETIQUETTE OF GIFT GIVING

basic shapes, then embellish with anything from lace and brown paper bags to popsicle sticks and pasta. Paper doilies, sequins, notary seals, even cake decorations can easily be glued to any type of wrapping. An excellent book that covers all the basics is *The Art of Gift Wrapping* by Jane Cornell; and authors Sandra Roth and Beverly Bieker demonstrate over one hundred imaginative wrapping ideas for all occasions in *Creative Gift Wrapping*.

Nonetheless, most of us have been doing our own rather utilitarian and mundane wrapping with gift wrap we purchase—usually at the last minute and with very little thought. Often the consequence is that the finished product conveys the message that the giver was preoccupied or in a hurry to find a gift, when in truth the giver spent much time selecting the appropriate gift for the occasion and the individual.

AVAILABLE
GIFT WRAPS

F ortunately for us, in the last few years gift wrap manufacturers have started to offer selections to match every personal
mood or lifestyle statement. The exciting and dramatic expansion of
designs and colors presents us with an astonishing range of choice
with which we should be familiar. Even ribbons are printed or woven
with teddy bears, ducks, Santas, stripes, hearts, rainbows, and messages. Although the classic patterns remain popular, most gift wrap
companies produce new collections several times a year. Interestingly,
these new designs follow the current fashions in both clothing and
home furnishings: the popularity of chintz for overstuffed chairs and
the increased use of men's-wear fabrics such as houndstooth checks
and herringbone patterns in women's clothing are reflected in the
same season's wrapping papers and ribbons. Currently, we can see
trends such as the fashion for passementerie reflected in Florentine
papers and gilded tassels, as well as high-tech in today's sleek, chic,
and shiny wraps.

In addition to being aware of the many choices available, you
should know which companies produce the types of gift wrap that
best express your lifestyle, your taste, and your personality. Some
firms specialize in a particular type of pattern. Stephen Lawrence,
for example, which targets the upscale, trend-setting market, specializes in geometric patterns. Company spokesperson Susan Rosenthal
predicts that these sometimes intricate patterns will become even

more popular in the next few years, along with the use of vivid, primary colors for most festive occasions. Coordinated printed ribbon completes the look. Contempo designs papers to appeal specifically to the fashionable. They commission the grapics of well-known artists such as Marimekko and Mary Quant and the work of modern wallpaper and upholstery designers. Many of their papers have a clay coating that give them deeper color and a shiny effect. From their recent collections such as "Lite-Hearts"™, which uses joyful muppets, bears, clowns—even numbers—Mylar paper with matte ink overlay, to romantic patterns of lace and roses, each wrap is intended to help you create a special mood for your gift presentation.

One company—WhimZdoodle, Ltd.—specializes in charming, whimsical papers and gift bags that are intentionally produced in very limited runs. These amusing papers can be found in selected gift shops, stationery stores, and museum gift shops.

Hallmark manufactures a great variety of styles and a broad range of colors and patterns. They, too, see more and more emphasis on a sophisticated, creative look. Their high-gloss solid colors give more leeway for one's own combinations and decorations. At the same time they continue to produce high-quality classics and many papers designed for specific groups such as children and for occasions such as weddings and birthdays. Hallmark's flat wrap packages, which include paper with coordinated ribbon and card, remain very popular with those who need gift wrap for individual occasions. Many people are more comfortable with a gift wrap that says "Happy Birthday" or "Bon Voyage."

An extraordinary wrap, which has been popular in Europe for some time, has recently been introduced in the United States by American Greetings. Metalized film, which has been printed with a design, results in a very shiny, soft material, making a bright and vibrant package. A Jillson and Roberts top seller is "Alligator Paper," in several colors with a texture that resembles the hide.

Also look in the next few years for PaperPlains, a young design firm, which now offers to major department stores a refreshing variety of all-occasion papers from stylish trompe l'oeil marble patterns to abstracted honeybees traversing a coral-colored sky. They soon plan to sell rolls under the private labels of select stores and eventually under their own label.

American manufacturers see some obvious trends in the immediate future. First, more convenience wraps and newer types of presentation vehicles—the decorated gift box, handled bags to hold unusual shapes, more small gift bags, and hard-handled containers.

The purpose is to make the gift wrapping process as effortless as possible, but keep the package stylish—lack of manual dexterity is no longer an excuse for presenting a poorly wrapped gift. Glossy gift totes from Gaylord specialties, Jillson and Roberts's "Wizard of Oz" tote bags, Collector's Gallery's decorated foil boxes stuffed with coordinating tissue, and Stribbons's "Complete Gift Box Ensemble" with its gift card and snap-on package decorations all make wrapping quicker and easier.

Another major trend is toward papers that allow more self-expression and individualized looks; people are demanding more choices and enjoy finding and using wraps in ways that reflect themselves. There is also an increasing demand for more elegant papers—special lavish foils and pearlescent wraps are being designed. For 1985 Christmas wrappers, Harry N. Abrams, Inc., produced the first two volumes of a new series of books called "Giftwraps by Artists." *Vienna Style* and *William Morris* each contain a brief history of the featured designer or school, in addition to striking designs that fold out into sheets of wonderful and unique wrapping paper. Abrams has continued this series.

The popularity of the business gift in many new situations has created a market for more tailored, subdued papers that are appropriate for both men and women and that look neither too masculine nor too feminine. There are still the classics and the perennial favorites—the popular stripes, hearts, and anything with a rainbow theme. But we seem to be getting away from symbolism; for instance, givers are choosing pretty pastel papers for bridal showers rather than wrap that specifies "For Your Wedding" or that pictures a bride and groom.

Although there are many lovely and unusual gift wraps used throughout the world, there are not very many imported gift wraps available to the American consumer. Some interesting and opulent-looking papers are shipped here from Italy, and Danish designs such as florals can be found in specialty stores throughout the country. I enjoy using papers that I find in other parts of the world. My favorite papers came from Nairobi—vivid, sweeping scenes of the African plains complete with wild animals; a repeated pattern of a stark black plane tree on a pale yellow background; a content pride of lions; and a very long-necked, quizzical giraffe. It's the sort of paper you save forever for that "special occasion" that seems never to come because you don't really want to give up the paper. Foreign gift wraps and cards are fun to collect and easy to pack: the perfect way to present your mementos and souvenirs to friends (rather than in a duty-free airport bag), and an inexpensive reminder of your trips.

Clearly, today's wide range of high-quality commercial gift wraps with sophisticated designs and easy-to-use materials puts the creation of attractive, interesting packages within everyone's reach.

Gift Wrapping Tips

- Tie or place a small related gift on the outside of a package. This means extra fun for children and a more distinctive gift for adults and can range from barrettes, stickpins, perfume, kitchen gadgets, or tiny sachets for women, to corkscrews, seed packets, novelty soaps, cologne, wristbands, or pocket diaries for men.

- Select the correct weight of paper for the package and the way you wish to wrap it: for example, it is difficult to wrap a very small package in heavy paper.

- Choose pattern size to correspond with package size: large, bold patterns belong on large packages.

- Develop your own personal way of wrapping—use of color, type or design of paper or ribbon, and use of unusual or special containers.

- Remember that a few words of personal sentiment are more appreciated than merely the signing of your name.

- Use different permanent or useful containers—baskets, bowls—or make one by covering a box with self-stick paper, plastic, or fabric.

- Tie fresh herbs, cinnamon sticks, feathers, or a fresh flower onto a package.

- Decorate or enhance very large gifts by adding festive streamers or ribbons.

- Wrap with go-togethers; for instance, personalized stationery in a monogrammed folder, a baby doll in a cradle or doll's truck, or pajamas inside a pillowcase.

- Use small gifts as gift tags or cards—you can label your message on luggage tags, giant lollipops, fans, bookmarks, key rings, address books, or in fortune cookies (carefully pull out the fortune and replace it with your own wish).

GIFT CARDS

Usually your reason for giving a gift is revealed in the message that your card communicates. The American public is spending about $3.4 billion a year on a very wide variety of greeting cards. Hallmark (40 percent of market), American Greetings (30 percent), and Gibson Greetings (10 percent) are seriously threatened by "alternative" cards.

Experts say that greeting cards mirror social changes more accurately and quickly than almost any other product. Thus, they now reflect modern trends such as fitness awareness, high technology, single-parent families, and a work force of executive women. From whimsical to goofy to specialized to risqué, these new commercial messages are used not just to remember important traditional occasions but for personal communication—often with a gift. American consumers, who exchanged more than 7 billion cards last year, should be aware of the range of card styles and messages that can give eloquent voice to the emotions and occasions of every segment of the population. It seems there is a card for every occasion—a second marriage, a successful diet, a new office, retirement, an adoption, kids getting braces . . . even a divorce.

Paper Moon Graphics was one of the first high-quality "alternative" card companies to leave the inside blank for people to write their own messages. The quality of art provides an additional reason to buy these cards. Maine Line, which produces humorous cards "for women, by women," represents the variety and complexities of modern women's attitudes and emotions. Editions Limited presents silk-screened images from famous artists such as Henri Matisse; Christian cards are designed by Paramount and by Jonathan and David, whose "Precious Moments" line includes appropriate Bible verses; many companies produce enticing animals or licensed Disney and other familiar creatures. Spanish cards for the growing Hispanic community and cards such as Hourglass Editions "Elderberries," which view senior citizens in a positive, caring light, address specific markets. Some card companies span the occasions with a special look—Curtis Swann's are elegantly embossed; and Manifestations, Inc., uses a metallic medium to create optical-illusionary art on their cards.

When art and captions aren't quite enough, some companies add other elements. You can personalize your card by inserting your own photograph into the picture frame Collector's Gallery has designed into their card. And some greeting cards are gifts in themselves: Sweetstop gives greetings in an apothecary jar filled with candies—your message carried by a pompom character; the Piano Card features a keyboard and the numbers to play a specific tune; a Valentine may come with its own sachet or candy; a card can also be a decorative paper sculpture; and the Great Northwestern Greeting Seed Company card encloses a natural ingredient in a small pouch—for example, for a birth congratulation, baby's-breath seeds with planting instructions.

Not every gift needs a memorable card. However, just about everyone who receives an unforgettable card keeps it for a while—a further reminder of your special thoughtfulness.

GIFT
PRESENTATIONS

Gift presentation involves more than the wrapping of a gift. Where, how, when, and under what circumstances a gift is given can be equally important. A truly notable example: The story of the legendary Trojan Horse has many elements of presentation including surprise. The Greeks had laid siege to Troy for ten years. Unable to take the city, Ulysses ordered that a huge wooden horse be built. After hiding Greek soldiers inside the horse and leaving it right outside the walls of Troy, the rest of the Greeks then pretended to sail away. The curious Trojans dragged the horse into the city. That night, the Greeks inside the horse opened the city gates to let the rest of their army in.

In gift presentation, **where** often means deciding whether the gift should be given in front of others. Is it quite personal? Is it a gag gift that is more fun when enjoyed by many? Would opening it in front of others please or embarrass the recipient? Some gifts, such as many business gifts, are better sent than delivered in person.

There are certain occasions, of course, where the setting and ambience are predetermined—Christmas morning around the Christmas tree. When you do choose a setting, it should relate to both the recipient and the occasion—a romantic restaurant, a zoo, an airplane, a party, a meadow, and so on.

How includes the wrapping, the card, and what you say when you offer the gift, as well as your attitude toward both the recipient and the gift. Too often, people who present gifts—whether at a large company retirement party or at an anniversary dinner for close friends—do not take time to think about the meaning of the occasion and the significance of the gift. The result is a very weak sentence or two about a "jolly good fellow" or, worse, someone's "better half."

When is usually dictated by outside factors—an event such as a holiday or a birthday party. For some people the surprise element can be very exciting—surprise parties, surprise gifts, or surprise in presentation, such as a special piece of jewelry in the centerpiece or dessert, or a child's gift under his pillow, with his favorite teddy, or in the back of his miniature red pickup truck. But do remember that there are people who dislike surprises and who would be most uncomfortable and unhappy with an unanticipated party or an unexpectedly generous gift.

In my business I occasionally have the opportunity to design really exciting presentations. Several years ago I was consulted by a Texas gentleman who wanted to give his wife a very distinctive birthday present. I learned that she decorated her home and dressed primarily in the color white and that he wanted to give her a car. On the afternoon of her birthday she was to go with a friend to their box at the football stadium to make some arrangements for the game the next day. When she arrived at the box, she found many of her friends and a beautifully catered lunch. The billboard flashed happy-birthday messages to her; music played over the loudspeaker; a custom-built white sports convertible was driven to the middle of the field. Wrapped in a gigantic white ribbon, it was driven by a handsome young man in white livery. The trunk was opened to display matching gold-monogrammed white leather luggage, which contained some fashionable clothing. Up in the box, her husband presented her with white driving goggles, gloves, and the key case.

For most of us, of course, this is fantasy; and in this instance, both the gift and the presentation were singular and dramatic.

Not every gift lends itself to an unusual or special presentation; but even the most modest gift can be enhanced with an interesting or attractive appearance. Every family has its share of young children who eagerly anticipate the semiannual visits of gift-bearing grandparents and favorite aunts and uncles. One of my biggest gift successes was the presentation of a used and rather worn-looking brown paper lunch bag to a six-year-old nephew who was surely expecting something more giftlike. Peering inside, he could see a sandwich bag containing a sandwich (an unusual offering to take from coast to coast). With a quick glance at his mother, a forced smile, and a deep sigh, he reached in to pull out an artificial bologna sandwich, which had a pad of colored paper inside. The sandwich went with him— wrapped in the same disguise—to his Indian Guide campout that weekend and then visited the first grade. Who knows how many six-year-olds almost ate paper bologna that week?

APPENDICES

SENDING GIFTS

There are many ways to get a gift from one place to another. Each requires certain containers, cushioning, sealing, addressing, and insurance; and each has different size and weight limitations.

General Tips for Preparing Your Packages

- Wrap and seal all packages securely: do not use household cellophane tape or masking tape. Nylon filament, strapping, waterproof, or pressure-sensitive tapes are acceptable.

- Make sure the contents are compatible with the container used: fiberboard boxes are best for anything over ten pounds. Liquid items should be placed into special, double, leakproof containers.

- Books, some items of clothing, and small packages fit into padded bags that can be purchased in various sizes at your local post office. Seal with staples and tape.

- Fragile items can be wrapped with plastic or padding; if you do not have Styrofoam beads or popcorn, pack newspaper around the contents.

- Avoid using string or rope, as it could snag on automatic sorting equipment.

- Insure your packages.

- Use permanent markers or typed labels. If you write in ink, cover the address with transparent tape so that it will not smear. Enclose an additional label, including return address, *inside* the package.

- Be sure to include the zip code.

To give you an idea of area coverage, requirements, and rates, following is some information about a few of the many services that can deliver your package.

United States Postal Service

The United States Postal Service has Express Mail service—next-day service—that is available 7 days a week, 365 days a year, for mailable items up to 70 pounds in weight and 108 inches in combined length and girth. Flat rates: up to 2 pounds, $10.75; over 2 pounds and up to 5 pounds, $12.85; 6-to-70-pound rates vary by weight and distance.

If your gift isn't already late, first-class or fourth-class mail will get there, too.

Parcel post service is available to most countries. Registration is available to all countries except Cambodia and North Korea. Country restrictions or prohibitions appear in the "Individual Country" listings of the *International Mail Manual*. Inquire at your local post office, as failure to investigate these limitations before mailing may result in seizure of packages at the country of address.

United Parcel Service

UPS delivers to any address throughout the forty-eight contiguous states, plus all points in Hawaii and Puerto Rico. You can send your packages by Next Day Air "committed morning delivery" (for more than fifty-four thousand communities), 2nd Day Air, or their regular service.

Federal Express

Federal Express offers overnight door-to-door services to and from thousands of communities across the United States, Puerto Rico, and Canada. Pickups in most areas are made Monday through

Saturday, with delivery scheduled the next business day. They will also provide different types of shipping containers: Overnight Tube—38″ × 6″ × 6″ × 6″—designed to accommodate up to 20 pounds and suitable for posters, fabrics, calendars, and unframed artwork; and the Overnight Box, 17½″ × 12½″ × 3″.

Priority 1 Service provides door-to-door early-morning service for packages weighing up to 150 pounds. Standard Air Service is one- to two-day service that costs significantly less than overnight service.

Federal Express serves over seventy-five countries, with two-day delivery to five major European cities—London, Paris, Frankfurt, Brussels, and Amsterdam.

International Commodity Restrictions

Many of the following items are totally prohibited by some countries:

Artwork, including drawings, paintings, sculpture, and ceramics
Jewelry, including watches, gems, and stones (cut or uncut, precious or semiprecious), industrial diamonds, and costume jewelry
Precious metals

Other notable restrictions that might apply to gifts:

Australia: entertainment films; aerosol products; CB radios; flammable nightwear; motorcycle helmets; toy firearms, reptile skins; seeds; TV sets
Belgium: ivory and ivory products
Bolivia: clothing; textile products; commercial films
Canada: ivory, processed or unprocessed
Channel Islands (U.K.): CB radios; wool; hops and hops' products; prison-made goods; stamps; whale by-products; wood
Chile: fabric; credit cards; airline tickets; precious metals; jewelry
Colombia: clothes; textiles; jewelry; precious metals
Costa Rica: all perishables; jewelry; precious stones; political literature of any kind
Ecuador: jewelry; precious metals; airline tickets; textile products; films; checks
England: wool; CB radios; hops and hops' products; prison-made goods; horror comics; whale by-products; wood; stamps; copyright works

France: personal health items; instruments for weights and measures; toys; jewelry; precious stones; precious metals

Hong Kong: lottery tickets

India: blank stationery (!); world maps

Ireland: wool; hops and hops' products; wood; whale by-products; copyright works; CB radios; horror comics; stamps; prison-made goods; therapeutic substances

Italy: leather; entertainment films; pictures; sculptures; antiques; electrical material produced or manufactured in Japan; textiles produced or manufactured in Far East countries

Japan: leather; toys; tableware; sprays or aerosols; knives; medical supplies; silk; feather or down items; clothing; garments and fabrics

Lebanon: calendars; slides; transparencies

Luxembourg: ivory and ivory products

Malaysia: seeds; jewelry and precious stones; safety equipment (crash helmets, safety belts, and so on)

Mexico: appliances; auto parts; books (school, medical, industrial); electronic parts; film of all kinds; powder, any type; videotape and cassettes

New Zealand: clothing; films; videotapes; CB radios; aerosol products; flammable nightwear; motorcycle helmets; toy firearms; reptile skins; seeds; TV sets

Norway: leather and leather products; synthetic textiles; wool or fur yarn; cotton thread and textiles; shoes made of plastic, rubber, or leather and textiles or soles, heels, and so on from Japan, South Korea, China, Mongolia, North Korea, Vietnam, and Taiwan; porcelain ware manufactured in Japan, South Korea, or Taiwan; bicycles; motorbikes; prams and parts thereof manufactured in Taiwan; toys and toy parts manufactured in Taiwan

Peru: jewelry; precious metals; textile products; airline tickets

Scotland: same restrictions as Ireland

Sweden: clothing; fabric

Taiwan: books; consumer, trade, or commercial magazines; undeveloped film; motion picture film

Thailand: ceramic items made with mercury; wireless communication equipment

Venezuela: jewelry; precious metals; textile products; films

Wales: same restrictions as England

GIFT
GUIDELINES

- Always keep the recipient in mind when selecting a gift: interests, dislikes, lifestyle, age, work, and so on. Please the recipient, not yourself.

- The manner in which a gift is presented is as important as the gift itself.

- Always include a personal message, even when the gift is sent from a store or ordered from a catalog.

- The unexpected gift is usually the nicest to receive and to give.

- Purchase the quality of merchandise you would like to have.

- Keep annual lists so that you do not duplicate any gifts (also of what you have received so that you don't give someone's gift back to him or her).

- Shop early for a gift occasion; if you are ordering by mail, ascertain that the product will arrive on time.

- Keep a selection of gifts to use for an unexpected hostess or thank-you gift, for children's birthday parties, and for forgotten occasions.

- When you see something "perfect" for a special person, buy it even though you may not need the gift for some time.

- It helps to have a gift calendar—a special calendar that alerts you to gift/card giving occasions such as birthdays and anniversaries.

- Keep gift mailing addresses together in a special book/place so that they are readily available for sending gifts and greeting cards.

- Answer relevant questions on the following gift forms to help you select individualized gifts.

The following forms are copies of those I use in my business: one is for exceptional personal gifts, the other for special business gifts. The questions are not necessarily meant to be answered in detail for each potential recipient but used as guidelines.

Personal Gifts

A GIFT
    FOR_____
    OCCASION_____
    PRESENTATION DATE_____
    RELATIONSHIP TO GIVER_____

AGE_____ HEIGHT_____ WEIGHT_____
HAIR COLOR_____ EYE COLOR_____ SKIN
                                                            COLORING_____
CHILDHOOD_____
_____

EDUCATION_____
_____

ENJOYABLE CLUB/ORGANIZATION AFFILIATIONS_____
_____

BUSINESS INTERESTS_____
_____

ASSOCIATIONS/HOBBIES/COLLECTIONS_____
_____

DOES RECIPIENT ENJOY SURPRISES?_____
CELEBRATIONS WITH MANY PEOPLE?_____
TRAVEL?_____

FAVORITES
COLORS_____ FOODS_____
FLOWERS_____ PLACES_____
SPORTS_____ STYLES_____
MAGAZINES_____ PEOPLE_____
TIME OF DAY_____ DRINKS_____
JEWELRY_____ ANIMALS_____
BOOKS_____ AUTOMOBILE_____
ARTISTS_____ VACATION_____
MUSIC_____ DANCE_____
DISLIKES_____
_____

CLOTHING SIZES_____
_____

- -

GIVER

WHERE WILL GIFT BE DELIVERED OR PRESENTED?_____
_____

DO YOU WISH TO INCLUDE TRAVEL OR A TRIP?_____
PRICE RANGE_____
ARE THERE ANY LIMITATIONS OR RESTRICTIONS CONCERNING THE GIFT
OR ITS PRESENTATION?_____
_____

ARE THERE ANY IDEAS OR ELEMENTS THAT MUST BE INCLUDED IN THE
GIFT OR ITS PRESENTATION?_____
_____

Business Gifts

A GIFT

FOR (INCLUDE TITLE)_____

BUSINESS_____

PRESENTATION DATE_____ OCCASION_____

    RELATIONSHIP TO GIVER_____

    APPROXIMATE AGE OF RECIPIENT_____ SEX_____

    MARITAL AND FAMILY STATUS_____

ENJOYABLE CLUB/ORGANIZATION AFFILIATIONS_____

_____

HOBBIES/COLLECTIONS/ASSOCIATIONS_____

_____

FAVORITE RESIDENCES—FARM, COUNTRY HOME, RANCH, SKI RESORT, ISLAND RETREAT, YACHT, ETC._____

_____

SPECIAL BUSINESS INTERESTS_____

_____

FAVORITE ACTIVITIES—SPORTS, HISTORICAL RESEARCH, MUSIC, TRAVEL, ETC._____

_____

IS THE RECIPIENT A SOPHISTICATED TRAVELER?_____ HAS HE/SHE TRAVELED TO THE UNITED STATES?_____

IS THE RECIPIENT A PRACTICING MUSLIM, HINDU, BUDDHIST, JEW, SHINTOIST, ROMAN CATHOLIC, ETC?_____

IS THE RECIPIENT A PARTICULARLY FORMAL OR INFORMAL PERSON?____

_____

INDEX

ABC's of Toys and Play, The (pamphlet), 318
Acknowledgment
  Arab ritual, 174–75
  of business deals, 206, 208
  of business gifts, 10–11, 111
  in China, 160
  phone calls for, 10–11
  psychological meaning, 9–11
  in Venezuela, 203
  of wedding gifts, 67–68
  see also Receiving gifts; Refusing gifts;
    Thank-you notes
Advent
  in Germany, 161
  in Venezuela, 201
Aged. *See* Elderly
Aguinaldos (Venezuelan Advent season), 201
Albright-Knox Museum (Buffalo, N.Y.),
    220–21
Alcoholic beverages. *See* Liquor, as gift
American foundation for the Blind, 219
American Greetings, 339, 342
American Kennel Club, 244
Animals
  Arab countries, why not to give animal
    sculptures, 174
  Chinese symbolism, 151–52
  oryx as gift, 176
  see also Pets; specific kinds
Anniversaries, wedding
  Arab, 173
  in Australia, 191
  in Chile, 208

first, 15
in France, 131
in Italy, 168
Jewish, 124
major, 71–72
older couples, 23, 71–72
in Soviet Union, 188
specific, 72–73
traditional customs, 72–73
younger couples, 72
Annulment of marriage, 68
Antimaterialism, Chinese, 150–51
Apartment gifts, 21, 253, 255–56
Aperitif, 240
Arabs
  anniversaries, 173
  birthdays, 173
  births, 173
  business gifts, 172, 174
  culture and tradition, 170–72
  falcon and oryx, 176
  funerals, 173
  holidays, 172
  hospitality, 171–72, 174
  'Id al-Fitr, 172
  New Year, 172
  presenting gifts, 173
  receiving gifts, ritual, 174–75
  special gifts, 175–76
  taboos, 173–75
  weddings, 172–73
  women, 174, 176
Archangel St. James' Day (Spain), 197

Archers, 282
Artists and art lovers, 295–96
Art Moderne, Musee de, 222
Art of Gift Wrapping, The, 337
Arts Décoratifs, Musée des, 222
Arts de la mode, Musée des, 222
Asprey gift boxes, 136, 276
Attorneys General, National Association of,
   236
Australia
   anniversaries, 191
   birthdays, 191
   business gifts, 191
   Christmas, 190
   Easter, 191
   hostess gifts, 191
   Mother's and Father's days, 191
   quarantine laws, 192
   Remembrance and Anzac days, 191
   Valentine's Day, 191
   weddings, 191
Awards, employees' service, 103

Baby gifts
   in Arab world, 173
   in Brazil, 206
   in Britain, 136
   in Chile, 208
   in China, 152
   in France, 130
   in Germany, 163
   Jewish, 121–22
   in The Netherlands, 194
   in Scandinavia, 179
   toys, 315
   in U.S., 55–58
   see also Children
Baby's Book of Babies, The, 216
Backpackers, 284–85
Baily's Hunting Directory, 136
Baldridge, Letitia, 119
Banquet, Chinese, 158–60
Baptisms. See Baby gifts
Bar accessories, 241–42
Bar/Bat Mitzvah, 20, 122
Barter, 6
Baskets
   Baskets as gift containers for flowers and
      plants, 227, 229
   Baskets Extraordinaire, 46
   Picnic baskets as wedding gift, 62
   Ultimate Basket, The, 92
Bastille Day, 17
Bath items, 46, 240–41
Bedtime Buddies (quilts), 316
Befana (Epiphany figure, Italy), 166
Belk, Russell, 6
Benefits, charity, 76, 91
Best man, gifts for, 69
Better Business Bureaus, Council of, 235
Bibles, 212, 215, 218

Bicyclists, 284
Birthdays
   adult, 60–61
   Arab, 173
   in Australia, 191
   Beethoven's, 17
   birthstones, 60, 306
   boss, gifts for, 100–102
   in Britain, 135
   children's, 59–60
   in Chile, 207
   in China, 152–53
   in France, 130
   in Germany, 163
   in Japan, 144
   in Korea, 183
   in The Netherlands, 194
   parties, 59–61
   pets', 17
   public officials, cards from, 23
   in Scandinavia, 178
   in Soviet Union, 189
   in Spain, 197
   in Venezuela, 202
Births. See Baby gifts
Birthstones, 60, 306
Bizarre Books, 213
Blind persons, 218–19, 269
Boat enthusiasts, 287–88
Bolivar, Simon, 204
Book-of-the-Month Club, 212
books, as gifts
   in Arab world, 176
   art books, 214
   Bibles, 212, 215, 218
   Bizarre Books, 213
   blank books, 215
   Book Call, 212
   Book-of-the-Month Club, 212
   children's, 213, 214, 215–17
   Christmas, 60
   coffee-table books, 213, 214
   in combination gifts, 213–14
   commissioned books, 214
   cookbooks, 212, 214, 218, 259
   encyclopedias, 213
   first or rare editions, 214
   Limited Editions Club, 214–15
   religious books, 212, 215, 218
   for speakers and writers, 212–13
   specialty bookstores, 211
   for sports fans, 280, 283
   on tape, 217–18
   for travelers, 213, 273–74
   for visually impaired, 218–19
Bordeaux cooking camp (France), 318
Born to Shop, 214, 273
Boss, gifts for, 97–98, 100–102, 141–42
   see also Executives
Bowlers, 284
Boxing Day (Britain), 134

Boy Scout items, 317
Braun, Pat, 226
Brazil
  baby gifts, 206
  business gifts, 206
  Christmas, 205
  Easter, 205
  funerals, 206
  host/hostess gifts, 205
  taboos, 206
  weddings, 206
Bread-and-butter gifts. See host/hostess gifts
Bribes, 10, 11, 111, 174, 198, 199
Bridal registry, 63, 64, 66–67, 123, 207
Bridal showers, 19, 65–66, 136
Bridesmaids, gifts for, 69
Bris, 121–22
Britain
  birthdays, 135
  Boxing Day, 134
  ceremonial gifts, 29, 294
  Christmas, 134–35
  Easter, 135
  host/hostess gifts, 136
  hunt weekend, 136
  Mother's and Father's Days, 135
  papal gift, 294
  philanthropy, 237
  Queen's birthday, 135
Bromeliads, 227
Buddhism, 12, 142
Buin tribe, 5–6
Business cards, exchanging
  in Arab world, 175
  in Japan, 137–38
  in The Netherlands, 195
  in Scandinavia, 179
  in Spain, 198
Business gifts
  acknowledging, 10–11, 111
  in Arab world, 172, 174
  in Australia, 191
  for boss, 100–102
  in Brazil, 206
  in Britain, 135
  in Chile, 208
  in China, 149–51
  for clients, 89–94, 110
  collections, office, 97–99
  company policies, 97–99, 104–105
  corporate outings, gifts at, 77, 93–94
  effectiveness of, 87–88
  employees, gifts for, 103–107, 201
  flowers, 226
  foreign. See Foreign gift-giving customs;
    specific countries
  in France, 131
  in Germany, 164–65
  guidelines, 88–89
  in Italy, 168–69
  in Japan, 137–48

joint, 97–99
in Korea, 184–85
logos, 90–91, 174, 199, 203, 206
multiple, 89–90
in The Netherlands, 195–96
new business opening, 95–96
premiums, 108–109
promotion, 21
"Protocol of Corporate Giving, The," 118
refusing, 11, 110–11
in Scandinavia, 179–80
secretaries, gifts for, 105
in Soviet Union, 189
in Spain, 198
special, 91–93
specialized applications, 110–11
taxes on, 94
tie-ins, 91
traditions, 89
in Venezuela, 203

Campers, 284–85
Candy
  chocolate, 309–10
  Valentine, 45–46
  Caplow, Theodore, 7
Cards. See Greeting cards
Carnevale (Italian pre-Lent festival), 167
Cartier, 332
Catalogs, 230–33
Cats. See Pets
Charisma, 213
Charity
  benefits, 76, 91
  gifts to, 110, 208, 234–37
Checks. See money, gifts of
Chesanow, Neil, 149
Children
  birthdays, 59–60
  books for, 213, 214, 215–17
  on car trips, 21
  Children's Day (Korea), 183
  Christmas and, 7
  clothing, 313
  get-well gifts, 272
  gifts from, 321–25
  infants, 315
  Japanese, gifts for, 142–43
  preschoolers, 316–17
  room, gifts for, 314
  school-age, 317–18
  toddlers, 315–16
  toys, 313–19
  in wedding parties, 69
  see also Baby gifts
Children's Book Council, 216, 217
Children's Choices (book guide), 217
Children's Video Report, 250
Chile
  anniversaries, 208
  baby gifts, 208

Chile (continued)
  birthdays, 207
  business gifts, 208
  Christmas, 207
  Easter, 207
  funerals, 208
  host/hostess gifts, 208
  saint's day, 207
  taboos, 208
  weddings, 207
China
  animal symbolism, 151–52
  antimaterialism, 150–51
  baby gifts, 152
  background information, 149
  banquets, 158–60
  birthdays, 152–53
  color symbolism, 152
  "face," 150
  host/hostess gifts, 156
  International Women's Day, 154
  jade, 306
  Labor Day, 154
  Lunar Festivals, 154
  New Year, 153
  numbers, meaning of, 152
  official holidays, 154
  pandas, gifts to U.S., 119
  photographs, as gifts, 157
  protocol in, 151
  receiving gifts, 160
  social gifts, 155–57
  student gifts, 153
  taboos, 157–58
  weddings, 153
  Western gifts, 154–60
  Youth Day, 154
Chocolate and chocoholics, 309–10
Christenings. See Baby gifts
Christmas
  in Australia, 190
  in Brazil, 205
  in Britain, 134–35
  business gifts, 89–90, 97–98, 100–102
  Campbell-Mithun Christmas Angel, 89
  children, 7
  in Chile, 207
  commercialization, 7
  couple's first, 15
  depression, post-, 14
  employees, gifts for, 104–105
  family and, 7
  in France, 129–30, 131
  in Germany, 161–62
  gifts with holiday theme, 49–50
  in Italy, 167
  in Japan, 143–44
  and Jews, 128
  in Korea, 183
  last-minute shopping, 50–52
  meaning of gifts, 7

  mistletoe, 223
  in The Netherlands, 194
  preparing for, 48
  religious tradition, 7, 12–14, 29, 43
  Santa Claus, 7, 43, 143, 162, 178
  in Scandinavia, 177–78
  in Spain, 197
  stocking stuffers, 78–80
  thank-you notes, 9
  in U.S., 43
  value of gifts, 8
  in Venezuela, 201–202
Chrysanthemums, 191, 198, 225
Chusok (Korean festival), 182, 185
City of New York, Museum of, 221
Clergy, 293–94
Clients, gifts for, 89–94, 110
Clothing
  for baby, 55
  for children, 313
  inappropriate, as gift, 9–10
  for outdoorspersons, 282, 284
  for pets, 301
Coffee-table books, 213, 214
Cognac, 240
Collections, gifts to start, 15–16
Collections, office, 97–99
College students, 21, 253–57, 299–300
Cologne, 46, 61, 133
Color symbolism, Chinese, 152
"Combination" gifts, 19–21, 213–14, 240–41
Comfortably Yours, 269
Commercialism, 7, 13
Communication, gifts as, 3–4
Condolence. see Sympathy
Congratulatory gifts
  in Germany, 163
  graduations, 19, 191, 208, 253–57
  in Japan, 145
  see also Baby gifts; Weddings
Connections (travel newsletter), 273
Consultants
  bridal, 66
  corporate gift, 112–13
Containers, as packaging, 334–35
Control, 10
Convalescents, 20, 145, 184, 270–72
Cookbooks, 212, 214, 218, 259
Cooks, 20, 21, 212, 214, 258–64, 287, 318, 323–24
Corporate gifts. See Business gifts
Countries, gifts between, 29, 30, 119–20, 203–204
  see also names of specific countries
Creative Gift Wrapping, 337
Creative Resources, 91, 92
Customers. See Clients, gifts for
Cyclists, 284

Dancers and dance enthusiasts, 298
Deaf American, 268

Deaf persons, 268
Death. *See* Sympathy
Debutantes, 311–12
Decoration Day (company, Larchmont, N.Y.), 228
Denmark. *See* Scandinavia
Día de la Hispanidad (Spain), 197
Direct Marketing Association, 230, 232–33
Disabled persons, 218–19, 265–69
Divers, 282
Dogs. *See* Pets
Donations, for charity events, 76
Dormitory residents, 21, 253, 255–56
Doubleday Large Print Home Library, 218–19

Earth-in-Space globe, 318
Easter
  in Australia, 191
  in Brazil, 205
  in Britain, 135
  in Chile, 207
  Fabergé egg, 30
  in Germany, 162
  in Italy, 167
  in Scandinavia, 178
  in Spain, 197
  in U.S., 38–39
800-FLOWERS, Inc., 227
Elderhostel, 24
Elderly, 16, 20, 23, 24, 218–19, 265–69, 343
  see also Nursing home patients
Embarrassment
  from inappropriate/expensive gift, 9–10, 11, 111
  from misinterpretation of gesture, 6
  from singing/dancing telegrams, 61
  from surprises, 61
Employees, gifts for, 98–99, 103–107, 179, 201
Employment. *See* Business gifts
Encyclopedia Britannica, 213
Engagements. *See* Weddings
England. *See* Britain
Entertaining. *See* Host/hostess gifts
Entrepreneurs, 95–96
Epiphany
  in Italy, 166
  in Spain, 197
  In Venezuela, 201–202
Eskimos, 6, 222
Evangelical Council for Financial Accountability, 236
Exchanges, 68
Executives, 278–79, 323
  see also Business gifts
Expensive gifts
  from acquaintances, 9
  in Arab world, 174
  and giver's status, 5–6, 8, 9
  refusing, 11, 111
  see also Extravagant gifts

Extortion, 10, 11
Extravagant gifts, 28–33
  see also Expensive gifts

"Face" (Oriental concept of honor), 146, 150
Falcon, as gift in Arab world, 176
Families
  in Brazil, 205
  gifts for, 250–52
  see also Children; Parents
Family Travel Times, 250
Fantasy gifts, 30
Farmer's Almanac, 213, 289, 290
FashionAble catalog, 269
Father Christmas
  in Australia, 190
  in Britain, 134
  in Scandinavia, 177
Father's Book, The, 218
Father's Day
  in Australia, 191
  in Britain, 135
  children's gift ideas, 322
  in France, 130
  in Germany, 162
  in Italy, 167
  in Japan, 144
  in Scandinavia, 178
  in Spain, 197
  tapes, as gifts, 218
  in U.S., 39–41
Favors, party. *See* Party favors
Federal Express, 348–49
Financial Crunch Banker's Dozen, 92
Finland. *See* Scandinavia
First editions, 214
Fishermen, 283
Fitness buffs, 286–87
Flattery, 10
Flower girls, gifts for, 69
Flowers
  arrangements, 225
  for birthday, 60
  in Birtain, 136
  for business opening, 96–97
  in Chile, 208
  800-FLOWERS, Inc., 227
  exotic, 224
  florists, working with, 227
  fragile, 224, 228
  in France, 131–32
  for funerals, 125, 131, 195
  garden, 225
  gardeners, 21, 29, 213, 289–92
  as get-well gift, 270
  as host/hostess gift, 131–32, 136, 195, 226–27, 258
  ikebana (Japanese arrangement), 225
  for men, 228
  miniature, 224
  in The Netherlands, 195

Flowers (continued)
  potpourri, 229
  as romantic gifts, 45
  selecting, 226
  silk, 228–29
  specific types, 191, 195, 198, 202, 223, 225, 226, 227, 228
  trends in, 224–26
  in Venezuela, 202
  when to give, 226–27
Folklore, gifts in, 6
Food, gifts of
  in Arab world, 174
  baskets, 20
  birthdays, 60
  as business gift, 89–92
  candy, Valentine, 45–46
  from children, 324
  in China, 156–57
  for chocoholics, 309–10
  Christmas, 51–52
  for families, 250–51
  in France, 132
  in Germany, 165
  homemade, 22
  as host/hostess gift, 259
  in Italy, 167
  in Japan, 140, 141
  for Jewish celebrations, 124–28
  as office gift, 98–99
  quarantine laws, 192
  repackaging, 22
  for sick or shut-ins, 265, 270
  Thanksgiving, 42
Footstools, custom-made, 92
Foreign gift-giving customs
  Arab countries, 170–76
  Australia, 190–92
  Britain, 134–36
  China, 149–60
  France, 129–33
  general, 117–20
  Germany, 161–65
  Italy, 166–69
  Japan, 137–48
  Korea, 181–86
  Latin America, 199–200
  Netherlands, 193–96
  philanthropy, 237
  Scandinavia, 177–80
  Soviet Union, 187–89
  Spain, 197–98
  see also Countries, gifts between
Foreign Gifts Act, 119–20
Forget-Me-Nots, 223
Fragrances, 46, 61, 133, 245
France
  anniversaries, 131
  baby gifts, 130
  Bordeaux cooking camp, 318
  Christmas season, 129–30, 131

French Farm and Village Holiday Guide, 274
  funerals, 131
  general gifts, 131–33
  May Day, 130
  Mother's Day, 130
  museums, 222
  Paris, travelers to, 276–77
  philanthropy, 237
  Statue of Liberty gift, 30
  Valentine's Day, 130
  weddings, 130–31
Franklin Library, 219
French Farm and Village Holiday Guide, 274
FTD florists, 226, 227
Fund raising, 110, 208, 234–37
Fund-Raising Counsel, American Association of, 237
Funds, office gift, 97, 98–99
Funerals. See Sympathy; under country names

Gags. See Joke gifts
Games, personalized, 93, 106
Gardeners, 21, 29, 213, 289–92, 323
Garden Game, 290
Gems
  anniversaries, 72–73
  birthstones, 60, 306
  enthusiasts, gifts for, 305–307
  famous extravagant gifts of, 29–30
General Foods Gevalia Caffe, 230
Germany
  Advent, 161
  baby gifts, 163
  birthdays, 59, 163
  business gifts, 164–65
  Christmas, 161–62
  festivals, 162
  gift-giving rules, 165
  Good Friday, 162
  host/hostess gifts, 164, 165
  Labor Day (May Day), 162
  Mother's and Father's days, 162
  Richtfest, 163
  St. Nicholas Day, 161–62
  weddings, 163
Get-well gifts, 20, 145, 184, 270–72
Gift certificates
  books, 212
  carriage ride, 24
  as housewarming gifts, 74
  as last-minute gifts, 50
  telephone, 24, 40
  as wedding gift, 64
  see also Money
Gift-giving guidelines, 351–54
Gift-of-the-month, 23, 50, 212, 230
Gilbert and Sullivan Operas, 219
Giri (Japanese concept of obligation), 138, 139, 145, 146

Girl Scout items, 317
Gladioli, 191, 225
God. *see* Religion
Godiva chocolate, 288, 332
Golfers, 285–86, 323
Good Friday, 162
Gourmet cooks. *See* Cooks
Graduations, 19, 191, 208, 253–57
Grandfather Frost (Russian St. Nick), 187
Grandparents, 20
Grandparents' Day, 4
Great Britain. *See* Britain
Great Maine Lobster Co., 90
Great Northwestern Greeting Seed Co., 343
Greeting cards
  business, 111
  New Year, Japanese, 142
  from public officials, 23
  trends, 342–43
Gucci, 169, 184, 185, 276, 285, 332
Guests, gifts for
  adults, 76–77
  children, 59–60
Guns, 282–83
Guy Fawkes Day (Britain), 135–36

Halloween, 41–42
Handicapped persons, 218–19, 265–69
Hanukkah, 126
Heads of State, 119–20, 203–204
Hearing impaired, 268
Hermès, 276, 286, 288, 332
Hermès ties, 29
Hideaway Report, The, 273
Hikers, 284–85
Historic Plant Center, 292
Holidays. *See* specific days
Holland. *see* Netherlands
Homemade gifts, 21–22, 49
Homeowners, 20, 213
  see also Housewarming
Horchow, Roger, 230–32
Horseback riders, 288
Hospitality gifts. *See* Host/hostess gifts
Hospitalized persons, 270–72
Host/hostess gifts
  in Arab world, 172, 174
  in Australia, 191
  in Brazil, 205
  in Britain, 136
  in Chile, 208
  in China, 156
  flowers, 131–32, 136, 195, 226–27, 258
  in France, 131–32
  general, 258–64
  in Germany, 164, 165
  in Italy, 167
  in Japan, 144
  in Korea, 182
  in The Netherlands, 195
  in Scandinavia, 178

  in Spain, 198
  in Venezuela, 202
Housewarming, 19, 20, 21, 74–75, 123
Hunting
  British weekend, 136
  gifts, 282

'Id al-Fitr (Arab feast), 172
Ikebana (Japanese flower arranging), 225
Ill persons, 20, 145, 184, 270–72
Inappropriate gifts, 245
  see also Taboos
Incentive gifts, 104
Independence Day, 17
India, 306
Indians. *See* Native Americans, gift-giving
  customs of
Industry and Trade Association, U.S.
  Commerce Department, 149
Inexpensive gifts, 25–27, 60, 63–64, 73
Infants. *See* Baby gifts; Children
Institute of Charity Fund-Raising Managers,
  237
Interaction (charity information agency), 237
Interfil, 237
"Interim" gifts, 81–83
International commodity restrictions, 349–50
International giving. *See* Countries, gifts
  between; Foreign gift-giving customs;
  specific country names
International Reading Association, 217
International Women's Day, 154, 188
Islam. *See* Arabs
Italy
  anniversaries, 168
  Carnevale, 167
  Christmas, 167
  Easter, 167
  Epiphany, 166
  funerals, 168
  gift-giving rules, 169
  hostess gifts, 167
  New Year, 166
  weddings, 168

Japan
  birthdays, 144
  Christmas, 143–44
  congratulations, 145
  get-well gifts, 145
  gift-giving and receiving protocol, 138–39,
    145–46, 148
  gifts to U.S., 120
  giri, 138, 139, 145, 146
  hostess/host gifts, 144
  ikebana (flower arranging), 225
  Japanese visitors abroad, 146
  New Year, 142–43
  ningen kankei, 138, 144, 146, 148
  Ochugen and Oseibo (seasons), 12, 13,
    140–42, 143

Japan (continued)
  packaging, 331
  record keeping, 148
  taraimawashi, 148
  weddings, 144
  wrapping, 147, 331
Jarvis, Anna, 28
Jewelry
  birthstones, 60, 306
  as extravagant gifts, 28–33
  as Valentine gift, 46
  see also Gems
Jews
  anniversaries, 124
  Ashkenazi Haggadah, The, 212
  baby gifts, 121–22
  Bar/Bat Mitzvah, 20, 122
  bookstores, Judaica, 211
  bris, 121–22
  Chagall's gift to, 30
  Christmas, 128
  Hanukkah, 12, 126
  Hanukkat Habayit (dedication of home),
    123–24
  Israel, planting trees in, 24, 122
  mourning ritual, 124–25
  Orthodox, 122, 123, 124–25, 128
  Passover, 127–28
  Purim, 127
  Rosh Hashanah, 125, 126
  Sabbath, 127
  Sukkoth, 125, 126
  weddings, 123
Joggers, 282
Joint gifts, 97–99
Joke gifts, 11, 60, 61

Kid-powered vehicles (KPVs), 316
Kitchen shower, 65
Korea
  birthdays, 183
  Children's Day, 183
  Christmas, 183
  Chusok (Harvest Moon Festival Day),
    182, 185
  funerals, 184
  gift guidelines, 185–86
  gifts to U.S., 120
  hostess/host gifts, 182
  names, 181–82
  National Folklore Day, 183
  New Year, 182–83
  Parents' Day, 183
  taboos, 185
  weddings, 184
  Westernization, 181
Kosher laws, 127–28
Kuriansky, Judith, 9–10

Labor, U.S. Department of, 319
Labor Day (China), 154, 162

Labor Day (Soviet Union), 188
Lamb International, 90
Lancôme cosmetics, 185
Lapidary Journal, The, 307
Large Print Books, 218
Latin America, gift-giving guidelines,
    199–200
  see also Brazil; Chile; Venezuela
Learning About Labels (pamphlet), 318
Learning Shirts, 316–17
Left-handed people, 320
Library of Congress, 219
Life cycle, gifts celebrating, 12–14
Lighthouse for the Blind, 219
Limited Editions Club, 214–15
Linen shower, 65–66
Lingerie shower, 66
Liquor, as gift
  in Arab world, 173
  bar accessories, 241–42
  general guidelines, 241
  gifts never to give, 245
  in Korea, 185–86
  in The Netherlands, 195
  in Scandinavia, 179–80
  in Soviet Union, 189
  types, 240
  in Venezuela, 202, 203
  wine, 240, 258–59
Louvre, 222
Love, Diane, 228, 229
Luggage, 276
Lunar Festivals (China), 154

Maiden names, brides keeping, 64
Mailing packages, 347–50
Mail order. See Catalogs
Man, Museum of, 220–21
Manifestations, Inc., 343
Manipulation, gifts as, 10
Marcus, Stanley, 29
Marriage
  maiden name retention, 64
  repeat, 66
  see also Anniversaries, wedding; Weddings
May Day, 16–17, 39, 130, 162, 188
Mexico, 120
Middletown Families, 7
Military personnel, 299–300
Mineral and rock enthusiasts, 221, 305–307
Ministers, 293
Mistletoe, 223
Modern Art, Museum of, 221
Money, gifts of
  acknowledging, 67
  appropriate, 238–39
  for birth/christening, 57, 122
  for Bar/Bat Mitzvah, 20
  for child, 59, 318
  foreign, 157–58
  for graduation, 255

Money, gifts of (continued)
  in Japan, 142–43, 145, 146
  in Korea, 184
  restrictions on amount, 59, 97–98
  in Scandinavia, 179
  for weddings, 64, 123
  see also Gift certificates
Monograms, 64
Month, gift-of-the, 23, 50, 212, 230
Monticello (Charlottesville, Va.), 292
Montreal Museum of Fine Arts, 222
Mother's Day
  in Australia, 191
  in Britain, 135
  children's gift ideas, 321, 322
  in France, 130
  in Germany, 162
  in Italy, 166
  in Japan, 144
  Jarvis's creation of, 28
  in Scandinavia, 178
  in Spain, 197
  in U.S., 39–40
Mount Vernon (Va.), 220–21
Mourning. See Sympathy
Movie buffs, 297–98
Moving, 20, 21
Museum gifts, 220–22
  see also names of specific museums
Musicians and music lovers, 221, 296–97
Muslims. See Arabs
Mythology, gifts in, 6, 344

Name day. see Saint's day
Names, maiden, 64
National Building Museum, 220–21
National Charities Information Bureau, 235, 237
National Council for U.S.-China Trade, 149
National Folkore Day (Korea), 183
National Library Services for the Blind and Physically Handicapped, 219
Native Americans, gift-giving customs of, 5, 6, 12
Natural History, American Museum of, 221, 318
Needleworkers, 303–304
Neiman-Marcus Christmas catalog, 29
Neiman-Marcus gift wrap, 334
Netherlands, The
  baby gifts, 194
  birthdays, 194
  business gifts, 195–96
  Christmas, 194
  hostess/host gifts, 195
  New Year, 194
  Sinterklaas (St. Nicholas), 193–94, 196
  weddings, 194
New business opening, 95–96
New neighbors, gifts for, 75
New Year

Arab, 172
Chinese, 153
Dutch, 194
Italian, 166
Japanese, 142–43
Jewish, 125, 126
Korean, 182–83
Russian, 187
Nicholas Shapes, Unlimited, 93
Ningen kankei (Japanese concept of relatonships), 138, 144, 146, 148
"No-gift" requests, 60, 73
Norway. See Scandinavia
Numbers, Chinese significance, 152
Nuns, 293
Nursing home patients, 265, 270–72

Obligation, 10, 138, 139
Occasions, creating, 16–19
Ochugen (Japanese holiday), 140–42
Octoberfest (Germany), 162
Office gifts. See Business gifts
Office-related gifts, 278–79
  see also Business gifts
Onomastico (name day, Italy), 167
Oral history, 23
Orthodox Jews. See Jews
Orvis Fishing School, 283
Oryx (Saudi antelope), 176
Oseibo (Japanese holiday), 12, 13, 140, 141–42, 143
Outdoorspeople, 284–85
Outings, corporate, 93–94
Overseas, gifts, 299–300

Packaging. See Wrapping
Pakistan, 119
Pandas, 119
Papal gifts, 293–94
Parents
  Christmas and, 7
  inappropriate gifts from, 9–10
  Parents' Day (Korea), 183
  see also Children; Father's Day; Mother's Day
Parent's Guide to Children's Reading, A, 217
Paris en Cuisine (reservation service), 276
Party favors
  adults, 76–77
  children, 59–60
Party gifts. See Guests, gifts for; Party favors; specific occasions
Passover, 127, 212
Passport (travel newsletter), 273
Pedersen golf clubs, 93, 285
Penhada (piñata), 202, 206
Perfect Setting, The, 214
Perfume, 46, 61, 133
Personal Family Record, 219
Personal satisfaction, 8
Personal services, 23, 24, 60, 63, 265, 270, 272, 322

Pet Cruises, 302
Pets
  bird dogs, 283
  birthdays, 17
  books on, 212, 244, 301
  Dogs for the Deaf, 268
  as gifts, 243–44
  gifts for, 301–302
  horses, 288
Philanthropy, 110, 208, 234–37
Phone calls, 10–11
Picnic basket, 62–63
Pierce, Frank N., 87–88
Pierpont Morgan Library, 221
Poetry tapes, 218
Polterabend (German wedding custom), 163
Popes, gifts to, 293–94
Portugal, gift to Britain, 29
Postal Service, 348
Potpourri, 229
Power, gifts and, 5–6
Precious stones. *See* Gems
Premiums, 108–109
Preschoolers. *See* Children
Presenting gifts, 344–46
President. *See* White House
Prestige, gifts and, 5–6
Price of His Toys, The (co.), 93
Priests, 293–94
Promises, gifts symbolizing, 81–83
Promotions, 108–109
"Protocol of Corporate Giving, The"
  (survey), 118
Purim, 127

Quarantine laws (Australia), 192

Rare gifts, 29–30
Reardon, Dr. Kathleen, 118
Receiving gifts
  Arab ritual, 174–75
  in China, 160
  discomfort, 9, 10
  graciousness, 9–11, 13–14
  in Japan, 145–46
  strangers, gifts from, 9
  "suspicious" gifts, 9
  wedding, 66–68
  see also Acknowledgment; Refusing gifts;
    Thank-you notes
Refusing gifts
  business, 110–11
  in China, 151
  explanation for, 11, 110–11
Registry, bridal, 63, 64, 66–67, 123, 207
Religion
  books, 212
  and Christmas, 7, 12–14, 29
  clergy, gifts for, 293–94
  greeting cards, 343
  and Halloween, 41–42

  see also specific holidays; specific religions,
    e.g., Buddhism
Remembrance and Anzac days (Australia),
  191
Restaurant Reporter, The, 273
Retirees, 20, 105–106
Returning gifts, 68
Revenge, gift-giving as, 6
Richtfest (German building ceremony), 163
Ring bearers, gifts for, 69
Rock and gem enthusiasts, 305–307
Romantic gifts, 44–47, 130
  see also Valentine's Day
Roscón de Reyes (Spanish Epiphany bread),
  197
Rosh Hashanah, 125
Runners, 282
Russia. *See* Soviet Union

Sailing enthusiasts, 287–88
St. George's Day (Spain), 197
St. Joseph's Day (Spain), 197
St. Nicholas, 161–62, 193–94, 196, 202
St. Patrick's Day, 16
Saint's day
  in Chile, 207
  in France, 130
  general, 59
  in Italy, 167
  in Scandinavia, 178
  in Spain, 197
  in Venezuela, 202
Santa Claus, 7, 43, 143, 162, 178
  see also Father Christmas; St. Nicholas
Santa Lucia's Day (Sweden), 177
Sarabeth's Kitchen, 98–99
Scandinavia
  baby gifts, 179
  birthdays, 178
  Christmas, 177–78
  Easter, 178
  funerals, 179
  gift-giving rules, 180
  host/hostess gifts, 178
  Mother's and Father's days, 178
  Valentine's Day, 178
  weddings, 179
Schwartz, Jack, 237
Scuba divers, 281
Secretaries, gifts for, 105
selectogram, 95–96
Sending gifts, 347–50
Sexual overtones, 11, 61, 111, 174
Sherry, 240
Shinto, 13, 142
Shipping, 347–50
Shogatsu (Japanese New Year), 142–43
Shopping by mail, 230–33
Shopping services, 112–13
Shower, baby. *See* Baby gifts
Shower, wedding, 19, 65–66, 136

Sick persons, 20, 145, 184, 270–72
Sierra Club, 285
Silk flowers, 228–29
"Simpatico," 199
Singing telegrams, 61
Sinterklaas (Dutch St. Nicholas), 193–94
Skiers, 281
Society Expeditions, 30
Solomon Islands, 5–6
Soviet Union
    alexandrite, 306
    birthdays, 189
    business gifts, 189
    ceremonial gifts, 119
    funerals, 188–89
    International Women's Day, 188
    New Year, 187
    October Revolution, anniversary, 188
    Spring and National Workers' Day, 188
    weddings, 188
Spain
    Archangel St. James' Day, 197
    birthdays, 197
    business gifts, 198
    ceremonial gifts, 119
    Christmas, 197
    Día de la Hispanidad, 197
    Epiphany, 197
    host/hostess gifts, 198
    Roscón de Reyes (Epiphany bread), 197
    St. George's Day, 197
    Saint's day, 197
    weddings, 198
Special touches, 22–24
Sports fans, 280–88, 323
    see also specific activities
Sports Scan, 281
Spring and National Workers' Day (Soviet
    Union), 188
Statue of Liberty, 30, 195–96, 333
Status, gifts and, 5–6
Stilton cheese, 136
Stocking stuffers, 78–80
Strangers, gifts from, 9
"Stripper-Grams," 61
Students, 21, 153, 253, 255–56, 299–300
    see also Graduations; office-related gifts;
    Teenagers
Studio Museum (Harlem), 221
Subscriptions
    for adults (gift from child), 322
    for children, 318
    for executives, 278
    for families, 250
    for graduates, 256
    for sports fans, 280
    for teenagers, 253
    travel publications, 273, 274
    see also individual publications
Sukkoth, 125–26
Superiority, demonstration of, 10

Superiors. See Boss, gifts for
Surprises, 61
"Suspicious" gifts, 9
Sweden. See Scandinavia
Symington, James W., 118, 119
Sympathy
    in Arab world, 173
    in Brazil, 206
    in Chile, 208
    in France, 131
    in Italy, 168
    in Japan, 145
    Jewish, 124–25
    in Korea, 184
    in The Netherlands, 195
    in Scandinavia, 179
    in Soviet Union, 188–89
    in Venezuela, 202

Table gifts. See Guests, gifts for
Taboos
    in Arab world, 173–75
    in Brazil, 206
    in Chile, 208
    food and drink, 259
    international commodity restrictions,
        349–50
    in Korea, 185
    kosher laws, 127–28
    in Venezuela, 203
Tape, books on, 217–18
Taraimawashi (Japanese social practice), 148
Taxes, business gift, 95
Teachers, 308
Teddy bears, 271, 313
Teenagers, 16, 19, 133, 253–54
    see also Graduations; Students
Telegrams, singing/dancing, 61
Telephone, thank-yous by, 10–11
Tennis players, 286, 323
Textile Museum, 220–21
Thanks. See Acknowledgment; Thank-you
    notes
Thanksgiving, 42
Thank-you notes
    in Arab world, 174
    business, 10–11, 111
    Christmas, 9
    content, 11
    in Germany, 165
    in Latin America, 200
    in Soviet Union, 189
    in Venezuela, 203
    for wedding gifts, 67–68
Theater-goers, 297–98
Three Kings Day. See Epiphany
Tiffany, 184, 286, 332
Tiffen, Gregge, 12–13, 14
Toddlers. See Children
Toy Manufacturers of America, 314, 318–19
Toys, 313–19

Travel and Leisure magazine, 274
Travelers, 16, 21, 213, 273–77, 299–300
Trees, planting, 23, 24, 122
Trivia Golf, 286
Tucker, Jo-Von, 230–31
Two-career families, 20

"Ugly American" syndrome. *See* Foreign
    gift-giving customs
Ultimate Basket, The, 92
Ultimate Golf, 286
Ultimate Householder's Book, The, 213
Unexpected gifts, 9
United Nations, 149, 221, 293–94
United Parcel Service (UPS), 348
U.S.S.R. *See* Soviet Union

Valentine's Day
    in Australia, 191
    in Britain, 135
    in France, 130
    gift suggestions, 44–47
    in Italy, 167
    in Japan, 144
    poetry tapes, 218
    in Scandinavia, 178
    in Spain, 197
    in U.S., 37–38
Varney, Stuart, 255
Vegetable Gardener's Book, The, 213
Venezuela
    Aguinaldos, 201
    birthdays, 202
    business gifts, 203
    Christmas, 201–202
    Epiphany, 201–202
    funerals, 202
    host/hostess gifts, 202
    penhadas, 202
    St. Nicholas, 202
    saint's days, 202
    taboos, 203
    weddings, 202
Visually impaired, 218–19, 269
Vuitton, Louis, 222, 276

Weddings
    Arab, 172
    attendants, gifts for, 69
    attendants, gifts from, 69–70
    in Australia, 191
    in Brazil, 206
    cancellation or annulment, returning gifts, 68

in Chile, 207
in China, 153
couple's gifts to each other, 68–69
encore (second or more), 66
in France, 130–31
in Germany, 163
gifts, when to send, 63
in Italy, 168
in Japan, 144
Jewish, 123
in Korea, 184
money as gift, 64
in The Netherlands, 194
in Scandinavia, 179
showers, 19, 65–66, 136
in Soviet Union, 188
in Spain, 198
in Venezuela, 202
see also Anniversaries, wedding; Bridal
    registry; Bridal shower
Welcome-to-the-neighborhood gifts, 75
West Germany. *See* Germany
White House
    Christmas ornament, 49
    diplomatic gifts, 119–20, 203–204
    greeting cards from, 23
    wrapping paper, 330
Who Lived Where in Europe, 273
Wine, 240, 258–59
Women
    in Arab world, 174, 176
    greeting cards, 342–43
    International Women's Day, 154, 188
    see also Mother's Day
Women's Travel Guide, 274
"Workacholic," gifts for, 15–16, 32
    see also Office-related gifts
World-Class Executive, The, 149
World of Stitches, The, 304
Wrapping
    available wraps, 338–41
    basic and creative, 336–37
    Japanese, 147, 331
    for shipping, 347–50
    as "signature," 330
    store wraps, 332–33
    tips, 341

Youth Day (China), 154
Youth Hostels, 276

Zodiac gifts, 60